To my mother

Guan, Zongshuang 關宗雙

汉字字源入门
修订本

The Origins of
Chinese Characters

Revised Edition

王宏源 著
Hongyuan Wang

社会科学文献出版社
SSAP SOCIAL SCIENCES ACADEMIC PRESS (CHINA)

目录　　CONTENTS

PREFACE

Unicode is the foundation of mathematical platform for human beings, and in math we trust that it is the basic for the Earth. Meanwhile, Unicode is a new gift from the West to the East, not only due to the huge quantity of the ideographic characters in East Asia, but also for the convenience it offers for editing or compilation, and survival of the Chinese dictionaries themselves.

Having acknowledged the profound significance of this universal standard, one idea about or opportunity for its application appears in front of us. If we include the Unicode for a character entry in a dictionary, by means of the code we can input the character in our computer immediately. For example, MS Word has a simple method: Internal Code Input Method. When we type in the Unicode *5B9D* for 宝, then press ALT+X simultaneously, the character 宝 shows up on our screen, and vice versa. Moreover, we can also try to hunt the *5B9D* for 宝 or *5BF6* for its traditional form 寶 in BableMap (Unicode Character Map for Windows), a web search engine, the Wiktionary, or even the unicode.org.

The Origins of Chinese Characters is a dictionary-like book of mine first published 25 years ago. In this revised edition, the primary job is to introduce Unicode as the reference for each character entry, allowing readers to make use of these electronic characters. The other revisions in this Unicode edition are: (1) Corrections to some errors in the original edition; (2) Additions and replacement for some character entries; (3) Additions of many glyph shapes; (4) Additions of page numbers for reference characters in the text, to facilitate quick search; (5) Additions of some Chinese and English contents for most entries. The modifications are under the original page format, and all the revisions are moderate. In the mean time, I removed the bibliography since this book is used for learning and teaching Chinese as a foreign language, instead of for studying the ancient Chinese writing itself.

Chinese writing system is the centralized embodiment of primitive thinking mode, mythology, aesthetic ideology and creation rules of ancient Chinese, however, the source and development of Chinese characters have been sometimes illusory or incomprehensible. For example, as a common character and abstract concept, 毒 dú *poison*, is confused sometimes with its two components: 生 shēng *to live*, and 母 mǔ *mother*. Is it originally from the legend of tasting the herbs or from the understanding that harmful and poisonous plants grow wildly? Meanwhile, some readers will find that the component 女 nǚ sometimes has a negative meaning, such as in 姦=奸 jiān *wicked*, 嫌 xián *disapproving* and 奴 nú *slave*. However, fortunately we have the word 好 hǎo *nice, good, fine*, combining 女子 nǚzǐ, that is *woman* or *female* literally.

I wrote this bilingual book, *The Origins of Chinese Characters*, around 1990 when I was a student in the Department of Physics, Tsinghua University. It was reprinted many times and translated into French in 1995 and German in 1996. After leaving the university, I was engaged in international trade, and then studied abroad, earning a degree in electrical and computer engineering from the University of Waterloo, and then ran a database company. However, I have always had a great interest in the ideographic characters, and editing *The Unicode Han Dictionary* is a hobby and took years of hard work. This revised Unicode edition is as another episode of my regular time-consuming work on the dictionary. I have really enjoyed the experience, and hope I can update and enlarge this book within a decade.

Harrison Hongyuan WANG

October. 20th 2018

序 言

　　《汉字字源入门》成书于 1990 年前后，当时作者系清华大学物理系的学生，在与来华学习汉语的外国学生交流讲授汉字起源的过程中，整理完成了这部英汉双语对外汉语教学辅助读物。该书是作者 30 年前以拆分汉字构件的方式，利用古文字的知识讲解汉字的一次尝试。书中虽然收字有限，解文释字也多有不足之处，但是由于该书是较早出现的一部采用汉字起源作为对外汉语教学的类字典读物，书中讲解的 641 个汉字字头具有构件属性，组字能力强，图书出版 25 年来多次重印至今，发行量大，销售面广，其英文部分并被译成法文和德文，具有一定的影响力。

　　这次《汉字字源入门》的修订出版，主要的目的是实现了"字宝"化改造，即在原书字头下加注 Unicode 编码。同时，"旧瓶"中装了些"新酒"，在保持旧稿版式、页码不变的基础上，全书内容有如下更动：（1）修改原版中的一些错误；（2）添加个别字头；（3）添加一些古文字字形；（4）对行文中的参考字，如出字头，则标注其所在的页码，便于读者快速翻检查验；（5）适量添加一些中英文内容，并在字头下引入一些相关联的衍生疑难字、游戏叠加字等，以增加趣味性。

　　半年来，作者利用 25 年前的旧稿修订《汉字字源入门》，感觉当年临摹字体、"剪刀加浆糊"出书的干劲没有变，面对汉字快乐的心态没有变，唯一改变的就是自己的年龄。当年拿到《汉字字源入门》样书时，年轻的作者在扉页上抄写下王国维《晓步》诗中的一句，在 25 年后的今天，情景和心境可能更贴切：

　　四时可爱唯春日，一事能狂便少年。

Harrison Hongyuan WANG

王宏源

2018 年 10 月 20 日于瀚堂

关于"字宝"

2000 年国际统一编码标准（Unicode）发布以来，对全球信息化的发展产生了重要影响。作者在十多年来依据 Unicode 东亚表意字符标准（Unicode Han）编撰字典的实践过程中，逐步形成了一个概念，即在纸质字典的字头附注 Unicode 编码数值。由于一个字符的编码完全等同于该字符，读者可根据编码，在电子编辑器上快速将编码转换为字符。作者将采用这种方法的出版物定名为"字宝"（Unicode Dictionary），"字宝"是字典在数字化时代的升级，是任意字符从纸质转化到电子设备中的桥梁，也是纸质字典在数字时代可以延续功用的有力武器。

大家在使用传统中文字典时，查询到任何字，不存在无法利用的问题，只要有笔和纸，就可以将其写出来。在数字化时代，读者在字典中查询到的字，如果属于生僻字，很多时候将其录入到电子设备中是困难的。"字宝"则是根据 Unicode 编码编撰的字典，读者将纸质字典上的 Unicode 编码输入到编辑器中，即可立即显示出字符，可以说利用"字宝"，任何字符都可以快速录入。作者在一年前出版的类字典著作《殷周金文字宝》一书中，首次明确提出此概念，并采用了"字宝"的形式，对 Unicode 发布的 2300 多个相当生僻的殷周金文隶定字，附注 Unicode 编码数值，使得读者在需要录入特定字符时，可立即获取之。

随着《殷周金文字宝》一书的出版，"字宝"这一概念引起了一些读者的兴趣。采用"字宝"这种方式，不仅对殷周金文隶定字这类生僻字符的"录入"有效，同样也可以将其引入到常见汉字中。作者进而萌生了将本人早期撰写的对外汉语教学辅助教材《汉字字源入门》一书，进行"字宝"化改造的想法。就对外汉语教学而言，常见汉字的录入对非汉语母语的学生来说也是难题，若采用"字宝"的方式，则可利用字符编码将汉字便捷地"录入"到电子文档中，《汉字字源入门（修订版）》中每个字头附带 Unicode 编码数值，就是作者这种构想的尝试结果。利用"字宝"，只需要开启 MS Word，输入字符编码，随即同时点击键盘中【ALT】+【X】两键即可。反之亦然，即光标在一个汉字字符后面，同时点击【ALT】+【X】，立即出现字符的 Unicode 编码。当然，读者亦可以下载安装最新版本的 Unicode 字符映射表，例如 BabelMap（Unicode Character Map for Windows），或者利用网络直接检索编码数值，以获取相应的汉字。

INTRODUCTION

This book is intended as a guide to the origins and histories of Chinese characters. Although it could be used as a Chinese etymological dictionary, this book is an attempt to find a new way to teach the practical ideography of Chinese to those whose native scripts are alphabet-based.

Writing is a system of conveying ideas by means of conventional symbol that form visible marks. These symbols are traced, incised, drawn, or written on the surface of materials such as tortoise shells, bones, stone, metal, bamboo, papyrus, parchment, or paper. Writing gives permanence to human knowledge and enables communication over great distances.

Writing grows out of pictures. This is as it should be, since the most natural way of communicating visually is through pictures. Some time in the Upper Paleolithic period, perhaps about 20,000 BC, early man in southern France and northeastern Spain drew sketches of his prey — horse, buffalo, deer and other animals — on the wall of his cave and colored them with earth and vegetable dyes. Several factors — some aesthetic, some spiritual or magical — may have led to the creation of these primitive drawings. This may have been the beginning of art, but it was hardly the beginning of writing. Such pictures do not represent writing because they do not belong to a system of conventional signs and their significance can be understood only by the man who drew them or by his family and close friends who had heard of the event depicted. However, genuine writing, whether it retains a pictorial form or not, serves purely to communicate.

In the process of using pictures to identify and recall objects or beings, complete correspondence is gradually established between written signs and objects or beings. These simple pictures contain only those elements that are important for the communication of meaning and lack the embellishments that are included in an artistic representation. Since these objects and beings have names in spoken words, a correspondence is also established between the written signs and their vocal counterparts. When individual signs are used to express individual words and syllables, it can lead to the development of a system of word signs; that is, script or logography. In logography, one sign or a combination of signs expresses one word or a combination of words. However, pure logography is not found in any known system of writing. It exists normally only in conjunction with syllabography or syllabic writing, as best represented in logo-syllabic writing.

Logo-syllabic writing, that is, writing with signs express that words and syllables, is found in the East, including continental Asia from the eastern shores of the Mediterranean Sea to the western shores of the Pacific Ocean. Egypt and the area of the Aegean Sea, at least in the pre-Hellenic period, are included within the orbit of Oriental civilizations.

This large area is home to seven original and fully developed logo-syllabic systems of writing: Sumerian in Mesopotamia, 3100 BC to AD 75; Proto-Elamite in Elam, 3000 to 2200 BC; Proto-Indic in the Indus Valley, around 2200 BC; Egyptian in Egypt, 3000 BC to AD 400; Cretan in Crete and Greece, 2000 to 1200 BC; Hittite in Anatolia and Syria, 1500 to 700 BC; and Chinese in China, 1300 BC to the present. Other logo-syllabic systems may exist, but at the present to the above list stands. The Proto-Armenian inscriptions discovered within the last few decades are too short and too little known to allow any safe conclusions. The mysterious Easter Island inscriptions are not writing even in the broadest sense of the word, as they are probably nothing but pictorial concoction for magical purposes. Finally, the systems of the Mayas and the Aztecs do not represent a full logo-syllabic writing system; even in their most advanced stages they never attained the level of phonographic development of the earliest stages of the Oriental systems.

Of the seven systems, three — Proto-Elamite, Proto-Indic and Cretan — are not yet deciphered. Consequently, modern understanding of the logo-syllabic systems is limited to the other four systems: Sumerian, Egyptian, Hittite and Chinese. Chinese writing is the only logo-syllabic writing system still in use today and it has developed a formidable degree of sophistication.

History does not throw much light on the beginning of Chinese writing. Chinese mythology attributes the invention of writing to *Ts'ang Chieh* 仓颉 Cāng Jié. It is said that he got his ideas from observing animals' footprints and birds' claw marks on the sand as well as other natural phenomena. We can divide the development of all Chinese characters into three stages, which overlap: Ideography, phonetic borrowing, and picto-phonetic writing.

Ideography is the earliest stage, the forerunner of writing. It consists of a drawing or a combination of drawings to represent the thing or action shown. The drawings are simple and give a clear impression as a memory-aid device. Samples of these devices can be found all over the globe. The following Chinese ideographic characters are good examples: 木 mù stands for a *tree*, 鱼 yú for a *fish*, 虫 chóng for a *snake*, and 射 shè, literally *to shoot*, is the combination of a hand and the bow and arrow. The number of ideographic characters in Chinese writing system is limited. However, the surviving ideographs have static and definite meanings with simple but distinctive strokes. They are basic and easy to understand and many of them, especially the pictographs of single objects, are used as *radicals* in the Chinese writing.

Ideography is a natural method, but a complete system of ideographs has probably never existed either in antiquity or in modern times. To create and memorize thousands of signs for newly acquired words and names is so impracticable that ideographic writing either can be used only as a very limited system, or it must be adapted in some new way in order to develop into a useful system.

Phonetic borrowing is the second stage. The number of function words and abstract nouns is very limited, but they are used frequently and difficult to draw or show. Therefore, signs for function words and abstract nouns were borrowed from the ideographs with similar pronunciation. Such signs should also be simple and distinct. A borrowed character should

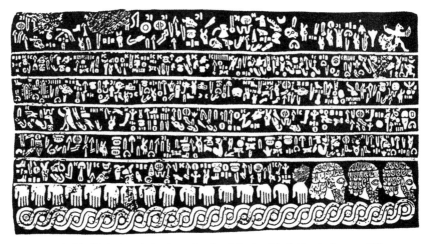

Copy of a hieroglyphic Hittite inscription from the site of Carchemish (*after Renfrew*, *p.* 48).
赫梯语象形文字(卡尔凯美什遗址)。

Word-Signs on Potsherds 陶器上的刻画符号

上：西安半坡　下：临潼姜寨

仰韶文化（5000~3000 B.C.）

马家窑文化（3300~2500 B.C.）

have few strokes; and if the borrowed ideograph was not obsolete, it should have its original meaning restored by adding an auxiliary element to distinguish the new character from its original borrowed pictorial form. These borrowed ideographs are called Phonetic Loan Characters (PLC) in this book. The phonetic loan characters can be regarded as symbols. However, in many cases there are semantic connections between the original and the borrowed forms. Let's see some examples:

北 běi, literally *north*, is borrowed from an ideograph of two figures back to back. The *north* may derive from the fact that early man sat facing the sun to the south with his back to the north, thus 北 běi is a PLC. The word for *back* is 背 bèi, adding a *human body*-radical below.

自 zì, literally *self* and *from*, is borrowed from the pictograph of a nose. Both *self* and *from* are difficult to express using drawings. Here, *self* may derive from a man pointing at his nose to express *himself*, and the character was also adopted to indicate the abstract concept *from*. 自 zì thus is a PLC. The word 鼻 bí, *nose*, includes the pictorial element 自 zì and a phonetic element 畀 bì below.

Finally, 枼 yè, meaning thin, derives from a pictograph of a tree with leaves, while 葉=叶 yè, meaning leaf, a *plant*-radical on the top. Note that since antiquity, many of the pronunciations have changed, so that the original *borrowed* and *returned* forms no longer sound alike sometimes.

The adoption of the borrowing method in the Chinese writing system was a watershed transition from memory-aid picture writing to practical logo-syllabic writing. As in the societies become more developed, more and more objects and beings were named more precisely. Therefore, picto-phonetic characters or pictophones emerged.

A picto-phonetic character consists of at least two parts: one part refers to the meaning of the character and is usually called the radical; the other, the phonetic element, gives the sound. In most cases, the phonetic element also has meaning value as a *picto-phonetic* element. The following examples are similar to rebus writing: 蝶 dié and 鰈 dié, literally butterfly and flounder, with the *worm* and *fish* radicals respectively, and the picto-phonetic element 枼 yè: thin. This is the last stage of development. Picto-phonetic characters comprise about ninety to ninety-five percent of all Chinese characters. Today, the number of characters is almost fixed. When the Chinese needed to introduce a word from another language, they use a combination of characters to form a new Chinese word, e.g., 吉普 jípǔ for *jeep*, 浪漫 làngmàn for *romance*, 歇斯底里 xiēsīdǐlǐ for *hysteria*, 激光 jīguāng in mainland China or 镭射 léishè for *laser*.

Whether borrowed or created, a character generally begins its life in Chinese with one meaning and its ancient pronunciation. Yet no living language is stagnant, and in time words develop new pronunciations or meanings and lose old ones. However, the forms of the ideographic characters are somewhat quiescent, especially the pictographs which derive the letters of Chinese from common objects or beings. This book will show you a large sample of these fascinating characters.

A look at the origins of the characters making up the Chinese writing system involves a look also at the origins of the Chinese civilization. The early history of both China and the Chinese dates from the Neolithic period (about 5000 BC) to the *Han* Dynasty (206 BC to AD 220), including the *Shang* Dynasty (1523 to 1028 BC) and the *Zhou* Dynasty (1027 to 221 BC). By the *Han* Dynasty, the number and forms of common characters were fixed on the whole.

Etymology is not an exact science. Often we are unable to discover the origin of a character, but more often there are multiple genetic stories for one character. Ingenious etymological theories are put forward frequently, some plausible and attractive, others wildly improbable. I have chosen the most likely explanations to be included in this book because the purpose of the book is not to introduce scholarly debates but to serve as a new way to learn Chinese characters. A picture is worth one thousand words. The origins and histories of Chinese characters should be not the missing piece in the Chinese puzzle, but a key to resolving the puzzle.

Some Chinese characters have been simplified as *Jianhuazi* 简化字, and these simplified forms are used in mainland China. But, the ancient form of Chinese characters must be referred to in such a book as this. And although the explanations for each entry are bilingual, they are not equivalent, the Chinese part being simpler with easy characters. For transcription, the Chinese phonetic, alphabet, or *pinyin* 拼音 as it is known, has been used with *four-tones* 四声 in this book.

INSCRIPTIONS

甲 **Shell and bone character** Inscriptions were carved on oracle bones with practical and angular strokes, *Shang* Dynasty.

金 **Bronze character** Inscriptions are found on bronze vessels of the *Shang* and *Zhou* Dynasties. Bronze characters derive from prehistoric picture writing, and their lines are smooth yet forceful.

古 **Ancient character** Inscriptions, which appear on the surface of bamboo, stone, pottery or ancient seals, were used mainly during the Warring States Period (475-221 BC).

篆 **Seal character** A kind of standard or decorative character which appeared in the *Qin* Dynasty (221-207 BC).

参 **For reference**

Hongyuan WANG

December 1991

Chapter 1

MAN 人类

The first inhabitants on Chinese soil whose remains are known to us were the race to which Yuanmou Man belonged 1,700,000 years ago. However, Peking Man is more famous, and it was the focus of worldwide attention in 1927. Peking Man was later and more "human" than Java Man. Peking Man's bones were firstly discovered by Professor Pei Wenzhong at *Zhoukoudian* near Beijing. Unfortunately, all the *Zhoukoudian* hominid remains disappeared when being transferred from Peking to an American ship during the Japanese invasion of China prior to the Second World War. In Chinese characters, the form of a standing man means "great", perhaps because standing was a great feat in man's evolution.

中国大地上埋藏有十分丰富的古人类化石和旧石器时代遗物,至今已发现的早、中、晚各个时期的地点共 200 多处,包括直立人、早期智人、晚期智人各个阶段的人类化石。这当中据认为最早的为距今 180 万年的西侯度文化(山西省)和距今 170 万年的元谋人*(云南省)。1927 年裴文中教授在北京周口店发现的北京人则是最早发现,最具有影响的中国直立人。不幸的是,大量极其珍贵的北京人遗物,包括五个头盖骨和其它骨和牙齿标本在太平洋战争爆发前,全部在几个美国人手里弄得下落不明。

Figures in rock art
岩画中所见人形

* 系根据古地磁学测定的数值。1983 年有人对此提出不同见解,认为元谋人化石年代不超过 73 万年,可能距今 50 至 60 万年。北京人距今 70 至 20 万年。

1.1 **Man's Body** 身体

rén

4EBA — man, person.

认=認rèn；從 **5F9E**=从 **4ECE**，
丛=叢cóng，苁，枞cōng；
众=眾zhòng.

A man, a figure in profile. The original form of 人 rén may reveal evolution from anthropoid apes to man. ☞ 亻 **4EBB** as radical.

人的侧视形。㐱，古文虞。㐱，古文盗。

tǐng

2123C — good; erect (archaic).

聽 **807D**.tǐng: listen；廷 **5EF7**，
庭，莛，蜓，霆tíng；挺，
艇，铤，梃tǐng.

A man standing on land. 挺tǐng: to erect; with a hand – radical which indicates a verb. 壬 **58EC**.rén is very close to 壬, and also a useful element in 妊，衽，任rèn，荏rěn. ☞ rén.1, tǔ.2.

人挺立于土地上。

wù

5140 — proud; upright; bald.

阢wù；堯 **582F**=尧 **5C27**，峣yáo；
浇jiāo；侥jiǎo；挠，蛲náo；硗，
跷qiāo；翘qiào；烧，桡，饶ráo；
绕rào；烧shāo；骁xiāo；晓xiāo.

A derivative of 人 rén.1 by adding a stroke on the man's head. 尧 yáo, a legendary monarch in ancient China around 2300 B.C., is also a useful phonetic.

人上一横。《说文》兀，高而上平也。从一在人上。尧，高也。从垚在兀上，高远也。杌，木无枝。檋杌，篆作橚杌。杌陧，不安貌，篆作黜陧、阢陧。

yuán

5143 basic, first, primary

阮ruán；玩，顽，完 **5B8C**，
烷wán；莞，皖，脘wǎn；沅，
园=園，鼋yuán；远=遠yuǎn；
埦，院yuàn.

Two strokes drawn on a man's head; a composite of the characters for man and above. ☞ 上shàng.195，人rén.1.

元字上从人头形，所以元即首（头）。元首二字重文迭义。"原来"一词原作"元来"，明灭元后，汉人忌讳"元"来，改为"原"来。

dà

大 甲 大 大 金 大 大 古 大 仐 公 篆 大 或体篆作 仆

5927 — big, great.

驮 tuó; 达 8FBE=達, 鞑 dá;
哒 dā.

A standing man with his legs apart and his arms held out.
正面直立人形。大的字形中可引申出一种胯下形，表示控制、掌握等意，参见家 jiā.82、衣 yī.25 等字。

Nourlange rock painting, Northern Territory, Australia. 澳大利亚土著岩画。

tài

太 甲 夵 金 大 古 夳 仐 篆 夳 夵 重文。或体篆作 仌

592A — greatest; too, over.

汰，酞，钛，肽，态=態 tài.

Shows one man placed over on another man. Later, the lower man was simplified as a dot. ☞ 大 dà.3.
人胯下一点。古文字大太一字。篆作夵，泰重文。

kàng

亢 甲

4EA2 — high, haughty; extreme.

伉, 抗, 炕 kàng; 杭, 航 háng;
沆 hàng; 坑、吭 kēng.

Derives from 大 dà.3, a standing man by adding stroke between the person's legs.

亢为大的加划衍生字。坑篆作 阬阬。

lì

立 甲

7ACB — stand; set up; exist; at once.

笠lì, 拉, 垃lā; 啦la; 泣qì;
位wèi; 翌, 翊yì.

Drawing of a man standing on land. 大 dà.3:

象人立于大地之上。立、位、莅古同字同音。

tiān

天 甲

5929 — overhead; sky; celestial; heaven, god; day, weather.

添tiān; 忝 5FDD, 舔tiǎn; 吞tūn.

A standing man drawn to emphasize the head or the vertex. 大 dà.3.

天即颠，即头顶。祅，俗开。焱 2164E＝燅 2168C，同皓。

shēn

身 甲

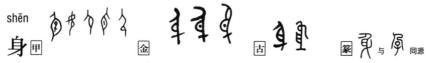

8EAB — body, life; personally.

丮 3406.yǐ: mirror image of 身.

躬 2B3EC, 俗影字。如影形随。

A side view of a man's body depicting the arm, prominent belly with navel and phallus. 身 shēn.4 is a radical that indicates the body or an action of the body. ☞ 殷 yīn.140.

象鼓腹的侧视人形。初文象大腹内有子，会妊娠之意。
后身字泛指人躯体，另造孕字，为妊娠专字。

jǐ

脊[篆] 脊 或 脊

810A — spine, backbone; ridge.

脊, 嵴, 瘠jí;
呂5442＝吕5415, 侣, 铝lǚ,
闾, 榈lú, 莒jǔ.

Drawing of a man's backbone and ribs. The lower part, 肉 ròu.128, is a radical indicating a person's body. Other useful character 吕 lǚ is believed as drawing of backbone, and a good phonetic as well.

脊《说文》本作𦟝，象人脊椎骨和肋骨形。重文从肉作𦡳。人一瘦，脊梁骨就突出了，故有"贫瘠"一词。

▶ The "X-ray" figure on a painted pottery plate, Banpo, the Neolithic.
半坡彩陶上的X光式人像。（采自《中国新石器时代陶器装饰艺术》，23页，文物出版社，1982年。）

wèi

胃[金]

80C3 — stomach

渭, 猬, 谓wèi;
膚＝肤fū; 喟kuì.

 [古] [篆] 或  [参] 甲骨文有𪚥字 或释胃

The upper part 𡇒 or 田tián.74 is said to be derived from a drawing of a stomach, and the dots or 米mǐ.45 stand for food in it. The lower 肉 ròu.128 is a radical indicating a man's body or body organs.

胃26785字上面的"𡇒211D2"源于胃中有米谷之形。

xīn

心[甲] [金] [古] [篆] 或

5FC3 — heart; feeling; center, core.

芯xīn; 沁qìn; 愛611B
＝爱7231, 嗳, 媛,
瑷, 暧ài; 蕊ruǐ;
憂＝忧, 優＝优yōu.

A primitive anatomical representation of a heart. There are two radicals derived from 心 xīn, a vertical 忄 5FC4 on the left side of a character, and a flat 小 E823 written on the bottom of a character such as 慕 mù and 恋liàn. Both of them are used in characters referring to emotions. The character double heart 忿 225F0.fǎn is uncommon, means rebellion.

象心脏轮廓形。在繁体字爱和忧中都用到了心。忿，同反。

5

yào

要

8981 — important; want to; must.

腰, 要 yāo: to ask, coerce.

Ancient pictographs of 要 yào showed two hands, 臼 jú, placed to indicate the midsection of the body. PLC, 腰yāo: waist, kidney; with the human body radical. According to Chinese tradition, the kidneys are the body's most important organs.

The second pictograph of 要 yāo portrays a woman being grasped by two hands, hence, the meaning "coerce". The upper middle part was an ancient phonetic element. Later, both the phonetic element and the hands merged in the character 西xī.59 and 女nǚ.27.

要是腰的初文, 象人双手叉腰以指示腰部, 腰乃一身之要。从女或与要挟的含义有关。古文字或释作娄 農。

shì

士

58EB — scholar-official; scholar, gentry; soldier; person.

仕shì: to be an official.

Drawing of a phallus. PLC. ☞ 牡mǔ: male (animal), 駐mǔ: stallion. Or it derives from a drawing of an ancient weapon.

象牡器之形。一说象斧钺之形。垚 **58F5**, 同牡。

jí

吉

5409 — favorable omen, good luck; propitious, auspicious; good; a surname.

佶, 诘jí; 髻jì; 洁, 结, 诘, 拮jié; 桔jú; 黠xiá; 颉, 撷xié.

A combination of 士 shì and a square.

《说文》吉, 善也。从士口。或曰士为男根之象, 口为女阴之象, 则整个字形表示男女交媾。喆=喆21547=囍, 同哲。喜2152F=喜20DAE, 同喜。

bǐ

比 [甲] ... [金] ... [古] ... 林 [篆]

6BD4 — to compare; liken to; ratio; next to.

妣，吡，粃=秕 bǐ；愍，狴，陛，庀，篦，毕=畢，毖=駜 bì；批，砒，纰 pī；琵，枇，毗，蚍 pí；仳 pǐ；屁 pì.

Shows two persons racing. ☞ 匕 bǐ.7.

象二人抬腿甩臂形，是比赛竞走赛跑的会意字。芘，古文比。毕，芘字之误，《康熙字典》臆造字。《说文》密也。二人为从，反从为比。林，古文比。

---

bǐ

匕 [甲] ... [金] ... [篆] [参] 妣 [精]

5315 — spoon.

叱 chì；牝 pìn: female.

Derived and simplified from 比 bǐ. Or drawing of a spoon. It is also a symbol for female. ☞ 妣 216A7=妣 bǐ; deceased mother, 牡 mǔ: male (animal).

匕是比字之省。或曰象人匍匐之侧形。

---

cǐ

此 [甲] ... [金] ... [古] ... [篆]

6B64 — this.

雌 cí；疵 cī；柴 chái；砦 zhài；赀，訾，觜，髭，龇 zī；紫，訾 zǐ；呲 zǐ；嘴 zuǐ.

A combination of the symbol for female 匕 bǐ.7 and a phonetic element 止 zhǐ.22. PLC, 雌 cí: female (animal), with the element of bird, 隹 zhuī. ☞ 雄 xióng: male, 匕 bǐ, 止 zhǐ.22.

此从匕止声。或谓从人从止，人足踩人之形，踩字初文。

---

yì

亦 [甲] ... [金]  [古] ... [篆]

4EA6 — also (literary form).

奕，弈 yì；迹 jì.

Drawing of a man with two dots indicating the two armpits. PLC. See below.

亦是腋字初文。人之腋下有两处，故引申义为复。参见夜 yì.8.

yè

夜 金 古  篆

591C — night, evening.

液，腋，掖yè.

A pictophone: 夕xī.33: night, is the meaning element, and 亦yì.7 phonetic. PLC, 腋yè: armpit, with the human body radical. ☞ 肉 ròu.128.

夕意亦声。鸟朝鸣曰嘲，夜鸣曰啼。

jiāo

交 甲 金 古 篆

4EA4 — to cross, intersect: meet, join: hand over: acquaintance: mutual.

郊，茭，姣，蛟，跤，鲛，胶=膠jiāo；
皎，狡，饺，铰，佼，绞jiǎo；较，
校jiào；效，校xiào；咬yǎo.

Drawing of a man crossing his legs. ☞ 大dà.3.

人两腿交互形。交会之交篆作这。从交之字或有小之意。狡，少狗。胶，小瓜。筊，小籫。

bèi

北 甲 金 古 篆

5317 — north.

背bēi: to carry on one's back；
背，褙bèi.

Shows two sitting back to back. PLC, 背bèi: to turn one's back on, the back of the body; with the human body radical. The Chinese emperor traditionally sat facing the sun to the south, with his back to the north. 悲kǒng: fear, 同恐, used in Buddhist sacred literature. ☞ 人rén.1, 匕bǐ.7, 肉ròu.128.

北为古背字，二人相背形。古人背北面南而坐，房屋坐北朝南而建。

zuò

坐 甲 古 坐 坐 坐 说文古文作 篆

5750 — to sit.

座zuò: seat；
矬，痤cuó；
挫，锉cuò.

A man sitting down on his knees, and later the glyph shows two persons 卪20A0E.zhuàn sitting on the ground 土 tǔ.74.

甲骨文坐字，象人跪坐于席上。后从卪从土。人坐则身体弯曲，故从坐之字多有曲折、不平之意，如剉，折伤，摧折，今用挫、锉字。莝，斩刍。嵯，山崩。痤，小肿。古坐字源于跪坐，跪即是坐，危是跪字初文。《上博简·四·柬大王泊旱.17》社稷吕逤2B429與，读若社稷以危欤。坐字或体较多：坐坐坐坐坐坐坐坐。

yǒng

永

6C38 — perpetually, forever, always.

泳，咏 yǒng.

Depicts a man swimming. PLC, 泳 yǒng: swim: with an additional water radical. ☞ 水 shuǐ, 人 rén.1, 彳 chì.

象人水中游泳形。彳是表示动作的符号。从永之字多有长之意。詠，长言。昶，日长。羕，水长。

jié

卩

5369 — archaic character

叩 kòu: kowtow; 節 = 节 jié, jié; 疖 jié; 即 jí.127.

Drawing of a kneeling or sitting man. ☞ 人 rén.1.

象人双膝跪坐形。古文字膝从卩作桼。叩问字篆作訆。卪 2A701.fú, 斩首之象，金文伐字。

ní

尼

5C3C — Buddhist nun.

妮 nī; 妮，泥，呢，怩，铌 ní; 旎 nǐ; 泥，昵，伲 nì.

参 孔子名丘，字仲尼，仲尼字篆作昵

Shows two people close together. PLC, 昵 nì: close, intimate; here the 日 rì, the sun, means warmth. ☞ 人 rén.1, 尸 shī, 匕 bǐ.7.

尼象两人相昵形。从尼之字多有迟滞之意。泥，水滞陷。詏，言不通。柅，车下止轮物。

Clan Insignias on Bronze Vessels

1.2 Face 面部

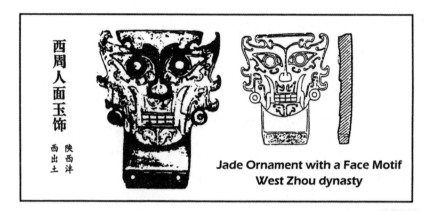

西周人面玉饰
陕西沣西出土

Jade Ornament with a Face Motif
West Zhou dynasty

---

xìn

參 甲骨文有 田字，音怕，鬼頭，或釋作囟。鬼、畏、禺从由。 从囟得聲

56DF — 囟门 xìnmén: fontanelle.
腦=脑，恼=恼，瑙nǎo；思，綗
锶sī；鰓，腮sāi；蔥xǐ；细xì.

Drawing of a human skull. 𦥯 nǎo, head with hair, is the ancient form of 腦=脑: brain, and 恖 sī: think, take the pictophonetic 囟 as an element for cerebrum.

人头颅形。恖、綗并从囟得声，今作思、细。

---

miàn

面甲 古

篆 㬎 圖，面 參 甲骨文 兒，古貌字。白象人面形

9762 — face; surface; aspect; side.
麵=面 miàn；湎，缅，腼 miǎn.

An attempt of drawing a man's face 百 shǒu, and 囗 wéi shows the range of face ☞ 目 mù.11: eye; 首 shǒu.11.

人面目形。《说文》本作圖或面。䩉 huì, 面肥貌。

---

yè

頁=页甲

金 古 篆 參 須

9801=9875 — page; leaf.
须 xū: heard, mustache;
嚣 xiāo: clamor.

A man drawn to emphasize the face. ☞ 首 shǒu.11.

强调人首的人形。顔 4B6D=䫂 2982C=警 29836.shǒu，人初产子。
又頯 2950A俗願。敦煌.P.2160《摩訶摩耶經》唯頯降法雨，
洽潤於枯槁。又贔，俗晶 bì。

shǒu

首 甲 金 古 篆

9996 — head; leader; first; a (song or poem).

道dào; 導=导dǎo.

An attempt of drawing a man's head, including the eye and the scalp. ☞ 目mù.11.

象人首侧视形，上部为毛发。猶，篆文首，省作百。

yāo

夭 甲 金 古 篆 参 妖，女子笑貌，篆作㛩

592D — tender, gentle; young.

祅ǎo; 沃wò; 误wù; 娱. 虞yú; 喬=乔qiáo.

A person walking or running, and the similar 矢zè shows the actions of the head. As an element, 夭yāo refers to facial expressions such as 妖yāo: seductively charming, and 笑xiào: to laugh. Meanwhile, 矢zè or 吴=吴wú: surname, is useful in 娱=娱yú: amusement, pleasure. ☞ 大dà.3.

矢，人倾头形。夭，人奔走貌，走字初文。妖怪字，篆作㛩。

máo

毛 金 篆

6BDB — hair, feather, down; wool; a surname.

牦，旄，氂máo; 笔=筆bǐ; 蚝háo; 耗hào; 尾wěi.

Drawing of a person's hair. ☞ 长cháng.28, 手shǒu.17.

毛发形。毳6BF3.cuì，鸟兽的细毛。氄fěi，毛纷纷。氂字很早就用同橇qiāo。《汉书》记载，大禹：过家不入门，陆行载车，水行乘舟，泥行乘氂。又北周天和二年 AD.567《华岳庙碑》有铭文：乘氂驾风。

mù

目 甲 金 古 篆

76EE — eye.

苜，钼mù; 盲máng; 看kàn, 从手下目; 省xǐng, shěng.

A man's eye, and it's a radical as well. Double eyes 眮4020.jù: look around, is interesting, and its variant 瞿 with a bird 隹zhuī.56 is a useful phonetic in 懼=惧jù: fear. ☞ 臣chén.159.

眼目形。眮，左右视。瞿，鹰隼之视。矍qú，走顾貌。㬮 7790.mò =㬰262F9，美目深邃。瞏25132.mié，目小。矒2525E.méng，目不明。

jiàn

見 = 见 甲 金 古 篆 参见篆作睍

898B=89C1 — to see; meet with; opinion.

觅mì; 蚬xiǎn; 苋, 现xiàn; 砚yàn; 舰=艦jiàn.

A man who opens his eyes to see. Compare with 看kàn: to look, the 目mù.11: eye, is under the hand 手shǒu.17, which means to use the eye. ☞ 人rén.1: man.

象人突出眼睛，前视有所见。觅或作𥄂=𥄂，俗作覔。

gèn

艮 甲 金 古 篆 参 金文限 限

826E — straightforward; tough.

根, 跟gēn; 痕hén; 很, 狠hěn; 恨hèn; 腿tuǐ; 退tuì; 限xiàn; 眼yǎn; 银, 垠, 龈yín.

A man looking back. 艮 or ☷2636 is one of the eight diagrams for divination used in *The Book of Changes* 《易经》, and it stands for mountain. ☞ 目mù.11, 人rén.1.

人回顾形。《说文》匕目为艮，七目为𥆞（真）。

tà

眔 甲 金 古 篆

7714 — and (archaic character).

懷=怀huái: to think of; 鰥guān: widower; widowered.

Picture of an eye shedding tears. ☞ 目mù.11, 泪lèi: tear.

象垂涕的眼形。眔《说文》作𥃲𥃲，众词与也。

zì

自 甲 金 古 篆

81EA — self, oneself: from; personal.

洎jì; 咱zán; 鼻bí.

Drawing of a nose seen from the front with nostrils and a bridge. PLC, 鼻bí: nose; pictophonetic, 畀bì.

鼻正视形。自、鼻古同字。

sì

四 甲 金 古 篆

56DB — four.

泗: nasal mucus, 驷:
a team of four horses,
牭: cattle at the age of
four, 柶sì; 恤xì.

The original form or number four is 三, just following the idea of
一、二、三. Later, 四sì, is borrowed from the drawing of the nostrils
and the sound of breathing, that is, when you blow your nose, you got
the number 4. PLC, 呬: breath.

四借鼻孔的形, 鼻息的声。三, 金文, 积画成四。呬罒, 古
文。囚図, 俗体。

kǒu

口 甲 金 古 篆

53E3 — mouth;
opening; stoma;
cut, hole;
population.

叩, 扣, 筘kòu;
曰yuē: say,
叫xuān: noisy,
哭kū: cry,
喪=丧sàng: lose.

A mouth with happy corners. As an element, is borrowed to represent
"speak" and "sound" which are difficult to depict. The square 口 is a wild
card, which generally appears in one of every five Chinese characters. In
some ancient writings, the square 口 is also represented certain round things
such as a pot 曾céng.124, a melon 瓜guā.44 or the head of a baby 子zǐ.26. But
in the modern character forms, these "squares" were replaced with 曰 or a
triangle 厶 in order to avoid the confusion with the "mouth". Meanwhile,
in the characters 蠚=圍wéi: surround, encircle; 聭zhēng: conquest; 甼dìng:
occupy, settle down; 或huò the original form of 域yù: region, the square 口
stands for the 邑yì.96 or city, town obviously. However, Chinese people
have the similar radical 囗wéi to be the element for the meaning of territory,
domain, or range.

口在汉字中出现的几率约为 20%, 不仅是表示语言和声音偏旁,
作为部件, 也用来表示圆形物体或疆域, 如品、员、邑、域。

gān

甘 甲 金 古 篆

7518 — sweet; willingly.

绀gàn; 坩, 苷, 泔, 柑, 疳gān;
蚶, 酣hān : intoxicated, heated
with wine; 邯hán; 钳=拑, 箝,
黚qián; 甜tián.

Depicts a mouth with something in it. ☞ 口kǒu.

口含美味之物。酣hān, 酒乐。甛tián, 美也。甚=
甚shèn, 尤安乐也。从甘。香=香xiāng, 芳也。从黍
从甘。楳méi=梅=呆=某mǒu.46, 酸果也。从木从甘。

shé

820C — tongue.

甜，恬 tián；栝 tiǎn；敌=敵 dí；
適=适 shì；昏，颳=刮=刮，
鴰=鸹 guā；聒=聒 guō；語=
话 huà；湉=活 huó；栝=括，
閼=阔 kuò。

A tongue protruding from mouth 口 kǒu.13.

伸出口外的歧舌形。舐 shì，以舌取食。舓，同猻 tà，狗
吃食。舐，古文舌。郭店楚墓竹簡《语丛四.19》若齿
之事舐。后舌与昏 guā 字混同，如颳、語、湉等，作刮、
话、活。舔舐，篆作西舓。嚥，囫囵吞下，篆作舓。

yán

8A00 — speech, world;
to say, talk, speak.

喭 yàn；信 xìn；狺 yín；
這=这 zhè, zhèi.

A combination of 一 yī.192 and 舌 shé, probably the above stroke is just
a symbol to indicate the silver tongue. ☞ 讠 8BA0 or 言 8A01 as radical.
誩 8AA9.jìng: argue, 譶 27B5B=嚞 8B76=譶 27BA6.là: speak quickly.

言是舌的加划衍生字。《说文》认为言从口辛 yǎn 声。

yīn

97F3 — sound; news; tone.

喑，喑 yīn；谙 ān；暗，
黯 àn: aterrimus；歆 xīn.

音 yīn.14 and 言 yán are cognate characters.

音言同源。从音之字多有黑、暗之意。窨，地室。暗，覆
盖。湆，幽暗潮湿。闇，闭门。䪭 4AAD=䪃 29418. ruǎn 五弦琴。

qiàn

6B20 — to yawn; owe; lacking.

吹，炊 chuī；坎，砍 kǎn；钦 qīn；饮 yǐn；
歡=欢 huān.

A man opening his mouth to yawn. ☞ 人 rén.1,
兄 xiōng.188.

象人张口打呵欠。欽 qīn，打喷嚏。㰥，古文欠。

cì

次 甲 ⋯ 金 ⋯ 古 蔺说文古文 汉印 篆 ⋯

14

6B21 — second; order, sequence; next; inferior, second-rate.

茨，瓷cí; 资，姿，咨，恣zī; 次，羡xiàn: envy, 盗=盜dào: steal.

Depicts a man sneezing or drooling. PLC. ☞ 欠qiàn.14.

象人张口打喷嚏。古文字次、次xiàn同字。次，慕欲口液也。羡 盗 从次。造次字篆作造赿。

duì

兊=兑 甲 金 古 篆

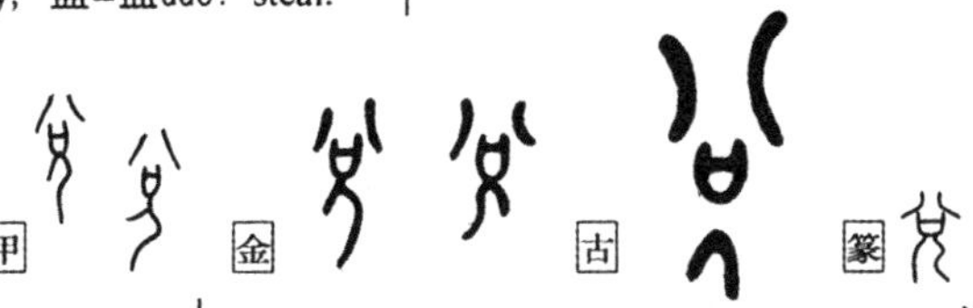

514C = 5151

—exchange, to cash.

锐ruì; 税，说shuì; 说shuō; 蜕tuì; 脱tuō; 悦，阅yuè.

Shows a man opening mouth to speak. PLC, 说shuō: to say. ☞ 人rén.1, 兄xiōng.188, 口kǒu.13, 八bā.85. 兊 duì or ☱2631 is one of the eight diagrams for divination used in *The Book of Changes* 《易经》yìjīng, and it stands for lakes and wet land.

兑表示人张口说话。八有分意，从兊之字多有解脱、开释之意。《说文》兊，说（悦）也。

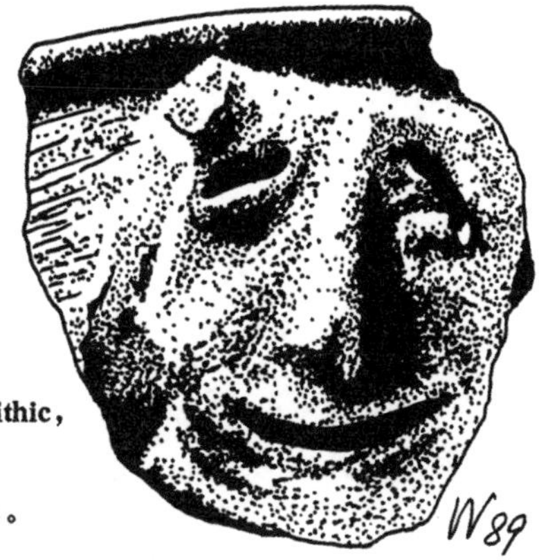

▶ **A potsherd with a human face motif, the Neolithic, Shaanxi Province.**

瓮口沿下堆塑人面像，仰韶文化，陕西扶风出土。

ěr

耳 甲 金 古 篆

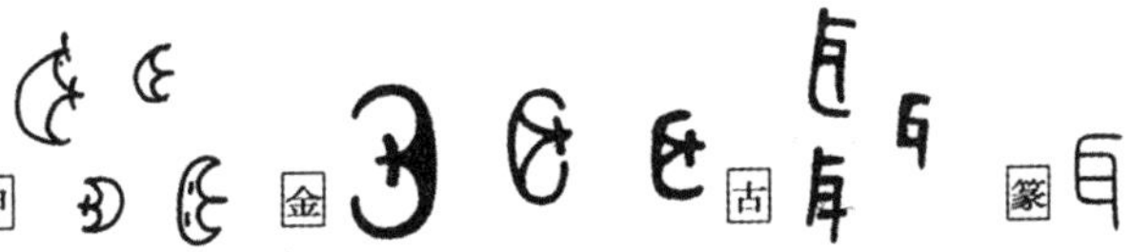

8033—ear.

饵，铒，珥ěr; 弭mí; 茸róng; 聶=聂，颞，镊，嗫，蹑niè; 摄，慑shè; 缉jī; 楫，揖jí; 葺qì.

Drawing of a person's ear. 耳ěr is a radical for auricular or hearing, and all the following characters, 聲=声shēng: sound; 聽=听tīng: hear; and 闻wén: well-known, news, take the 耳 as element.

象耳形。耳，聽=听字初文。耵tīng，俗听。用耳为听。聑tiē，妥帖。咠qì，聂语，附耳私语。刵èr，断耳。聊liáo，耳鸣。耴zhé，耳垂。耿gěng，耳朵贴着面颊。𦗏zhé，耳竖貌。

méi

眉 甲 金 古 篆 参 媚

7709 — eyebrow.

湄, 镅, 猸, 楣: lintel (over a door), 鹛: babbler, 嵋méi; 媚mèi.

Drawing of an eye with an eyebrow 尸. ☞ 目mù.11.

象目上眉毛形。蝞mèi，古代传说中的一种蛊虫，似虾，寄生龟壳中，食之颜色有爱媚。

ér

而 甲 金 古 篆

800C — moreover; and.

耍shuǎ; 耐nài: pondering about.

而ér was derived from a drawing of a beard. PLC. 髵ér: beard. ☞ 须xū: beard and mustache. Someone believes that 而ér is a drawing of scalp, taken from an enemy in battlefield.

下巴上的胡子。或以为象剥离倒置的头皮形。上古有剥敌方头皮的风俗，用以炫耀或挑衅。古战场取耳为聝 805D，取首为馘 9998。

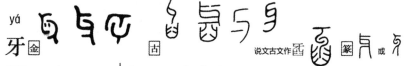

yá

牙 金 古 说文古文作𠈃 篆 或

7259 — tooth.

芽, 蚜yá; 呀ya; 呀, 鸦yā; 雅yǎ; 砑, 迓, 讶yà; 穿chuān.

Portrays a pair of molars.

一对臼齿咬合形。𠈃，古文牙从臼。𠈃𠈃𠈃𠈃邪，並同古文牙。琅邪yá，也作琅琊，郡名。邪xié正之邪，篆作衺。

chǐ

齒 = 齿 甲 金 古 篆

9F52＝9F7F — tooth; gear.

啮niè: to gnaw.

The glyph 𤘈 is from the drawing of frontal incisors. The upper part 止 zhǐ.22 is a phonetic. 齿 is a radical. ☞ 口kǒu.13.

口中门齿形。后加止为声符，𤘈为古齿字。

16

1. 3　Hands and Feet　手与足

▶ **Handprints in rock painting**
岩画中所见手印

1. 3. 1—Hands　手

shǒu

手 金  古 篆

624B — hand.

掰 bāi: break off with
the fingers and thumb;
拜 bài: 看 kàn, 从手下
目, 或从 臶 声作 鞊;
扒 pá 手 = 扒手: thief.

Drawing of a left hand with five fingers. In prehistoric cave or rock art, the painted hands were mostly left hands, since early artists usually preferred to use their right hands to paint, leaving only the left hands to copy. ☞ 扌 624C as radical, 毛 máo.11: hair.

象手之形。史前艺术中凡出现手的形象时多为左手，这是因为先民使用右手来画左手的形状。𦳊 21D24 𡥀 200BF，并古文手。

yòu

又 甲 金 古 篆

53C8 — also, too.

驭 yù: to drive (a carriage):
叕 zhuó; 缀 zhuì; 辍 chuò.

Shows the right hand and it's action. PLC. ☞ 寸 cùn, 右 yòu.20, 有 yòu.128. 叐 355B = 友 53C8.yǒu: friend.

右手侧视形。叐，同 嚣、龆，籀文若，择也。

cùn

寸 古 篆

5BF8 — cun, a unit of length
= 1/3 decimeter; very short.

村 cūn; 忖 cǔn; 衬 chèn;
守 shǒu; 狩 shòu; 讨 tǎo;
肘 zhǒu; 纣 zhòu.

Derived from 又 yòu, and the short stroke or dot indicated the width of a finger, an ancient unit of length. Today, the lengths of cun, 尺 chǐ.18: chi and 丈 zhàng: zhang are approximately double.

寸源于又，短横或点表示一个手指的宽度，即远古时期一寸的长度。村，篆文作邨。

chǐ

5C3A — *chi*, a unit of length (=10 cun).

迟=遲chí; 咫zhǐ: eight *cun* in *Zhou* Dynasty.

Indicates a hand-span. Similar to the British who used the foot for measuring, early Chinese used the hand and arms to measure. The *chi*, one hand-span, is a basic unit of length. ☞ 寸cùn.

布手知尺。人左手拇指和食指拃开的长度为尺，也即为尺字之象。古文字或借用斥字作尺字。尺在尸部。

zhàng

4E08 — *zhang*, a unit of length *(=10 chi)*; fathom; measure.

仗，杖zhàng.

The combination of 十shí: ten and 又yòu.17: action of hand. 丈 zhàng meant ten hand-spans, or the fathom of two arms as a unite of length for early Chinese. ☞ 尺chǐ.18, 又yòu.17.

《说文》丈，十尺也。即十尺（拃）之意。丈是人横向伸开两只手臂的宽度，等于十拃。仗篆作杖。丈在一部。

bā

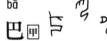

5DF4 — to hope earnestly; be close to.

芭，吧，笆bā; 吧ba; 把，钯，靶bǎ; 耙，爸bà; 葩pā; 杷，爬，耙，琶pá.

Shows a hand palm down. The traditional explanation is that 巴bā derives from the drawing of a python. PLC.

象巴掌形。一说巴象蛇形。巳22033，同巴，碑别字。肥féi 字本从肉从 ？作肥，古文肥字或从女作 妃，即妃字，从巴的肥字是俗写。巴在己部。

bái

767D — write.

百，柏bǎi; 柏，伯，泊，舶，铂，箔，泉，魄bó; 啪pā; 帕，怕pò; 拍pāi; 珀，迫，粕，魄pò.

A thumb. PLC. 樂yuè.178: stringed instruments, with the glyph of finger in the upper middle part. 白 is a radical.

象拇指之形。拇为将指，居首位，故白古文同伯仲之伯。一说象人面貌之形。帕，同白。晶 xiǎo，明。

dù

度 甲 金 古 篆

5EA6 — measure; limit; spend, pass; consideration; degree, a unit of measurement for angles, temperature etc.

渡, 镀dù; 度, 踱duó.

The essential part of 度dù is 又yòu.17, the hand action. The hand was an important unit of measurement. 庶shù.118 without the bottom dots, as the phonetic, was from 石shí.175.
☞ 尺chǐ.18, 庹tuǒ: fathom.

从又石声, 用手拃量之意。砭, 古文度。㦤, 忖㦤。

sì

寺 金 古 篆

5BFA — temple.

特tè; 等děng; 待dài; 诗shī; 峙, 痔zhì; 時=时, 鲥shí, 莳; 侍, 恃shì.

A derivative of meaning element 又yòu.17: hand, or its variant 寸cùn, and the phonetic 之zhī.23: foot, or later 止zhǐ.22: stop. The phonetic is also the meaning for the PLC 持chí: to hold, grasp; with a hand-radical. The picto-phonetic 止 was incorrectly substituted by 土tǔ.

寺从寸之聲, 是持的本字。古文从又之声。㞢=志, 从心之声。

yú

舁 篆

8201 — (of two or more persons) to carry.

舆, 與=与yú; 与, 屿yǔ; 譽=誉yù; 興=兴xīng.107.

Shows two persons (four hands) carrying something together. The upper part 臼jū is shown two hands, and as a radical, it was merged into the similar 臼jiù.79. The lower part 廾=収gǒng is also a radical for the meaning of using two hands. ☞ 舉=举jǔ: to lift, raise, with a bottom hand-radical 手shǒu.17, and 兵bīng.160.

四手抬物。《说文》舁, 共举。从臼从収。臼、収, 二人四手。

fǎn

反 甲 金 古 篆

53CD — to turn over; in the opposite direction.

返fǎn; 販, 畈, 饭fàn; 扳bān: pull; 阪, 坂, 板, 钣, 版, 舨bǎn; 皈guī; 叛pàn.

Shows a hand climbing up a cliff. PLC.
☞ 樊fán.22, 厂hàn.38, 又yòu.17.

以手攀崖。经典用作翻转义, 或借其音。

zhǎo

722A — claw, talon, paw.

抓zhuā; 爪 zhuǎ; 蚤=蚤 zǎo: flea.

Shows a hand grabbing something. It is a radical indicating grabbing, written at the top of a character. PLC, 抓zhuā: to grab, catch. ☞ 丑chǒu, 又yòu.17, 叉=爪, finger nail, 又chā. 巵=睪 chà, the sound of clawing.

象覆手形。仉 zhǎng，姓，系爪字的讹变。𧶛，古文得，从手抓贝。

lì

力

529B — power, strength, ability, force.

荔=協: to do sth. jointly, 脅=胁 xié; 历=歷 lì.

Glyph of a man's arm. It is also said to be an plow. ☞ 又yòu.17.

传统的解释为力象人手及臂形。一说力象耒的侧视形，耜字初文。使用耒掘土耕地须用力。持帚为妇，田力为男。加=刕=从。荔=協=协，同力。趰 xiàn 走貌。嫐 xiàn 好貌。

yòu

右

53F3 — right.

佑: to help, 祐: to bless, protect (family, people) yòu.

Derived from 又yòu.17 by adding 口kǒu.13 as a symbol in order to distinguish from 又yòu. PLC, 佑: to help.

右源于又，又右同字。《说文》右，手口相助也。

zuǒ

左

5DE6 — left.

佐zuǒ; 差chā, 槎chá; 差chà; 差chāi; 瘥chài; 差cǐ; 搓, 磋, 蹉cuō; 嵯cuó; 嗟jiē; 隋, 隨=随suí; 墮=堕duò; 橢=椭tuǒ; 髓suǐ.

Shows the left hand 屮 zuǒ. 工gōng.102, in the lower part, is a symbol of a tool. PLC. ☞ 佐zuǒ: an assistant; with a person-radical, 又yòu.17.

屮象左手形，金文加言、口、工，系记号，以区分左、右二字。差，籀文左。𢀳，古文差。

zhēng

爭＝争 甲 古 金文静

722D＝4E89 — to contend, strive, dispute.

挣，峥，狰，筝，睁，铮 zhēng；
挣，诤 zhèng；净，静 jìng.

Shows two hands coiling rope. PLC, 絟 zhēng: coil rope, with a radical 糸 mì.93. ☞ 爪 zhǎo, 又 yòu.17.

象两手持绳盘绕之形。或谓象两手争物之形。

yuán

爰 甲 金 古 篆

7230 — then, therefore.

援，媛 yuán；媛 yuàn；
锾 huán；缓 huǎn；暖 nuǎn.

Shows a person holding a stick or rope to rescue another person. PLC, 援 yuán: to pull by hand; help. ☞ 爭 zhēng, 又 yòu.17.

象两人以物相援引形。

gōng

厷 甲 金 古 篆 参 肱

53B7 — forearm (archaic).

宏: great, 弘, 泓 hóng；郊 qiè；
雄 xióng: male, imposing.

The 厶 sī in the character shows a man's biceps. PLC, 肱 gōng: the forearm; with a human body radical 肉 ròu.128.

臂上肱部。《毛公鼎》有厷厄一辞，讀若鞃軶，用皮革裹衬之軶。《師詢簋》叐厷先王，股肱先王。

dòu

鬥＝斗 甲 篆

9B25＝6597
— to fight.

鬧＝闹 nào: noisy, stir up trouble.

Shows two people wrestling. 鬥 is a radical, but Chinese prefer to use 門 mén.135 to replace it, and in 1964, 鬥 is simplified as 斗 dòu.122, with all its variants 鬭、鬫、鬪、鬮、鬦、鬬、鬧、鬩、鬨、閗、鬥、鬧、鬭、鬪、鬩、鬧、鬮 merged into 斗 dòu.

两人打斗形。《说文》鬥，两士相对，兵杖在后，象鬥之形。

chā

叉 篆

53C9 — fork, cross.

杈chā; 祃, 又chǎ;
汉, 杈chà; 钗chāi.

A hand, with the dots indicating the fingernails. ☞ 又yòu.17.

象手叉取物形。"一"表示手指所叉取之物。义，同叉。

chǒu

丑 甲   金   古   篆

4E11 — number two of the
duodecimal cycle; a clown.

妞niǔ; 扭, 忸, 狃, 纽, 钮niǔ.

Drawing of a claw. PLC, 扭 niǔ: twist, with radical of
hand 扌. ☞ 又yòu.17, 手shǒu.17, 爪zhǎo.

从又作屈指用力形。忸怩字篆作恧。

fán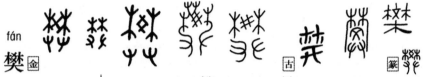

樊 金   古   篆

6A0A — a surname;
bird cage.

樊=矾fán; 攀pān.

Climbing the hedge 棥 fán by hands. 棥 is the phonetic as well. The
lower 大dà.3: derives from a depiction of both hands 廾=収gǒng. PLC,
攀pān: climb; with a bottom radical of 手shǒu.17: hand. ☞ 林lín: forest.

用双手攀爬藩篱。棥，藩屏。礬=鄨fán，古乡名。

1.3.2—Feet 足

zhǐ

止 甲   金   古   篆

6B62 — to stop; only.

址, 芷, 趾, 祉zhǐ;
扯chě; 企qǐ; 志zhì;
寺sì; 齿chǐ.

Footprint. PLC, 趾 zhǐ: toe. It's a radical for foot or movement.

象人足有趾形。踄=蹼=㴽=崇=坒=澁=澀=涩。址，俗址=
癶 bō。登發从癶。

▶ **An inscription of foot on a pottery
fragment, Shang period.**

陶文·止。商代。

zhī

之 甲 金 古 篆

4E4B — to go; of.

芝zhī.

Foot 止zhǐ.22 on the ground, that is on the way to go. 止 is the phonetic as well. Later 之 was borrowed to be a function world.

从止从一。以足踏地，会出行意。

zú

足 甲 金 古 篆

8DB3 — foot; enough, ample.

促cù; 捉zhuō, 浞 zhuó; 龊chuò; 猚què.

A foot and leg. The upper square could be supposed as a symbol to distinguish with 止zhǐ.22. ☞ 正zhèng, 疋pǐ.

象形。疋 shū 足同源。跰=踚=龊 chuò，齐谨貌。龊chuò，行疾也。俗居从足作屄，当作踞。

bù

步 甲 金 古 篆

6B65 — step, pace, stage; to go on foot.

频pín; 涉shè; 陟，骘zhì.

A pair of footprints. Note the "big toes" of the footprint. ☞ 止zhǐ.

一对足印形。𣥂=走=步。步从止少，日本加丶简化作歩。半步为跬=蹞 kuǐ。歲=戨=㞸=半=半=岁=岁，从步戍声。

zǒu

走 金 古 篆 参

8D70 — to walk, go.

陡=阤=屴dǒu; 徒 = 徢 = 赳 = 辻tú; 赱=走=走.

歪=歪 shows a man walking, 夭=夭 yāo.11, swinging his arms, with a footprint between the legs. Meanwhile, 奔bēn: to run quickly, scamper, has three footprint symbols under a running man. It is interesting that a trend in modern art portrays motion by using repeated forms, such as Marcel Duchamp's *Nude Descending a Staircase, No. 2.* ☞ 大dà.3, 止zhǐ.

人摆臂行走。宗泽《早發》眼中形势胸中策，缓步徐行静不哗。

1.4 From the Womb to the Tomb 人的一生

▶ Fuxi and Nüwa, the primordial ancestors of China. Rubbing of a stone from a tomb, Han Dynasty

伏羲女娲图。南阳画像砖。汉代

bāo

包甲 金 古 篆

5305 — to wrap up; to include; package.

苞，炮，孢bāo；雹báo；饱bǎo；抱，刨，鲍bào；泡pāo；炮，刨，咆，庖，袍páo；跑pǎo；泡，炮，疱pào.

Shows a baby 巳 sì in its mother's womb 勹bāo. PLC, 胞bāo, womb, the placenta of a child. ☞ 孕yùn: to be pregnant, pregnancy.

象在母亲腹中的胎儿形。包裹字篆作勹。

sì

巳甲 ...金 ...古 ...篆

5DF3 — the sixth of the twelve Earthly Branches.

氾，祀sì.

A human embryo. PLC. ☞ 子zǐ.26, 已jǐ: oneself and 已yǐ: already.

象胎儿形。《说文》包，象人裹妊，巳在中，象子未成形也。

yí

台金 古 ...篆

53F0 — I; happy (archaic).

怡，贻，饴，诒yí；冶yě；治zhì；臺＝台，抬，鲐，佁，邰，骀，苔tái；胎，胎tāi；笞chī；始shǐ；殆，怠，迨，骀dài.

The combination of 目yí and 口kǒu.13.

☞ 以yǐ, 胎tāi: embryo, 始shǐ: beginning.

《说文》台，说也。从口目声。

24

yù 育＝毓 甲 金 篆 育＝毓

80B2＝6BD3 — to give birth to; to rear, raise, bring up; education.

流, 硫, 琉, 旒, 锍, 鎏liú, 梳, 蔬, 疏shū.

Childbearing. The baby is inverted 云tū and the dots represent amniotic fluid. 毓 yù is the ancient form of 育yù.

☞ 每měi, 肉ròu.128, 子zǐ.26.

母产子。婴儿顺产时头先出现，故从倒子云＝㐬＝充，下方的点代表分娩时流出的羊水。

hòu 后 金 后 古 后 后 篆 后 参 后母戊鼎

540E — queen.

逅hòu; 骺hóu, 垢, 诟gòu.

Derives from 毓yù, see above.

古文字后、司、毓同字。《后母戊鼎》后母戊。或释司母戊、姤戊，藏国博，系目前最大的商周铜鼎。又《后母姒康方鼎》姒嬠。姒从女从司、厶二聲。亦作幻㛚姒。姒嬠，周文王正妃，史书称太姒。

yī 衣 甲 金  古 篆

8863 — clothes, coating; afterbirth.

依, 铱yī; 哀, 锿āi; 亵xiè.

Perhaps the drawing depicts the essential part of the human afterbirth. According to the traditional explanation, this character is a picture of an ancient jacket. 衤 is a radical for garments. ☞ 裔 yì: descendants.

衣字下部或指衣胞。传统的解释为象上衣交衽形。

chū 初 甲 金 篆

521D — at the beginning of; first (in order); original; a surname.

Shows a knife 刀dāo severing the umbilical cord. ☞ 衣yī: afterbirth.

初表示用刀割断脐带。忉，古壮字。忉卦，可怜。

25

zǐ

子 

5B50 — son, child

好hǎo; 孕yùn; 仔, 籽zǐ; 仔zǐ; 字zì.

A baby wrapped in swaddling clothes with two arms free. ☞ 字zì: to give birth to (archaic); the upper radical 宀 mián derived from 大dà.3.

象婴儿在襁褓中两手舞动之形。粤字孖 mā，双生子，对，双。孖叶，手铐。孖褦，关系。孴=孖=[illegible] nì，聚集。孨jí，未详。

ér

兒=儿 

5152 = 513F — son.

倪，霓，猊，鲵ní; 睨nì.

A traditional explanation says that 兒=儿ér shows the boneless opening in a baby'a skull. 儿rén is a radical as well. ☞ 囟xìn, 儿=人rén.1.

小儿头大而囟门未合之形。亮=亮=亮下从儿rén，人处高则明。

kǒng

孔 

5B54 — hole, aperture; a surname.

吼hǒu; 乳rǔ; 扣kōu; [illegible]=朗; [illegible]=嚣.

Shows a baby sucking the breast. ☞ 乳rǔ: milk, breast.

孔可能源于婴儿吮 shǔn 乳之形。古文孔训大。《老子》孔德之容，惟道是从。又表示孔雀。《楚辭·九歌·少司命》孔蓋兮翠旍，登九天兮撫彗星。𡥉，喃字。𩿨𡥉，窟窿。

bǎo

保 

4FDD — to protect, defend; to keep, maintain; to ensure.

葆，堡，褓bǎo; 煲，褒bāo.

A man carrying a baby on his back. ☞ 人rěn，子zǐ.

象人负子形。《说文》保，养也。《鮑子鎛》[illegible]子佳，读若保吾子姓。楚简有賲冡一辞，亦作保冡、[illegible]冡，读若宝蓍，筮具名。

nǎi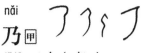

乃 甲 金 古 篆

4E43 — to be (written).

A simple depiction of breast. PLC, 奶nǎi: breast, milk.

奶，艿，氖nǎi; 鼐nài; 仍réng; 扔rēng; 秀xiù.

象妇女乳房侧面形。

mǔ

母 甲 金 古 篆

6BCD — mother; female.

A mother during her breast - feeding period. ☞ 每měi.180.

姆，拇mǔ; 毒=毐dú.

象女子突出乳房，表示已哺育过子女的妇女。

fū

夫 甲 金 古 篆

592B — man; husband.

Portrays a man with a hairpin in his hair. The hairpin was a sign of ritual initiation. ☞ 大dà.3.

趺，呋，肤=膚，麸fū; 扶，芙，蚨fú.

男子戴发簪形。发簪是接受成人礼的标志。扶=伴。

nǔ

女 甲 金 古 篆

5973 — woman.

A woman squatting down with hands crossed in front of her body.

钕nǔ; 汝rǔ; 妆zhuāng; 好hǎo.

交手屈膝跪坐的女子形。妠 nuán，争吵。妾，同姣。

▶ **Rock painting · Copulation**

岩画·交媾图

bèi

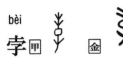

孛

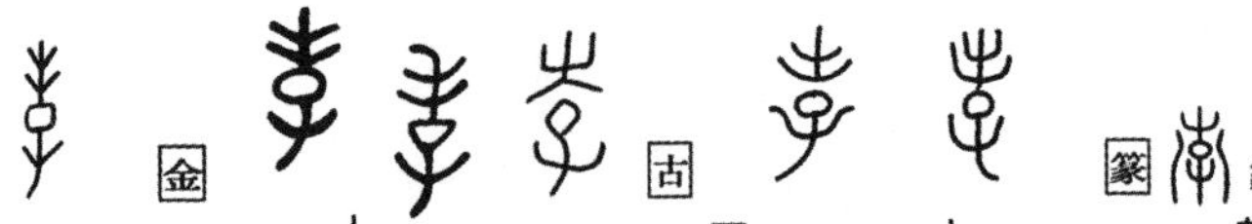

篆作 南21947

5B5B — comet.

勃，脖，渤，鹁bó；饽bō；孛，勃，悖bèi；荸bí.

A combination of 子zǐ.26 and 丰 fēng.76. PLC, 勃 bó: vigorous, exuberant. Or a comet with its tail and coma.

从子从丰，是孩童生长发育蓬勃向上的形声兼会意字。

cháng

長=长

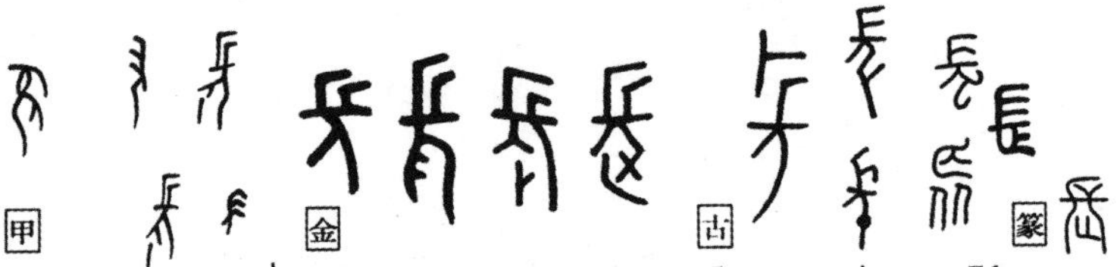

9577= 957F — long.

张zhāng；怅chàng；伥chāng；长：elder，涨zhǎng；帐，胀，涨zhàng.

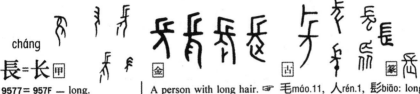

A person with long hair. ☞ 毛máo.11，人rén.1，髟biāo: long hair, is a radical referring to hair or hairstyles.

象人长发之形。后在字形中加杖以示长者。镸镺夫光兵宂兊皃𩬍兂夾尻兴並古文长。

kǎo

考

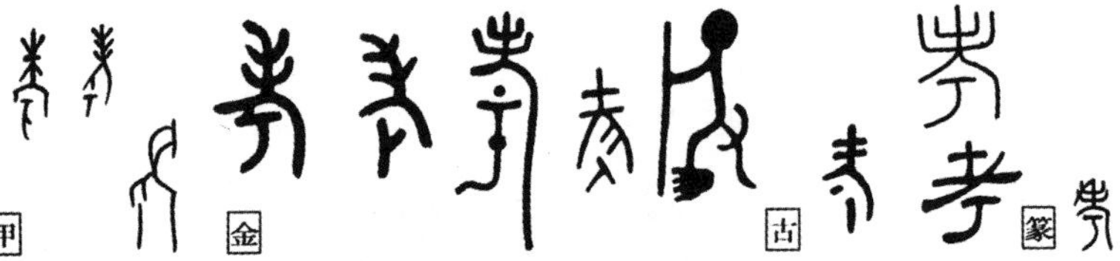

8003—deceased; father; to test, examine; investigate.

烤，拷，栲kǎo；铐kào.

Shows an old man leaning on a stick. 丂 kǎo is the stick in the character. ☞ 老lǎo，朽xiǔ: decayed, senile.

老耄长者策杖形。老、考二字同源。

lǎo

老

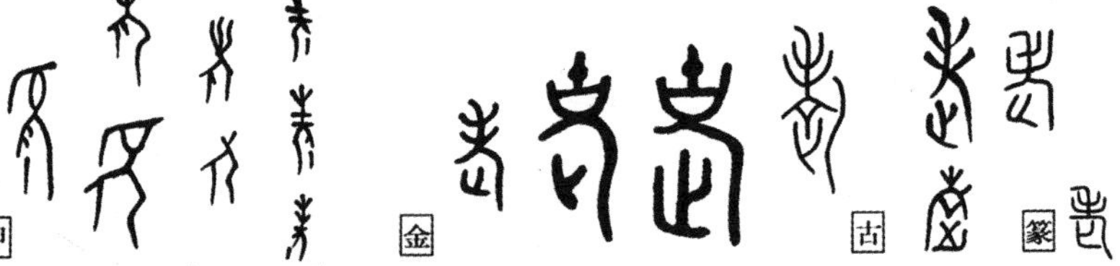

8001 – old (in age); become old.

佬，姥，铑lǎo.

Derives from 考 kǎo, see above. 老lǎo or 耂 8002 is a radical for senile.

甲骨文倚杖老者一般认为是考字。可确定的老字最早见于《辛中姬鼎》子孙用享孝于宗老。䎜 439C.mào 同耄。𦓈 264C8.xiòng 同[illegible]，老弱。𦓋 264CB.wàng 未详。[illegible]老並俗。《玉篇》[illegible]，古文老。

xiào

孝 金  古 篆

5B5D — filial pierty; mourning.

哮xiào; 教jiāo; 教, 酵jiào.

Shows an old man supported by his son. ☞ 老lǎo, 子zǐ.26.

象子扶侍老者之形，表示孝敬长辈。養，金文孝从食。

shòu

壽=寿 金 古 篆

58FD＝5BFF — a person's age; birthday celebration; something burial or having to do with burial.

籌，俦，畴chóu; 祷dǎo; 涛tāo; 铸zhù.

The upper part of 寿shòu is a drawing of an old man, and the bottom shows a hand holding a wine vessel. The middle part was an ancient phonetic. ☞ 寸cùn.17.

手持酒器向老者祝寿。《说文》壽，久也。从老省壽聲。𦓐𦓎𦕤𦕫𦕬晨𦕪，古文壽。儔𦕭，俗。

▶ A man and a woman buried close together, the woman's skeleton is flexed. The Neolithic, Gansu Province.

男女合葬墓（甘肃永靖秦魏家 M105）。齐家文化，新石器时代。（采自《新中国的考古发现和研究》，124 页。）

shī

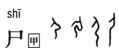 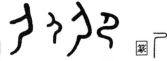

尸甲　金　篆

5C38 — corpse, dead body.

屄bī: vaginal orifice;
屌diǎo: penis;
屎=尿=骹sóng: semen;
尾wěi: tail;
启dǔ: anal orifice (archaic).
琚, 裾, 湨, 腒, 椐, 居jū;
鋸, 据, 倨, 踞 jù; 涃 gǔ;
崛, 刷, 掘 jué; 堀, 窟 kū;
苣, 鶋, 屈qū.

The glyph shape of 尸shī shows a man bending his knees. Actually 尸shī is a archaic character for Eastern *Yi*, the subject peoples from the East part of China, and a radical referring to a person's body or action as well, and the common 尸shī: corpse, is from its tranditional form 屍shī with a meaning component 死sǐ: die, death, dead. Meanwhile, unlike 尸, 居jū and 屈qū themselves are good phonetics.

☞ 人rén.1, 尼ní.9, 尿niǎo.139.

象屈膝的人形。尸、夷古同字，指古代屈膝臣服的东方部落之人。死、屍（尸）为古今字。

xiān

 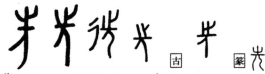

先甲　金　古　篆

5148 —earlier, before, first.

酰xiān; 跣, 铣xiǎn;
宪=憲xiàn; 洗, 铣xǐ;
选=選xuǎn.

先xiān is a combination of a man 人rén and an upward footprint 止zhǐ.22, indicating a forefather who has passed away.

止在人上，表示逝去的先祖。㲹xióng. 204D9 同㲭，老弱。

jiàng

降甲　金　古　篆

964D — to fall, move to a lower place.

绛jiàng; 降xiáng: to vanquish, surrender.

Borrows two downward footprints to represent a man descending a ladder or stairs. As a polyphone, 降xiáng is a variant of 夅xiáng, the two footprints downward, which has the meaning of going down, that is 降jiàng. In the ancient glyph shapes, 夅xiáng is perfered to integrate with the ladder, standing for the derection of motion.

☞ 阜fù.96, 止zhǐ.22, 步bù.23.

用在石阶边的两个指向下方的足印表示下降的动作。夅xiáng 有下、大的含义：浲hóng，同洪，水泛滥；绛jiàng，大赤；隆，省作隆，丰大也。

$\mathfrak{Chapter}$ 2

NATURE 自然

2. 1 Mother Nature 大自然

▶ A bird in the sun. Rubbing of a brick
from a tomb in Henan. Han Dynasty.
东汉画像砖 • 太阳鸟。河南南阳出土。

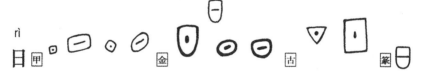

65E5 — sun; day.

晶jīng; 昌, 猖, 娼, 菖, 鯧chāng;
唱, 倡chàng; 曧=曧huǐ.

Sun. The dot in the sun stands for sunshine, not a sunspot.
☞ 口kǒu.13: mouth and 月yuè.33: moon, month.

象太阳形。中间一点表示日光。曡 2AC48 未详。

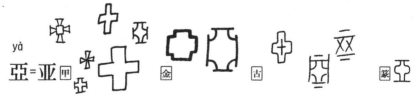

4E9E= **4E9A** — second;
Asia.

垭, 娅, 氩, 哑yā;
哑, 痖yǎ; 恶, 垩è;
恶 ě, wū, wù.

Chinese believed that the earth was square and the sky round, 亚yà
indicates the square earth with its four corners occupied by pillars.
These pillars were said to prop up the sky.

天圆地方。亚指方形的地，四角被支撑苍天的柱子占用去了。
被美国人从蔡季襄手里骗走的长沙子弹库楚帛书，其四角绘
有四棵树，即以树隐喻柱子。娅，连襟；俹，倚靠。

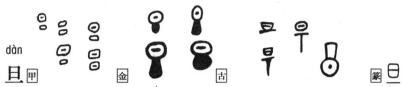

dàn

旦 甲 金 古 篆

65E6 — dawn, morning.

蛋，但，担=擔 dàn；胆=膽，
疸 dǎn；担 dān；祖，坦，钽 tǎn.

A depiction of sunrise. ☞ 日 rì，丁 dīng.

日出。古文字从日丁声。二简字元旦=圆蛋。

xīng

星 甲 金 古 篆

661F — star.

惺，猩，腥 xīng；
醒 xǐng.

The ancient form of 星 xīng was a drawing of a cluster of stars with the phonetic 生 shēng.40. ☞ 晶 jīng: brilliant, glittering.

象天上的群星，生为声符。瑆=瑆 xīng，玉光。叠叠叠，並古文星。〇，武则天所造星字。

mò

莫 甲 金 古 篆

83AB — no (written).

漠，寞 mò；摸 mō；摹，模，
膜，馍 mó；模 mú；募，墓，
幕，暮，慕 mù.

The 日 rì: sun setting in the woods. Later, the 林 lín: forest symbol was replaced by 茻 mǎng: grassland. PLC, 暮 mù: dusk, evening; with a lower sun-radical.

日落林木草丛中。《说文》莫，日且冥也。从日在茻中。

yuè

月 甲 金 古 篆

6708 — the moon; month

刖 yuè；钥=鑰 yào，yuè：胢=
阴=陰 yīn. 朤=朗 lǎng.

Drawing of the moon, a new moon. ☞ 日 rì.31，夕 xī.33.

象蛾眉月之形。从月之字或有折断、分离之意：刖，
绝；拐，折；朗，断足；明，墉耳；间=间，隙。

xī

夕 甲 金 古 篆

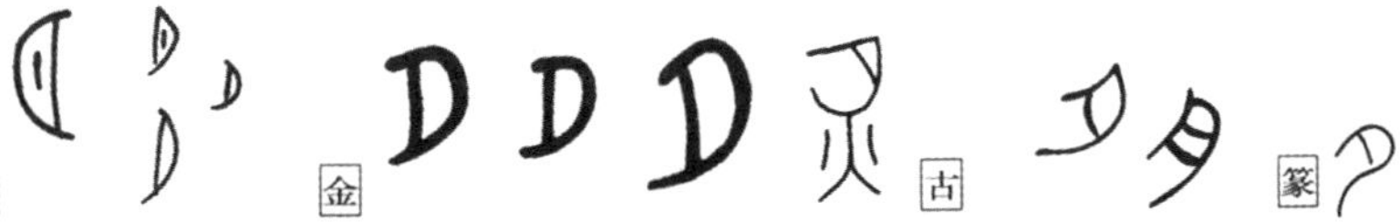

5915 — sunset, evening.

汐，穸，矽xī.

The ancient glyph of 夕xī and 月yuè was the same, later people use the dot 月yuè for moon, and 夕xī for the night or evening.

古文字夕月同形。后省去点以与月相区分。外，从月得声。炙，讀若夜。从火从夕，會夜以火照明意。好盗壶：日炙不忘。

gèng xuān

亙 & 亘 甲 亙 金 亙 篆 亘 参 恆

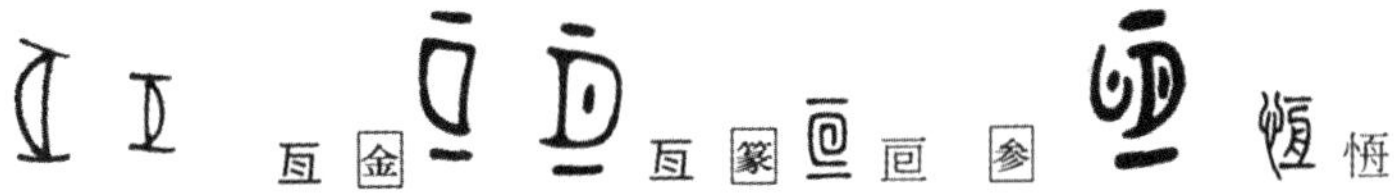

4E99 4E98

亙: the quadrature of the moon.

恆=恒=恒héng: constant;

亘: to extend, stretch.

宣xuān; 垣yuán.

亙=櫃=亙=亙gèng showed the moon between two strokes indicating its waxing and waning phases constantly. Or the middle 月yuè: moon, derives from a boat, thus, the two horizontal strokes represent the banks. 亘=亘=亘 xuān should be the same, with the 回=回 huí: returning, circle, in the middle. Today people prefer to use 亘 for both. PLC. ☞ 月yuè, 舟zhōu.

亙从二从月。表示月亮圆缺恒定的变化。《诗经·小雅·天保》如月之恒。亙，亙字之误。亘 xuān，从二从回。今亙、亘並作亘。

míng

明 甲 金 古 篆 朙

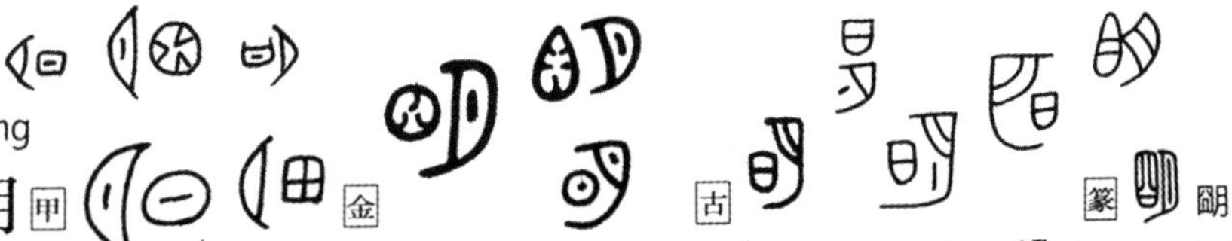

660E

— bright; clear.

盟míng; 盟，萌méng.

明míng is a combination of the sun and the moon. Perhaps 明míng recorded a prehistoric supernova observed near the lunar crescent. ☞ 日rì, 月yuè.

《说文》朙，照也。从月从囧。明，古文朙从日。朙、明，以月光照进窗户而会光明意。

míng

名 甲 金 古 篆

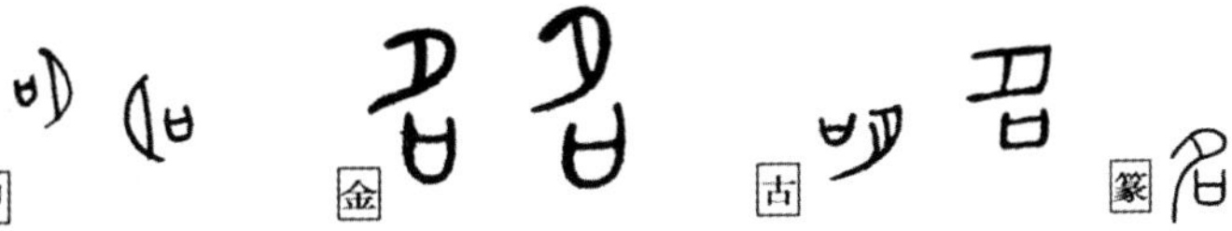

540D — name; fame, reputations; famous.

茗，铭míng; 酩mǐng.

At night 夕xī, people can't see each other's faces to recognize, but use mouth 口kǒu.13, ask or report their names.

从口从夕。夜间看不清对方面孔，而询问或自报姓名之意。

yún

雲=云 96F2 = 4E91 —cloud.

芸，耘，纭yún；运=運，酝=醖yùn；魂hún；昙，坛=壇tán.

A cirrus cloud. The upper part, the two short strokes 二 2011E, is the ancient form of 上 shàng: upper, implying the sky.

象回转的云形。雲2E996 同云。靐4A3A=靐duì，云貌。靐291D4.nóng，云广貌。邧，篆作郧。

bīng

仌=冫 51AB —ice (archaic).

寒 hán: cold.

Two bronze ingots 吕 lǚ.105. It is a radical referring to coldness, because of the feeling of touching the bronze. ☞ 冰 bīng: ice.

仌源于吕，铜锭。《说文》仌，冻也。象水凝之形。氷，俗冰。冰，古文冰。霳21B1C. lín，同凛。

▶ **Inscriptions on an oracle bone：*Today it will rain. Is the rain coming from the west? the east? the north? or the south?***

卜辞：癸卯卜：
今日雨？
其自西来雨？
其自东来雨？
其自北来雨？
其自南来雨？

yǔ
雨 甲

96E8 — rain.
屚=屚=漏lòu:
to leak.

Shows rain pouring from the sky. It is an upper radical as 2ED7 for many characters denoting certain types of natural phenomena.

象雨点自天而降之形。霂霝霿霒求霂峫澟灥，或古或俗。

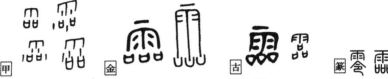

líng
零 甲

96F6 — (rain) fall; zero.
靈=灵，椛，酃líng。
霝 971D，雨零。雺luò，
雨零。霝，雨零。零，
餘雨。

霝=零líng is the combination of 雨yǔ: rain, and the 川 líng for the sound of rain, or another phonetic 令líng was used. Later, 零líng was borrowed to indicate the important number *zero*.

从雨从口令声，雨落下的声音。明代开始借零表示数字 0。

shēn
申 甲

7533 — to state, express; the ninth of the twelve Earthly Branches; a surname.
伸，呻，绅，砷shēn；神795E.shén；
审=審shěn；畅chàng。

An attempt to draw a bolt of lightning. PLC, 電=电
7535.diàn: lightning, electricity; 神 shén: god, divinity.

象闪电形。引申为神灵。鼺2C3CD，未详。

léi
雷 甲

96F7 — thunder.
擂，镭，累léi；累，
蕾，儡léi；擂，
累léi；螺，骡luó。

Ancient forms of 鼺24CF3=靁 9741=雷léi depict lightning accompanied by peals of thunder. Later, the symbols for thunder were reduced to 畾 757E.léi as a phonetic, which was topped with the radical for rain. The modern 雷léi is simplified with one 田tián. ☞ 申shēn, 雨yǔ.

雷古从申从雨。靐霺雷霻靁畾畾朋畾靐畾畾并古文雷。

shuǐ

水

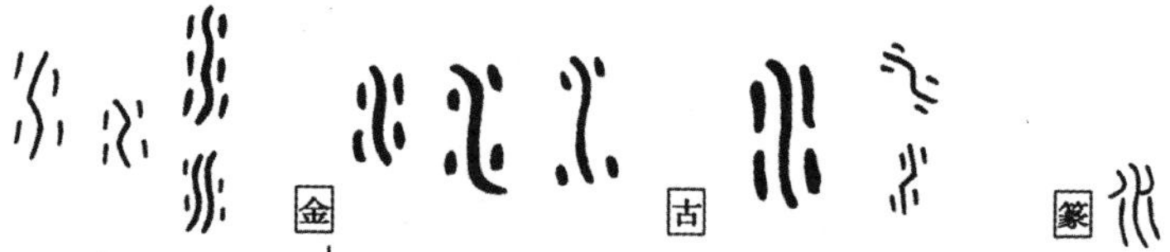
甲
金
古
篆

6C34 — water; river.

尿niào, suī: urine; 汆cuān; 淼 miǎo: immense.

A stream with four dots representing the drops of water or pebbles on its bank. ☞ 氵 6C35 as radical.

象水流之形。沝 6C9D，同水。㵘3D58.màn，大水。[illegible]=[illegible]=阴阳。

qì

气

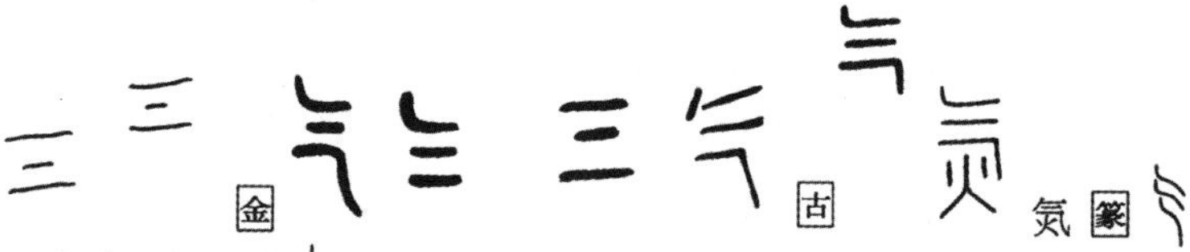
甲
金
古
気
篆

6C14 — gas; air; breath; smell, odour.

气qǐ; 汽, 迄, 讫qì.

Shows clouds in thin parallel layers or vapor on the surface of a lake. PLC, 汽qì: steam, vapor.

象云层或水面蒸气形。氣篆作 ，與 同。雲氣之氣篆作气，道教书籍中，气字作炁 7081。

chuān

川

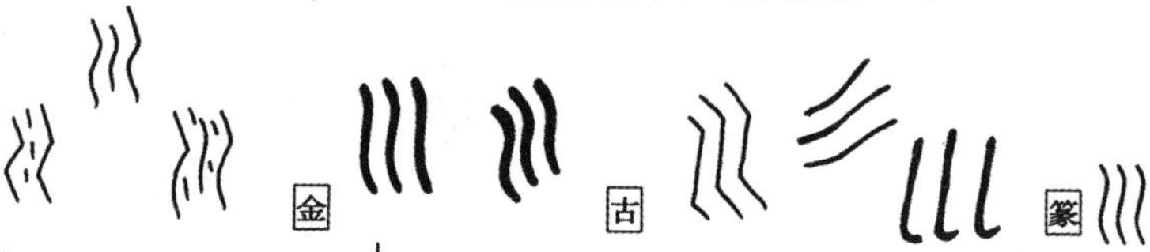
甲
金
古
篆

5DDD — river.

巛chuān; 钏chuàn; 顺shùn; 巡, 驯xún; 训xùn; 圳zhèn.

A river.

象两岸间水流之形。

huí

回

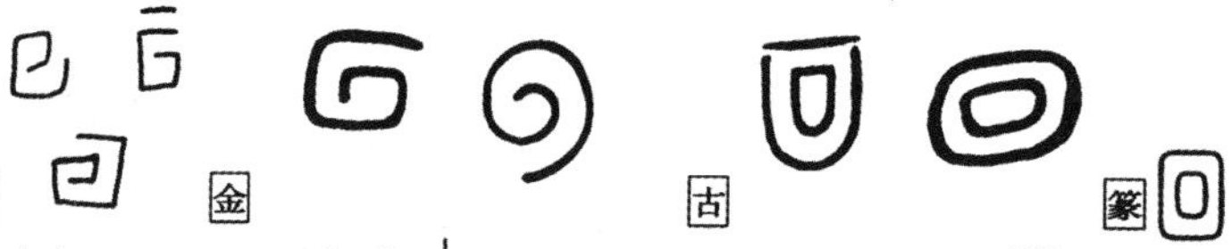
甲
金
古
篆

56DE — circle; to return, go back.

洄, 茴, 蛔huí.

Shows a whirlpool or eddy. PLC, 洄: (of water) whirl.

象水回流形。回又作囬囘囬。㺯，对回民的蔑称。

zhōu

州

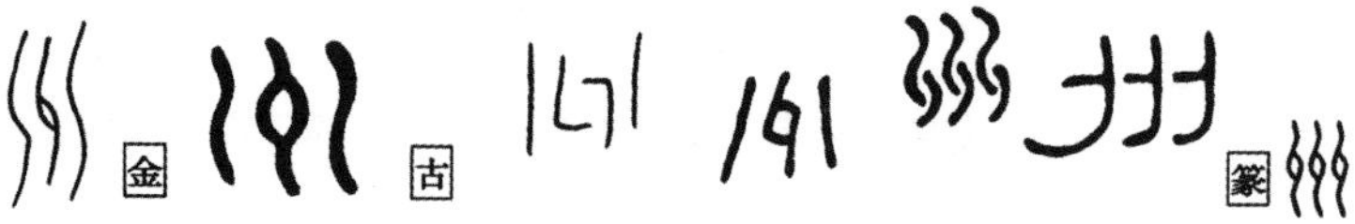
甲
金
古
篆

5DDE — state, an administrative division.
洲zhōu; 酬chóu.

Depicts an island in the middle of a river. ☞ 洲zhōu: continent.

河心绿洲。𨙩239D3 �𬳇223DD 㳶20097 巛20113 巜200D5 剑206CF 巛206B4，并古文州。洲，篆作州。

quán
泉甲  古 篆  参 𬭁環 钱铭

6CC9 — spring.
腺: gland,
線=线 xiàn.

Shows spring water flowing from a cave or the mouth of a spring.

泉水从泉眼或山洞里流出。𣹭𣹭或并同泉字，游戏字。𤽆𤽆㟖𡾥 㵾㵘㘈㘈，或古或俗。金文习见𬋿2C256字，从泉𬭁省声。或释泽，或读薄。又《楚缯书》有亡𤽆一辞，或读渊。钱贝篆作泉贝𤽆𧴪。

yuán
原金 古 篆 原

539F — original; unprocessed; to excuse, pardon; plain; a surname.
源，螈yuán; 愿，愿yuàn.

Shows a spring flowing from the face of a cliff. PLC 源yuán: fountainhead; source. ☞ 厂hàn, 水shuǐ, 泉quán.

泉水从山崖边流过。原为源字初文。篆文作𬏠20AD0。

shān
山甲 金 古 篆 山

5C71 — mountain, hill; a surname.
舢shān; 疝，汕，讪shàn;
灿=燦càn; 籼，粐，仙 xiān.

A Mountain with three peaks. It's a radical.

象山峰并立之形。屾5C7E. shēn 二山。㟆21DC8 同㟆，俗㵵。又㟆屾 kāchá，山名，在山东沂源大张庄。

qiū
丘甲 金 古   篆

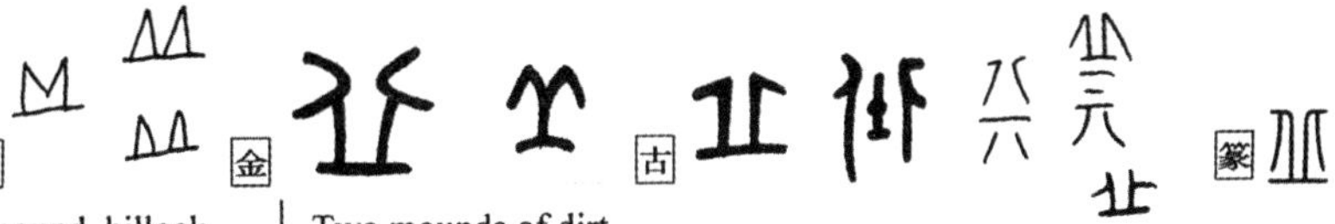

4E18 — mound, hillock, dune; a surname.
邱，蚯qiū; 岳yuè.

Two mounds of dirt.

两丘突起形。𠀼北𡊋𠀓北𡉻坴坵𡊤，或古或俗。或避孔子讳作𠀓。岳飞后人避难改姓为岴21DA6. yò。

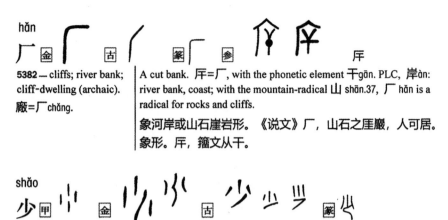

hăn

厂 金 古 篆 参 斤

5382 — cliffs; river bank; cliff-dwelling (archaic).
廠=厂 chăng.

A cut bank. 斤=厂, with the phonetic element 干 gān. PLC, 岸 àn: river bank, coast; with the mountain-radical 山 shān.37, 厂 hăn is a radical for rocks and cliffs.

象河岸或山石崖岩形。《说文》厂，山石之厓巖，人可居。象形。斤，籀文从干。

shăo

少 甲 金 古 篆

5C11 — few, little, less.

少shăo; 抄, 钞chāo; 吵, 炒chǎo; 杪, 眇, 秒, 渺, 缈miǎo; 妙miào; 挲sa; 沙, 砂: grit, 纱, 裟, 鲨shā; 娑, 挲suō; 劣liè.

The four dots in the glyph may represent sand. PLC, 沙shā: sand; with a water-radical 水shuǐ.38 implying the location of the sand.

少从四点。缈miǎo，戸政俗字。

xiăo

小 甲 金 篆

5C0F — small.

雀què, qiāo; 尘=塵chén; 尖jiān; 肖xiào; 肖, 消, 逍, 宵, 霄, 硝, 削, 销xiāo.

Three dots. ☞ 少shăo.

小从三点，从少省。𣌭21B90，同小。

2.2 Flora 植物

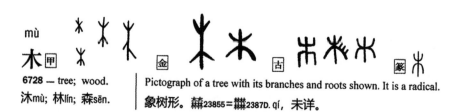

mù

木 甲 金 古 篆

6728 — tree; wood.
沐mù; 林lín; 森sēn.

Pictograph of a tree with its branches and roots shown. It is a radical.

象树形。𣖀23855=𣏟2387D. qí，未详。

zhū

朱 甲 金 古 篆

6731
— vermilion, bright red; cinnabar, a surname.

侏，珠，株，诛，铢，蛛zhū；殊，姝shū.

The dot or a horizontal stroke indicates the trunk of a tree. PLC, 株zhū: stem of a plant. ☞木mù.38: tree, 干gàn.64.

木字中间加指示符号圆点，株字初文。伐木为株，从朱之字多有斩、短之意：如诛、珠、侏儒、蜘蛛、锱铢。又殊，死也；𢧵、𣪠、𣫍，杀也。木心赤色，从朱之字亦有红意：硃，丹砂；袾，朱衣；絑，纯赤色；㝃，深红色。

bĕn

本 金 古 篆

672C — the root of a tree; origin, foundation.

苯bĕn；笨bèn；钵bō；体=體tǐ.

The roots of a tree emphasized by an additional short stroke near the base of the character. ☞ 木mù.38.

《说文》木下曰本。从木，一在其下。𣐺𣐺𣐺，古文。

mò

末 金 古 篆

672B — end; minor details.

沫，抹，茉，眜，妺，秣=䬴mò；抹mǒ，mā；韎 mèi.

Constructed like 本bĕn, 末mò shows the branches of a tree emphasized by a short stroke on the top. ☞ 木mù.38, 未wèi.

《说文》末，木上曰末。从木，一在其上。从末之字或有微、弱之意：沫，泡沫；眜，目不明。

wèi

未 甲 金 古 篆 参 𫭆 族徽

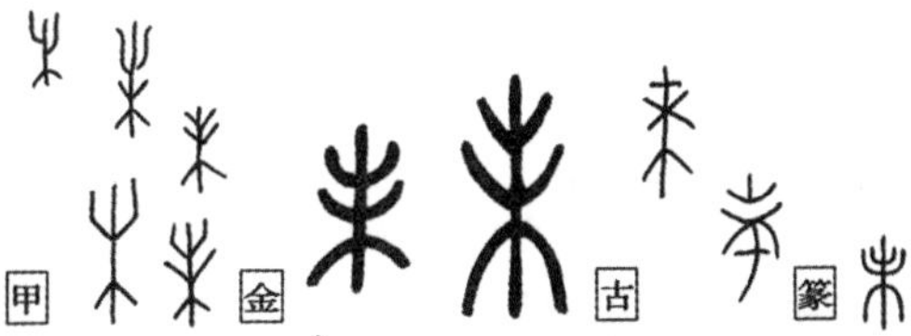

672A — the eighth of the twelve Earthly Branches; to have not.

味wèi；寐，昧，妹，眛，魅，寐mèi.

Derived from 木mù with twigs. PLC, 味wèi: taste. Tender leaves are more delicious.

《说文》未，味也，象木重枝叶也。重枝叶则鲜嫩味美。𫭆2BB46=種=种，种子的种字会意初文，以植物种子包于口中而胚芽未发，会种子意。李仲璇修孔子廟碑：瑶光佽彩，秝弈於上龄。若水嘉祥，扶蕀於季葉。秝弈，赫奕，名声显赫。

shēng

生 _甲

751F — grow; give birth to; unripe.

牲，笙 shēng；眚 shěng；胜 shèng；
旌 jīng；性，姓 xing.

A seedling growing on land.

象草木生出地面形。省 xǐng 字古文字从生，小篆从目，生省声。毒＝莓＝毒，害人毒草，往往而生。

duān

耑 _甲

8011 — beginning; extremity.

揣 chuāi；踹 chuài；喘 chuǎn；
端 duān；瑞 ruì；湍 tuān；
惴 zhuì.

A seedling breaking through the soil. ☞ 不 bù.41，而 ér.16.

植物初生，小苗破土上出之形。从耑之字多有疾、直之意：喘，疾息；湍，疾瀨；遄，疾速；端，直也；褍，衣正幅。

cǎo

艸 _古

8278 — grass.

屮 chè；茻 huì；茻 mǎng；
芬＝芬 fēn.

Grass. 草＝艸，and 早 zǎo.193 is a phonetic. ⺾ **8279**＝艸 is the radical for grasses and plants.

草是形声字。荷花茎藕蓬莲苔，芙蓉芍药蕊芬芳。

yè

枼 _甲

67BC — thin (archaic);
bedplate 牑.

蝶，碟，谍，堞，
揲，喋，蹀，牒，
鰈 dié.

A tree with its leaves shown. It's a picot-phonetic element, with the meaning *thin*. PLC, 葉＝叶 yè: leaf, with an upper plant-radical.

象树枝叶形。枼，牑，薄。从木 mù.38 世 shì.191 声。从枼之字多有薄义：蝶；碟；鰈，比目鱼；堞，女墙；牒＝䐑，薄切肉。

cái

才 _甲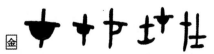

624D — ability, talent, gift; people of a certain type; simplified form of 纔 7E94: just; only.

闭bì; 材, 财, 裁cái; 豺chái; 存cún. 哉, 栽zāi; 载zǎi; 戴dài.

The traditional interpretation is that 才 cái is a depiction of a germinating seed breaking through the soil. PLC.

种子胚芽出土形。在 zài.5728 从土才声。㦵22994=㦵=㦵 zāi 从戈才聲。《说文》才，艸木之初也。

bù

4E0D — not.

钚bù; 杯=盃bēi.

The root of a germinating seed. PLC. See below.

种子萌芽时的胚根形。不杯，即丕显，金文习语，指光明正大。

pī

4E15 — big, great (written).

邳, 坏pī; 呸, 胚pēi; 苤piě.

With the addition of a bottom stroke, 丕pī is a derivative of 不bù. PLC, 胚pēi: embryo.

丕为不的加划衍生字。

Stages in the germination of a corn seed.
玉米种子萌芽示意图。

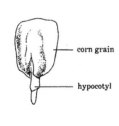

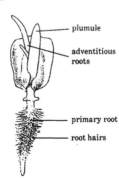

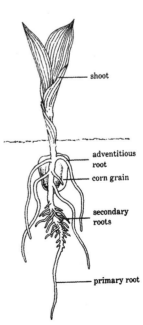

corn grain

hypocotyl

plumule

adventitious roots

primary root

root hairs

shoot

adventitious root

corn grain

secondary roots

primary root

Flowers

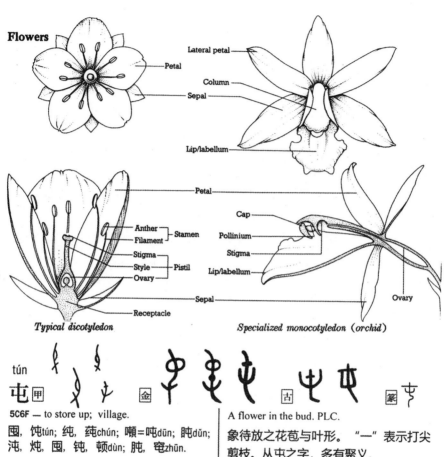

Lateral petal
Column
Sepal
Petal
Lip/labellum

Petal
Cap
Anther
Filament — Stamen
Pollinium
Stigma
Stigma
Style — Pistil
Ovary
Lip/labellum
Sepal
Ovary
Receptacle

Typical dicotyledon   *Specialized monocotyledon*（*orchid*）

tún

屯 甲   金   古   篆

5C6F — to store up; village.

囤，饨tún；纯，莼chún；噸=吨dūn；肫dūn；
沌，炖，囵，钝，顿dùn；肫，窀zhūn.

A flower in the bud. PLC.

象待放之花苞与叶形。 "一" 表示打尖
剪枝。从屯之字，多有聚义。

chūn

春 甲   金   古   篆

6625 — spring; life
vitality; love, lust,
stirrings of love.
椿chūn；蠢chǔn.

A combination of 林lín: forest or 艸cǎo.40: grass, 屯tún: bud and 日rì.31:
the sun. 屯 was also a phonetic. Later, 屯 and 林 were merged as 夫.

从林或草日屯，屯亦声。 蓄，篆。冀眘睧音，古。 眘睿睧，俗。
蠢chún，义未详。王国维：四时可爱唯春日，一事能狂便少年。

huá

華＝华 金

83EF＝534E — flourishing, prosperous; brilliant.

哗＝譁, 骅huá; 哗huā; 桦huà.

A flower with an upper plant-radical. ☞ 草cǎo.40.

象花形。華篆作䔢20336 蕐26F93。农历 2 月 12 日为花朝，又叫百花生日。

róng

榮＝荣 金

69AE＝8363 — to grow luxuriantly; to flourish; glory, honor; a surname.

嵘, 蝾róng; 劳láo; 莺yīng; 营, 茔, 荧, 莹, 萤, 萦, 濚, 溁, 滢yíng.

A bouquet, 熒2C287＝ 241FE consisting of two flowers. The bottom element, 木mù: tree, is a later addition.

从从木。象花木形。 ＝熒，并古文荣。
王国维：最是人间留不住，朱颜辞镜花辞树。

píng

平 金

5E73 — flat, level; calm; impartial; to level.

评, 枰, 鲆, 坪, 苹＝蘋píng; 抨, 怦, 砰pēng; 秤chèng.

Floating duckweed. PLC, 萍píng: duckweed.

象浮萍形。

má

麻 金

9EBB — hemp, flax; pockmarks; benumbed, having a tingling feeling; a surname.

嘛ma; 摩mó; 魔huī; 糜, 縻, 靡, 蘼mí; 靡mǐ; 磨, 麽, 蘑, 魔mó; 磨mò.

Drawing of two hemp plant, *Cannabis sativa*, used for the tough phloem fiber. Perhaps 广guǎng.98 pictograph of a shed, implies storing hemp in a shed after harvest. 朮pìn shows the fiber of hemp, and 林pài, double 朮.

广下剥麻形。林强调麻类植物的韧皮部分，其纤维系古人衣料纺织的主要原料来源。

43

guā

瓜 金 古  篆

74DC — melon.

呱, 胍 guā ; 呱, 孤, 苽,
觚, 眾, 泒 gū; 狐, 弧 hú.

A melon or gourd on the vine. It's a radical for melon or gourd.

藤蔓上结瓜形。在木曰果，在地曰蓏。莃，大瓜；㼎，
小瓜；瓠，葫芦；瓣，瓜实；㼌 yǔ, 瓜实繁多而弱。㼎，
俗㼎。

lái

來=来 甲  金 古 篆 参 麥 麦

4F86= **6765**
— to come.

莱, 崃, 徕, 涞,
铼 lái: 睞, 赉 lài;
麰 móu: barley;
麥 9EA5=麦 9EA6.
mài: wheat.

A ripe wheat plant. PLC, 麥mài: wheat, and a radical as well, with an element 夊 suī denoting a footprint downwards. Wheat and barley originated in West Asia, and early Chinese believed that wheat is a precious gift from heaven. Early *L* and *M* was very similar; since 来lái is simpler and *COME* is an everyday verb, then 来 and 麦 were exchanged.

象一株成熟的麦形。古人认为小麦乃天所来也，是和红薯同等重要的天赐之物。来为麦形，麦从夊，会来意。来、麦互借是由于古代汉语发音中 L 与 M 不分和常用来字的缘故。

qí

齊=齐 甲  金  古 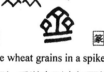 篆

9F4A= **9F50**— neat, uniform; on a level with; simultaneously; all ready; a surname.

荠, 蛴, 脐 qí; 跻, 薺ⁿ; 济, 挤ⁿ; 剂,
济, 鲚, 荠, 霁ⁿ; 齋=斋 zhāi

Wheat in the ear, or the wheat grains in a spike. PLC.

象小麦吐穗整齐之形，后世字形中加两横画以示平整。刘墉：粗茶淡饭布衣裳，这点福让老夫消受；齐家治国平天下，那些事有儿辈担当。

hé

禾 甲  金 古 篆

79BE — rice; standing grain, cercal.

和, 盉, 穌 hé; 香xiāng.126.

A ripe rice plant. It is a radical for cereal plants.

象谷穗低垂的稻谷之形。

mǐ

米甲 古

7C73 — rice; shelled or husked seed; metre.

籹, 脒, 眯mǐ; 咪, 眯mǐ; 迷, 逃, 醚, 糜, 麋mí; 屎shǐ; 粥zhōu: gruel, porridge.

An attempt to draw grains of rice. The 十 may be a mnemonic symbol. ☞ 糣phở: rice noodle or *Pho*.

象米粒形。粣, 俗粖, 即粄, 屑米饼。粲, 榮字俗讹。糣phở.2C5BE, 喃字, 从米頗声。米粉。館糣: 米粉店。糣辅: 牛肉粉。

guǒ

果甲 金

679C — result; if indeed.

蜾, 裹guǒ; 踝huái; 棵, 窠, 稞, 颗, 髁kē; 课kè; 裸luǒ.

A tree bearing fruit. PLC, 菓=果: fruit. ☞ 木mù.

树上结果之形。金文果字或作果中有实形。猓=猓=猓chuǎ, 树分叉。猓又音 hū。

cì

束甲 金

673F — thorn, prickle.

刺cì: splinter, to stab.

A plant with thorns or prickles. ☞ 木mù. 棗=枣zǎo: jujube, Chinese date; 棘jí: thorn bushes; brambles.

象有芒刺的植物。棘, 同棗。棘, 同棘。

lì

栗甲 古

6817 — chestnut.

傈, 溧, 篥lì.

A chestnut tree. ☞ 木mù.

象栗树形。篆文从卤作栗3B9A, 古文从三卤作栗2387C。

45

mǒu

某 金 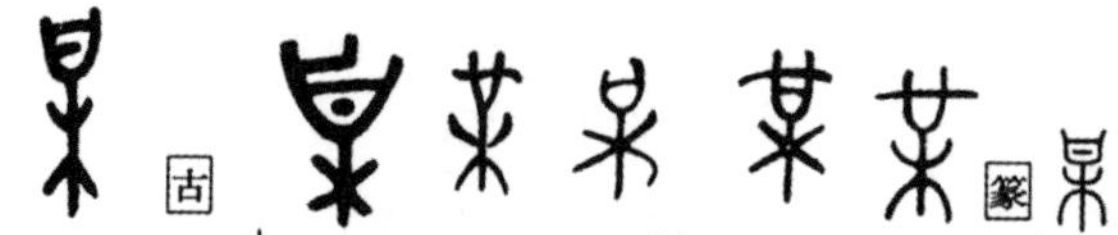

67D0 — certain, some.
谋móu; 媒, 煤méi.

A combination of 甘gān.13: sweet and 木mù.38: tree; the character may indicate a kind of fruit. PLC, 楳＝梅méi: plum.

某从甘从木，表示酸果。槑 69D1 呆 233C1，並古文梅。

zhú

竹 甲 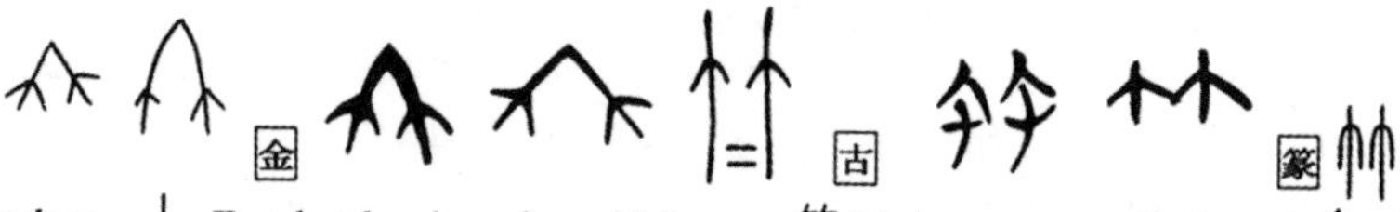

7AF9 — bamboo.

Two bamboo branches with leaves. 竹zhú is an upper radical. And 个 gè: individual, drawing of one bamboo branch, half of 竹zhú.

象竹枝叶形。竻2E14B. duk，从二竹。古壮字。竹篾。𥷹25DF9. sè 或 shā，𥴒25D12.zhì 或 jí，並义未详。元·郑采《题复古秋山对月图》木森森兮竹𥴒𥴒。

2. 3 Fauna 动物

2. 3. 1—Aquatic Animals, Reptiles and Insects 水生动物，爬行动物和昆虫

yú

魚＝鱼 甲 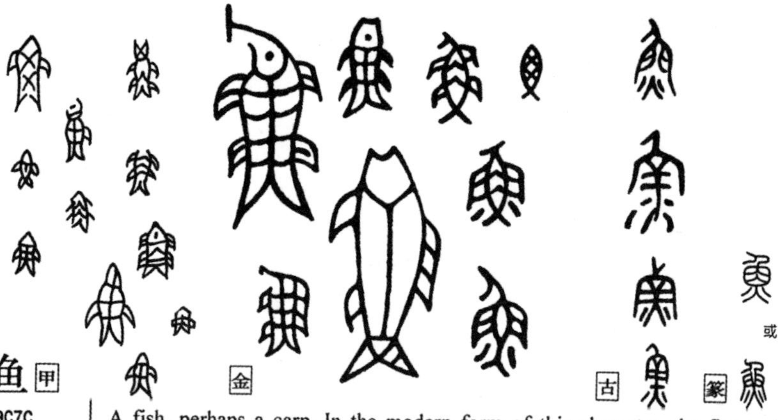

9B5A＝9C7C — fish.
渔yú: to fish.

A fish, perhaps a carp. In the modern form of this character, the fins and scales are simplified into the element 田tián, and the four dots at the bottom derive from the tail fin. ☞ 龟guī.47, 燕yàn.57.

鱼的侧视图。䲆4C86＝𩺰＝鲜。𩺰29EB0. wú，大鱼。䲜4C9C.yè，鱼盛。又𪺚2AE9A 𫙐2B650 𣿡23FE1 𤀯2402F 䰻4C3B，並同渔。

bǐng

丙 甲 金 古 篆 丙

4E19 — the third of the Heavenly stems; third.

柄，炳bǐng；病bìng。

The tail fin of a fish. PLC.

象鱼尾之形。一说象器物底座之形。

bèi

貝=贝 甲 金 古 篆 貝

8C9D= 8D1D— shellfish; cypraea, cowry; a surname.

狈，钡bèi；坝bà；败bài；瞁yīng: necklace.

The ventral view of a cowry shell. Cowry shells were used as money in the early stages of civilization; thus, this pictogram is a radical to money, property or treasure.

宝贝的腹视图。矗屓=颏屃 bìxì，碑首盘龙。

guī

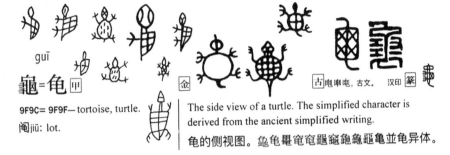

龜=龟 甲 金 古 汉印 篆

9F9C= 9F9F— tortoise, turtle.

阄jiū: lot.

The side view of a turtle. The simplified character is derived from the ancient simplified writing.

龟的侧视图。龜龟畾龟龟龜龜龜龜龟並龟异体。

▲ Detail from the inside of a bronze vessel, a turtle motif

青铜器铭纹·龟

▲ A clay vessel with a fish motif. Banpo, the Neolithic

半坡彩陶盆·鱼。仰韶文化

chóng

虫 甲 金 古 篆 參

866B — insect, worm.
融 róng; 虫 huǐ:
蟲 87F2=虫 chóng;
蚰 45B5=昆 kūn.

A snake or worm. 虫 chóng is a radical used in many characters meaning for worm or insect.

象虫形。虫，古虺字，毒蛇。蟲1964年简化作虫。蚰kūn，与虫、蟲同，与昆通。蚰也是部首，从蚰之字现多从虫。昆篆作𦐮，《说文》同也。昆虫，篆作蚰蟲。昆弟之昆篆作𦥑。

tā

它 甲 金 古 篆

5B83 — it.
铊 tā; 舵 duò; 蛇 shé, yí.

A cobra-like snake. PLC, 蛇 shé: snake, serpent. ☞ 虫 chóng.

"它"字刻画一条蛇的轮廓，是蛇字初文。

yě

也 甲 金 古 篆

4E5F — oh, also, as well.
池, 弛, 驰 chí; 地 de, dì;
他, 她 tā; 迤 yí, yǐ.

An attempt of drawing a vulva. It is then borrowed to be an interjection. PLC.

《说文》也，女阴也。象形。或象人张口呼号形。

měng

黽=黾 甲 金 古 篆

9EFD=9EFE — frog.
黾 miǎn, mǐn; 绳 shéng; 蝇 yíng;
鼍 tuó: Chinese alligator;
鼋=鼋 yuán: soft-shelled turtle.

A frog. 黾 měng is a radical for certain reptiles or insects. 鼅鼄=蜘蛛 zhīzhū: spider. ☞ 龟 guī.

象大腹的蛙形。《说文》蝇𪓑，蟲之大腹者。又蛙，篆作鼃𪓑。黽勉篆作恾勉 𢢀 𢢍。

lóng

龍=龙 甲 金 古 篆

9F8D = 9F99

—dragon.

茏，咙，泷，珑，
栊，胧，砻，聋，
笼lóng；陇，垄，
拢，笼lǒng；
宠chǒng；庞páng；
袭xí.

The dragon is a frequetly used symbol in China. It is a remnant of ancient tribal totems. The original form of the dragon may have been a snake used as a totem by a powerful clan. This clan conquered weaker clans whose totems were deer, tigers or even fish, The dragon, which bore many features of these other creatures, eventually appeared as a new unified emblem for the new and larger clan or nation, The dragon in China indicates an emperor, the *yang* , or even a bridegroom.

象龙形。龍字的龙头音zhuāng，立源于龙角，月源于张开的龙口。

龖=龘dá，飞龙。龘，同詟 zhé，言不止。

wàn

萬=万 甲 金 古 篆

842C= 4E07

—ten thousand; myriad; absolutely; a surname.

壾dǔn；厉，疠，励，砺，粝，蛎lì；迈mài.

万俟 mòqí: two-character surname.

A scorpion with pincers, a segmented body and curved tail tipped with a venomous sting. Later, the pincers were simplified into a grass-radical. The stroke on the tail indicates a numeric value and the lower surrounding strokes may be a form of the hand element suah as 离.68. *Wan* is a peculiarly Chinese number unit, which also appears in the American Indian languages. ☞ 十shí.193, 百bǎi, 千qiān.

象蝎之形。全世界只有中国人和印第安人以万做为计数的单位之一。甲骨文里发现的最大计数为三万。对史前人来说，能数到万，确实象蝎子那样可怕。

qiú

求 甲 金 古 篆

6C42 — to request; to try; demand.

俅，逑，球，赇，裘qiú；救jiù.

A caterpillar or millipede. PLC, 蚯qiú: myriapod.

多足虫。蟊27494＝蛷272DB＝蚯。

2. 3. 2—Mammals　哺乳动物

zhì

8C78 — an insect without feet or legs (mentioned in ancient book).

蚔=豸。辵犭，俗豸。

A jackal, with an open mouth, fangs, legs, and a tail. Its relation to the insect described in the ancient book is unclear. 豸 is a radical in some characters referring to beasts. ☞ 肉ròu.128.

象野兽形。或以为即豺字初文。獬豸字篆作解廌 觧 廌 。

bào

豹

8C79

— leopard, panther.

A leopard with its spots shown. The right - hand part 勺sháo derives from the outline of a leopard's back and its spot (a dot). See above.

象身上有花斑点的豹形。从豹之字，大多生僻。貛，同貆zhuó，飞鼠。碥，同砲。哟，誇。傄、葯bào，人名用字。潊，未详。

néng

能

80FD — can, ability.

熊xióng.

A bear. The claws 匕 are placed on the right in the vertical positioning. Compare the mouth and fangs in this character with those in 豸zhì and 鼠shǔ.50. PLC. 熊xióng: bear, raging (flames); with a lower fire-radical. 熊 is derived from *roasting a bear*. ☞ 肉ròu.128, 龙lóng, 火huǒ.

象张口行走的熊形。羆，古文熊。船骵，俗熊。

shǔ

鼠

9F20 — mouse.

竄=窜cuàn: to flee; 撺蹿, 镩cuān.

A mouse with an upturned mouth and teeth, and a long tail.

象牙齿发达长尾巴老鼠形。鼠，金文一。中山王方壶：曾亡（无）鼠夫之栽（救）。

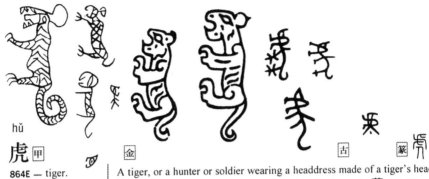

hǔ

虎 [甲]　[金]　[古]　[篆]

864E — tiger.

唬，琥hǔ；彪biāo.

A tiger, or a hunter or soldier wearing a headdress made of a tiger's head 虍hū. 虍hū is a phonetic as well as a radical for tiger. ☞ 蒙méng.70.

象虎形，后借用戴虎头头饰的人形为虎字。虍虝虎，俗虎。

lù

鹿 [甲]　[金]　[古]　[篆]

9E7F — deer.

漉，辘，麓lù；镳biāo；
龘＝麤＝塵＝尘chén；

A deer, the upper part is the deer's eye and antlers, and the lower part, 比bǐ, represents the deer's legs. ☞ 能 néng.

象形。龘＝麤＝麁＝麤，同粗。㒼麻庵庶廉麜，並俗鹿。

mǎ

馬＝马 [甲]　[金]　[古]　[篆]

99AC＝9A6C — horse, steed, a surname.

码，玛，犸，蚂mǎ；吗má, mǎ, ma；
蚂，妈mā；骂，蚂mà；闯chuǎng；笃dǔ.

The upper part of 马mǎ represants the horse's eye and mane, and the lower part its legs and tail.

象形。客家方言詩：五行車馬驫驫走。

51

tù

兔 甲 金 古 篆

5154 — hare, rabit.

堍tù; 逸yì; 冤yuān.

A rabbit with a long ear.

象兔形。甲骨文兔字与㲋chuò、毘形近易混。毘即麛 mí，幼鹿。赴疾字篆作[illegible]fù，同趕，急疾。

xiàng

象 甲 金 古 篆

8C61 — elephant; to image; to resemble, seem, like.

像，橡xiàng.

An elephant with its tusks, trunk and ears shown. In prehistoric times, there were a lot of elephants in northern China, but they disappeared gradually, When one person had seen the rare beast, he might then have given a glowing account of his adventure to his friends, who could only have imagined the animal.

象形。《匡卣》有象躱一辞，讀若象樂，大象歌舞。古代北中国大象日渐稀少，以致于需要通过图像来想象这种抽象的怪物了。

niú

牛 甲 金 古 篆

725B — ox; a surname.

件jiàn; 犇 bēn.

The front view of an ox's head with horns. ☞ 牢láo.83.

牛头前视形。[illegible]guǐ，牛声。牪 yàn，牛伴。犇，同群。

yáng

羊甲　〔金〕　〔古〕羊篆羊

7F8A — sheep.

佯，洋，徉，烊yáng；養=养，
氧，瘍=痒yǎng；恙，樣=样yàng；
咩miē: baa, bleat; 鮮xiān，姺庠
祥，翔，详xiáng；譱=善shàn。

Drawing of the long face, beard and horns of a ram.
☞ 鲜xiān.54，羞xiū.71，羌qiāng.70.

羊字源于对羊双角和长脸的刻划。

羴=羶=羺=羴=羶=膻 shān。

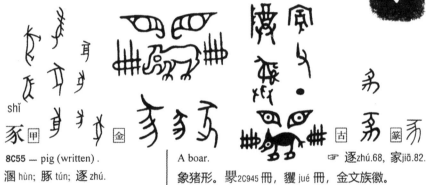

shǐ

豕甲　身　〔金〕　〔古〕豕篆豕

8C55 — pig (written).

溷hùn；豚tún；逐zhú.

A boar.　☞ 逐zhú.68，家jiā.82.

象猪形。𥅻2C945冊，貜jué冊，金文族徽。

▶ A pig-shaped clay kettle. Excavated at
Dawenkou, the Neolithic. High 21.6 cm.

夹沙红陶兽形器·猪。大汶口出土。

hài
亥 甲 金 古 篆

4EA5—the last of the twelve Earthly Branches.

氦，骇hài；咳hāi；孩，骸hái；该，赅gāi；劾，阂，核hé；核hú；颏kē；咳hé；刻kè.

Supposedly a cognate of 豕 shǐ: pig, PLC.
亥为豕的变形。或曰象植物根荄形，荄字初文。

▶ Rubbing of a pig motif from a Neolithic clay vessel, Hemudu culture.
黑陶猪纹方钵拓片。河姆渡文化。

quǎn
犬 甲 金 古 篆

72AC—dog.
吠fèi：bark, yap；莽，蟒mǎng；猋=飙biāo.

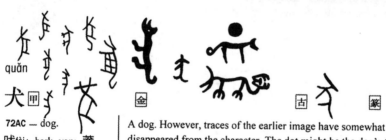

A dog. However, traces of the earlier image have somewhat disappeared from the character. The dot might be the dog's tail. It's a radical as 犭 on the side.
象狗形。狺3E5C.yín，犬相吠。

xiān
鲜 金 古 篆

9C9C—delicious；fresh.
鲜，藓xiǎn；癣xuǎn.

The combination of a fish 鱼yú.46 and a ram 羊yáng.53.
鱼和羊的组合，表示味道鲜美。鱻4C86 鱻9C7B 并同鲜。

nüè
虐 甲 金 古 篆

8650 — cruel; ill-treat.

瘧=疟 nüè; 謔 xuè.

Shows tiger clawing. The lower part is the tiger's claw. ☞ 虎 hǔ.51, 又 yòu.17: the action of hand, notice the direction of the hand 彐.

虎足反爪伤人，表示肆虐。篆文虐作 虐 虐 虙 處。《詩·衛風·淇奧》善戲謔兮，不爲虐兮。

jiǎo

角 甲

89D2 — horn; angle; corner; cape.

角 jué; 确=確 què.

An ox horn. 角 jiǎo is also a radical. ☞ 解 jiě.87.

象牛角之形。用=角，音禄。姓。觹=觽 xī，解结器。《說文》觹，佩角，銳耑，可以解結。《詩·衛風·芄蘭》曰：童子佩觹。

lì

麗=丽 甲

9E97=4E3D — beautiful.

俪 lǐ; 骊、鱺、丽、鸝 lí; 逦 lǐ; 灑=洒 sǎ; 醨、曬=晒 shài; 釃 shī.

A deer with beautiful antlers, or possibly a giraffe. PLC.

象鹿有双角，表示美丽和匹配。禒丽丽丽，古文麗。

sì

兕 甲

5155 — male rhinoceros.

Picture writing of a rhino.

象犀牛形。兕 20485，古文兕。兕 27C3D 兕 24261，篆文兕。

2.3.3—Birds 鸟类

niǎo

鳥＝鸟 甲

9CE5 = 9E1F
— bird.

萄 niǎo; 鳴 míng: the cry
of birds.

A bird with a beak or bill; the lower four dots represent the talons and feathers. It's a radical such as 鵝＝䳘＝鷲＝鸞＝鵝 é: goose, and 鳴 21219.é: a caged bird used to bring other birds to the lure.

象鸟形。《客家方言詩》二鳥鵤 2A15D鷲2A23C 林外飛。

wū

烏＝乌 金

70CF = 4E4C —crow, black.

於，嗚，鎢 wū; 隖＝塢 wù；
於，瘀，淤 yū; 於 yú.

A crying crow. The traditional interpretation of this character's meaning is that the crow is too black for its eye to be seen.

象仰天鳴叫的烏鴉形。烏、於二字同源分化。

zhuī

隹 甲

96B9 — short-tailed bird.

椎，錐 zhuī; 椎 chuí; 崔，催，摧 cuī; 璀 cuǐ；
翟 dí，zhái; 堆 duī; 碓 duì; 淮 huái; 集 jí; 進
＝进 jìn; 雀 què，qiāo; 誰 shéi，shuí; 售 shòu;
睢 suī; 隼，榫 sǔn; 推 tuī; 维，惟，帷，
唯 wéi; 唯 wěi; 隻＝只 zhī; 稚，雉 zhì; 準＝
准 zhǔn.

Other glyph of a bird, especially for short tailed bird. It is both a radical and a phonetic, generally used in characters benoting birds and fowl. ☞ 鸟 niǎo, 佳 jiā: beautiful, good, and 讎 96D4.chóu: a pair, a couple.

隹象鸟形。雧 96E5.zá，群鳥聚集。雦 96E6＝
雧 96E7，古文集。

yàn

燕 [甲] [古] [篆]

71D5
— swallow.
燕yān.

A flying swallow carrying a twig in its bill.

飞燕衔枝。《说文》燕，玄鸟也。籋口、布翄、枝尾。象形。鷰，古文燕从妟声。嬿=嬮 yàn，美也。讌，俗宴字。爩xuě，人名用字。糯yoen，韩国字，米粉。

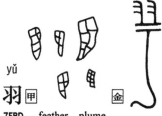

yǔ

羽 [甲] [金] [古] [篆]

7FBD — feather, plume.
翅chì: wing, shark's fin; 扇，煽shān; 扇，骟shàn; 翔xiáng; 栩，诩xǔ; 習=习xí; 翊，翌yì.

The ancient pictograph is a picture of a bird's wing. The modern 羽yǔ comes from a drawing of two pulmes.

象鸟羽形。翗，篆文。翻，同飞。又喃字。鸃翻：鸭绒。

fēi

非 [甲] [金] [古] [篆]

975E — no, not; wrong, errors.
扉，蜚，绯，菲fēi; 腓féi; 诽，翡，菲féi; 痱féi.

Shows the flapping wings of a bird. PLC.

鸟振动双翅。从非之字或有红意：绯，帛赤色；翠鸟赤而雄曰翡；菲草花紫赤色；痱，热赤疮。

fēi

飛=飞 [古] [篆]

98DB=98DE
— to fly.

A flying bird. ☞ 升shēng: to move upward.

飞鸟形。飛飛，并古文。飝飞卂，并俗飞。悲bay，从飞悲声。飞。飰 pích，鸟羽。并喃字。飝 bân，岱喃字。飞。

fèng

鳳=凤

9CF3＝51E4
— phoenix.

A bird with a beautiful crest and plumes. The surrounding element 凡fán is a phonetic. ☞ 凡fán.106, 鸟niǎo.56, 风fēng.

象头上有羽冠的鸟。翍翄翄鵬鵠翵，並古文凤。瀜féng，水聲。

瑪媷麯騆颷偑鎁fèng，鷢xiāo，並人名用字。

▶ Inscriptions on a oracle bone; *The phoenix stops (the wind falls).*

卜辞·凤止＝风止

fēng

風=风

98A8＝98CE — wind.

枫，疯，砜fēng；讽fěng；岚lán；飒sà.

Derived from 鳳=凤fèng, with the lower 鸟niǎo: bird, replaced by 虫chóng: worm. It's a radical as well. PLC. ☞ 凤fèng.

风源于凤，假借。飈qiǎng，乱风；又音 xiāng，风声。飍xiū，惊风。飍pōu，同飈，风吹貌。

zào

喿

55BF — chirp of birds.

操cāo；缲，臊sào；臊sāo；澡，藻zǎo；噪，燥，躁zào.

Three *mouths* 品 pǐn on the tree 木 mù.38 imply the songs of birds. ☞ 口 kǒu.13.

树上鸟鸣声。《说文》鸟群鸣也。从品在木上。

huán

崔 [甲]  [古]

8411 — eagle-owl.

觀=观 guān; 觀=观 guān; 灌, 罐,
鸛 guàn; 歡=欢, 獾 huān;
權=权, 顴 quán; 勸=劝 quàn;
護=护 hù; 獲=获, 镬, 蠖 huò;
劃 huō; 舊=旧 jiù.

Glyphs show a kind of eagle-owl, great horned owl, with
the meaning element 丫=艹 guǎi: ram's horn. ☞ 隹 zhuī.56,
雚=鸛 guàn: stork.

象长耳猫头鹰。《说文》雚，鸱属。从隹从丫，有
毛角。所鸣，其民有祸。又萑 zhuī，草多貌。今
萑、雚形近不分。雚，从萑叩声。

huò

霍 [甲] [金] [古] [篆] 靃

970D — suddenly; quickly.

藿 huò; 攉 huō.

Shows birds flying quickly in the rain. ☞ 雨 yǔ, 隹 zhuī.56.

《说文》靃，飞声也。雨而双飞者，其声靃然。古文字
或从雔=靁 zá、从雔 chóu，后从隹作霍。

cháo

巢 [甲] [金] [古] [篆]

5DE2 — nest.

撢, 剿 chāo, jiǎo; 缫 sāo.

A bird's nest in a tree. ☞ 木 mù.

木上有巢形。樔，古文。巢 jiǎo，未详。

xī

西 [甲] [金] [古] [篆]

897F — west.

牺=牺, 硒. 茜, 栖 xī;
栖 qī; 茜 qiàn.

A bird's nest. PLC. ☞ 巢 cháo.

鸟巢形。卤卤卤卤，籀文。卤，篆文。日既西落，倦
鸟归巢。

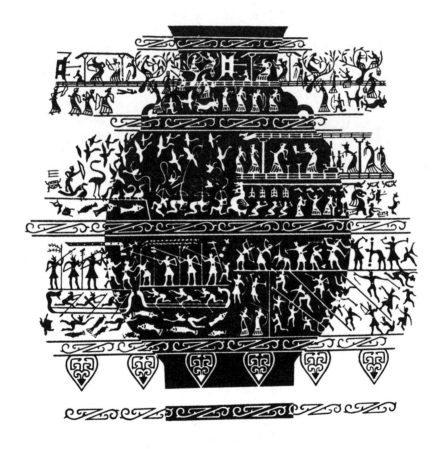

Design on a bronze wine jar, Warring States Period.

战国铜器图案。

Chapter 3

HUNTING AND AGRICULTURE 狩猎与农耕

Progress from a hunting and gathering way of life to the domestication of plants and animals is called the Food-Producing Revolution. This occured during the Neolithic period. Great improvements in the manufacture of stone implements are associated with this change. In this chapter, the entries will show us a panoramic view of the struggle of early Chinese to survive.

从采集渔猎靠天吃饭,到发明农业和畜牧业控制食物的生产过程是人类经济生活中的一次大跃进,这一跃进被考古学家们称之为新石器时代革命。这一章中的汉字将向读者展现一幅三千多年前中国人为生存而斗争的生动的全景画。

Hunting and harvesting. Rubbing of a brick from a tomb. Sichuan Province, Han Dynasty.

汉代画象砖·弋射收获图。成都杨子山出土,46cm×42cm。

3. 1   Hunting   狩猎

Five bowmen. Rock painting of Levant, Spain, the Stone Age.
五个弓手。西班牙列文特岩画，石器时代（自《世界美术史》第一卷，109 页）。

3. 1. 1—Animal's Footprint   躔

biàn

91C6 — archaic form of 辨biàn: to distingguish, differentiate.

悉: to be familiar with, 蟋xī; 釋=释shì: to explain.

The footprint of an animal. See below. ☞ 采 cǎi.78.

For prehistoric people, the discovery and recognition of animal prints was important for both hunting and avoiding the dangers of prowling beasts. If a hunter found an animal's footprint with which he was familiar, he could explain to his son or partner what kind of animal was nearby. The assistant would look carefully at the foofprint, and could learn the skills of tracking.

动物足印形。采系古辨字，与采易混。

　对史前先民来说，在打猎中发现和识别动物的足印是十分重要的。当一个猎人发现一种他所熟悉的动物足印，他可以向他的儿子或助手解释周围有何种动物，并决定追猎或逃避；而晚辈则会将这种足印仔细审视一番，从而学到狩猎技巧。

fān

番  古

756A — a course, a turn; aborigines.

幡，翻，蕃fān，蕃，蹯fán；播bō；潘pān；蟠pán.

A combination of an animal's footprint and a symbal of hunting: 田tián. PLC, 蹯fán: animal's footprint; with a foot-radical 足zú.
☞ 采biàn，田tián.74，留liú.87，畜chù.65.

兽足谓之番，采象其爪掌。这里"田"可理解为一个表示狩猎的符号。蹿，番或体。𤲃，古文番。

shěn

審=审 古 寀, 古文 窨, 古籀文 篆

5BE9=5BA1 — to look closely at.

妽，瀋=沈shěn.

May depict a hunter (legs shown) standing over and examining an animal's footprint carefully. ☞ 大dà.3，家jiā.82，番fān，申shēn.35.

猎人弯腰审视胯下的动物足印。宀象胯下形，参见大、家。

◄ Some footprints of carnivorous animals.
几种肉食动物的足印。
1. badger　2. wolf　3. tiger　4. bear

► Some footprints of hoofed animals (mostly herbivorous).
马类和几种常见偶蹄类动物的足印。
1. wild ox　2. antelope　3. ram　4. deer
5. wild boar　6. horse　7. ass
（采自尤玉柱:《乌兰察布岩画中的动物》，《乌兰察布岩画》,326页。）

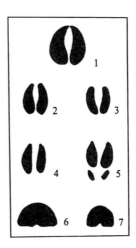

3. 1. 2—Tools for Hunting   打猎工具

yā

4E2B — branch or fork (of a tree).

Pictograph. │ gùn: stick rod, stands for tree trunk, and ∨=八 bā.85: eight, a symbol for separating or broken.

象树杈枝枒。俗作桠=桠。鬌鬒、髫環、髫妷，同丫鬟。

gàn

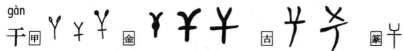

5E72 — to do; to fight; trunk.

干: to offend, 奸, 肝, 竿, 酐gān; 杆, 秆, 赶, 擀gǎn; 斡, 幹=干, 盰gàn; 岸àn; 犴hān; 旱, 汗, 捍, 悍, 焊hàn; 妍, 歼jiān; 刊kān; 轩xuān; 讦jié.

The dot (later a horizontal stoke) indicates the stem of a tree branch. Branches were used as perhistoric weapons for both hunting and war. ☞ 丫yā, 单dān.

用一点（一横画）指示树杈的枝干，枝干作为原始工具，用于打猎和战争。干犯字篆作干。干求字篆作迀。干戈字作戰。罕篆文从网作罕 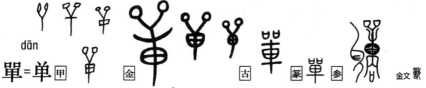。

dān

55AE＝5355 — single, one.

殚, 箪, 郸dān; 掸dǎn; 瘅, 惮, 弹dàn; 婵, 禅, 蝉, 单（单于）chán; 阐chǎn; 单（姓）, 掸（族）, 禅（让）shàn; 蕲, 弹tán;.

金文 歡

A prehistoric weapon made from a tree branch with stone knives and a net (or shield) attached to it. PLC. ☞ 戰＝战zhàn: to fight, 戈gē, and see above.

系有石刀的树杈，中间的田可能表示网或盾牌。

wǎng

7F51 — ancient glyph of 網 =网wǎng: net; reticular.

罔, 辋, 惘, 魍wǎng.

A net. As an upper radical, the form of 网wǎng is flattened as ⊓.
☞ 罔wǎng: deceive, cheat; 亡wáng.

象网形，网是一个返朴归真的好简化字。

▶ A boat-shaped clay kettle with a net motif. Excavated at Beishouling, the Neolithic.

船形陶壶·网。北首岭遗址出土（4840—4170 BC）。

W 91.2

bì

畢=毕 [甲]

7562＝6BD5

— to accomplish.

哔，跸，筚bì；棄字本作𣂸，从畢.

𣂸=畢 shows an net made from a tree branch, the upper 田tián.74 is a symbol of hunting. ☞ 单dān、事shì.67 and 禽qín.68.

𣂸象一种用树枝做的网，后加符号田，表示狩猎。畢業篆作𢿙業。𢿙，𢿙盡也。《诗·小雅·鸳鸯》鸳鸯于飛，畢之羅之。

xuán

 [甲]   [金]

玄 [甲]

7384 — abstruse; mystic; dark; a surname.

痃xuán；泫，眩，炫xuán；弦，舷xián；牽=牵qiān.

 [古]   [篆]

The glyptic 串.20D53 stands for bolas, a throwing-weapon made with two stone fastened to the ends of a rope, see below. PLC.

绳球象形。绳球为一种在长绳或皮条两端系有石块的狩猎工具，用来投向猎物（如鹿），以缠绕猎物的腿等处。

chù

 [甲]   [金]

畜 [甲]

755C — domestic animal, livestock.

搐chù；蓄xù: to store up, to harbour；畜养xùyǎng: raise (domestic animals).

 [古]   [篆]

A combination of 玄xuán: bolas, and 田tián.74.

玄田为畜。甲骨文从胃省，以牲畜 chù 胃有草谷蓄 xù 积，会畜 xù 养意。蕌，或体。犝猪，俗。

3. 1. 3—Fishing and Hunting   渔猎

◀ **Rock painting · Hunting.**

岩画·射猎

gǔn

鯀＝鮌 甲 金 古 篆

9BC0＝9CA7— name of a legendary ancestor.

A hand fishing with a line. ☞ 鱼 yú.46, 系 xì.190 or 糸 mì.93.

钓鱼之形。鲧是夏禹父亲的名字，传说中最早开始建造城市的人。漫溽鮫鮫歔并同渔。金文渔从奴作舁 2B650 或从 ⌐⌐ 从鼺作 鼺 2AE9A。

shòu

獸－兽 甲

7378＝517D — beast.

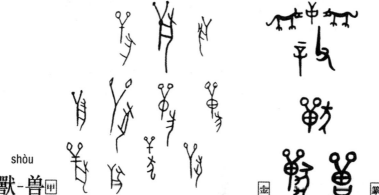

A combination of 干 gàn or 单 dān.64: a prehistoric weapon, and 犬 quǎn.54: dog. 兽 shòu: beast, and 狩 shòu: hunting, had the same origin. The modern character 狩 shòu is a pictophone.

干犬会狩猎意，引申为狩猎对象。古文 獸猏 一字。

shǐ

史 甲

53F2 — history.
吏lì; 使, 驶shǐ.

A hand holding a hunting weapon. 史shǐ: history, 事shì: affair, 吏lì: official, and 使shǐ: to use, are cognate characters. See below.

史象手持叉网形。史，吏，事，使四字同源。叟嫂旋，古文事。

gǎn

敢 甲

6562 — dare, venture; bold, brave, courageous, daring.
猴hān; 撖, 譀 hàn; 闞＝阚 kàn.

Depicts catching a boar with a branch-net. ☞ 豕 shǐ.53.

用叉网捕捉野猪。《说文》敢，进取也。敢叔叔敢敢敢敢並敢古文字。

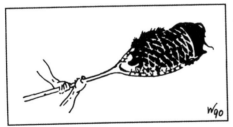

◀ **Catching a boar with a branch-net**
敢·用叉网捕获野猪

zhuō

卓 甲

5353 — outstanding.
桌zhuō; 绰chuò; 婥chuò;
悼dào; 掉diào; 淖nào;
棹, 罩zhào.

A man with a net. The upper part is supposed to be the simplified form of a bird. Later, a phonetic 早 zǎo.193 was introduced. PLC, 罩zhào: to cover; topped a net-radical. ☞ 畢bì.65.

构形不明。或象网罩物形。罩亭帛阜帛並古文。卓，俗卓。

67

qín

禽 甲

79BD — bird, fowl.

檎, 擒, 噙qín.

A hand holding a net. The upper 今jīn is a phonetic element, thus, 禽qín is a pictophone. It is also a PLC, 擒qín: catch, with a hand-radical.

手拿捕鸟网形, 擒本字。《说文》禽, 走兽总名。从厹, 象形, 今声。

lí

離=离 甲

96E2=79BB — to leave, be away from; off, away, from; without, independent of.

篱, 漓, 璃, 缡lí; 魑chī.

Shows a bird 隹zhuī being taken from a net.

用手取出网内的鸟儿。可能是指鸟儿离开了伙伴, 简省的离字中, 鸟儿彻底离开了。

zhī

隻=只 甲

96BB=53EA — only, just, merely; single, lonely.

枳, 咫zhǐ; 织=織 zhī; 职zhí; 炽chì; 识, 帜zhì; 识shí.

A hand 又yòu.17 grasping a bird 隹zhuī.56. PLC. ☞ 雙=双 shuāng: a pair.

手抓获一只鸟形。《说文》隻, 鸟一枚也。从又持隹。

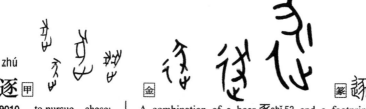

zhú

逐 甲

9010 — to pursue, chase; to expel; one by one, progressively.

A combination of a boar 豕shǐ.53 and a footprint 止zhǐ.22. It represents hunters chasing or driving a boar. ☞ 辶chuò.

猎人追逐驱赶野猪。篴 dí, 同笛。

tuàn

象 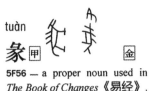 甲 金  古 篆

5F56 — a proper noun used in *The Book of Changes* 《易经》.

掾yuàn; 缘, 椽yuán; 椽chuán.

Drawing of a dead boar. PLC. ☞ 豕shǐ.53.

长牙野猪形。鬵=盉li、瓢。古文原字作邍、遵,从象从夂从辵,以于原野追逐野猪,会平原意。彐=彑,象之头。希=帚=帘=鶓=彖、夂=貗、彘、彖=彖诸字从彑。

---

duì

隊=队 甲 金 古 篆 叄  篆

968A=961F — row, line; team, group.

坠zhuì.

隊=队 shows a boar being driven over a cliff 阜=阜fù.96. PLC, 墬=坠zhuì: to fall. Here 土tǔ.74: soil. indicates the bottom of the cliff, meanwhile 豕shǐ.53 and later 隊suì.86 as phonetics as well.

隊表示驱赶野猪坠下山崖。古文字队、阝,并释作=隊,为坠字初文。《说文》隊,从高隊也。从阜豕声。

---

xiàn

臽 甲 金 古  篆

81FD — pit (archaic).

谄chǎn: to flatter; 馅: filling, stuffing, 陷xiàn; 阎yán; 焰yàn; 掐qiā: to pinch.

A man setting a trap. The dirt clods and pitfall were replaced with the element 臼jiù.79: mortar. PLC, 陷 xiàn: to sink, get stuck.

人挖陷井之形。古文字或象人陷坎中,指陷埋人牲以祭。

---

dài

隶 金 古 篆

96B6 — under the jurisdiction; a person in servitude.

逮dǎi; 棣dì; 隸=隶lì.

A hand seizing an animal's tail. PLC, 逮dǎi: to capture; 逮dài: to arrest, reach. ☞ 又yòu.17, 辶chuò.141.

手抓住猎物的尾巴,会逮意。

méng

8499 — to hoodwink, cheat, dupe, deceive; unconscious.

蒙: to cove, 檬, 朦, 曚 méng; 蒙 měng: the Mongol nationality.

Depicts hunters disguising themselves in animal skins. Later, radical 艹 cǎo.40 added. ☞ 冒 mào.130, 豕 shǐ.53.

猎人用动物的毛皮伪装自己。以接近猎物。《说文》作冡，加草的蒙指王女，即大女萝草。后与冡同。

qiāng

7F8C — an ancient nationality in China, the Qiang nationality, living in Sichuan Province.

A man with a ram headdress. ☞ 羊 yáng, 儿 = 人 rén.1.

头戴羊角的人形。羌族是中国古代较大的民族。

jiāng

59DC — a surname.

A woman with a ram headdress. ☞ 羊 yáng.53, 女 nǚ.27.

女人头戴羊角形。姜为羌族女子之称。也是羌族、羌姓之称。

Bushman's rock painting · Hunter disguised in an ostrich skin.
伪装成鸵鸟的猎人正在接近猎物（自《世界美术史》第一卷 296）。

xiū

羞甲 金 古 篆

7F9E — shy, bashful; shame;
to feel ashamed.

馐xiū: delicacy, dainty.

A hand catching a ram. 丑chǒu. 22 derives from 又yòu.17:
action of the hand . PLC. ☞ 羊yáng.53.

羞象手抓羊形，有进献和美味之意。

---

zhì

雉甲 古 篆

96C9
— pheasant.

To shoot an arrow at a bird 隹zhuī.56. 矢shǐ.152 is
also a phonetic.

象箭射鸟形。𨿘28FD8，古文雉。

**Shooting · Rubbing of bricks from
tombs. Han Dynasty.**

汉代画像砖·射猎。

---

zhì

彘甲 金 古 篆

5F58
— boar.

To shoot an arrow at a boar. 比bǐ is the glyph of the
boar's claws, and the 矢shǐ.152: arrow, is also a phonetic.
☞ 彖tuàn.69, 雉zhì, 能néng.50 and 鹿lù.51.

象箭射中野猪形。野猪中箭倒地，故彘在古文字
中用同墬=坠。

3.2 Agriculture 农业

At different times and in numerous places, many plants and animals have been domesticated. China is one of the original centers of agriculture, and dependence on millet and rice is characteristic of Chinese Neolithic agriculture. It has been suggested on somewhat speculative grounds that foxtail millet (*Setaria italica*) was cultivated before 6000 BC in the Yellow River basin and the loess highland of northern China. By 5000 BC rice (*Oryza sativa*) had probably been domesticated. This took place around the drainage area of the Yangtze River and the south eastern coast of China. Wheat and barley were introduced to China before 1300 BC, and the soy bean, perhaps around 1100 BC.

Setaria italica, foxtail millet

狗尾草,粟

中国是世界上农业起源中心之一,早在七、八千年以前就已进入相当繁荣的农耕阶段。中国考古发现的大量谷物遗存中,可以以粟(包括黍)和稻为代表。黄河流域广泛种植的粟,俗称小米,一般认为是由中国人首先从狗尾草驯化而来的。长江流域和东南沿海一带则在七千年以前,已经开始栽培稻谷,这在世界范围内属于最早的。伴随着农业的产生和发展,人类的定居生活也就更加稳固,往往形成大规模的聚落,为城市和国家的出现打下了基础。

3.2.1　Farmer's Tools　农具

"Slash-and-burn" may have been a principal feature of prehistoric farming. Chinese prehistoric farming implements were mainly made from stone, wood, bone and clam-shell. Bronze was an important material for making sacrificial utensils and weapons, not common farmer's tools.

中国原始的农具主要是用石、木、骨、蚌壳等物制成的，就是到了青铜时代，这种状况也没有很大的改善。因为青铜在古代中国有更重要的用途——祭祀与战争，只是到了铁器时代，大规模的毁林种田才得以实现。

lěi

耒金

8012 — plow.
诔，邦lěi；莱lèi.

An ancient plow. It's a radical in characters referring to farming.
一种下端歧出的翻土农具。

chén

辰甲

8FB0 — the fifth of Twelve Earthly Branches; celestial bodies; time.

宸，晨chén；唇chún；娠shēn；蜃shèn；振，赈，震zhèn.

Farmer's sickle made of clam-shell. PLC, 蜃shèn: clam; with a worm-radical. 辰chén as a phonetic has the meaning "to move" in certain characters, since someone believes that the glyph is from a caterpillar. ☞ 农nóng.75, 蓐rù.75.

商代以蚌壳为镰，在蚌壳上穿上孔并用绳索缚于拇指，用以掐断禾穗。或曰辰象蠕虫形。从辰之字多有动意。

3.2.2—Farming　农耕

· · · · ·

chǔ

楚甲

695A — name of ancient kingdom; pang, suffering; clear, neat; a surname.

礎=础chǔ；憷chù.

The combination of 林lín: forest, and 疋pǐ: variant form of 足zú.23: foot. 楚chǔ shows man marching into the virgin forest. 足zú is also a phonetic. ☞ 正zhèng.160.

楚4802=楚字以足向林，表示拔除荆棘，征服森林。

tǔ 土甲 金

571F — soil, earth; land; native.
吐, 钍tǔ; 吐tù; 肚dù; 杜dù;
社shè: the god of the land.

A dirt clod in a field. The upper cross represents the clod.
☞ 士shì.6.

象地面上的土块之形。

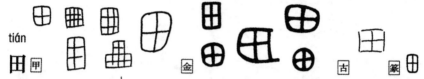

tián 田甲 金 古 篆

7530 — field, cropland;
a surname.

畋: to hunt, 佃, 钿tián;
佃, 甸, 钿diàn;
男nán; 亩mǔ; 界jiè.

A picture of the farmland with low earthen embankments between fields. It is also a symbol for hunting. ☞ 番fān.63, 畜chù.65.

象农田分割之形。一说象古代田猎战阵之形。畕, 比田也。
畾=畾léi, 田间也。雷léi.35, 古作畾。

jiāng 疆甲 金 古 篆

7586 — border;
territory.

僵, 缰jiāng.

畺 **757A**=疆 emphasizes the boundary ridges between fields 田tián. The bow, 弓gōng.150, was used for measurement; 土tǔ: land, is a meaning element.

田地间界线, 弓为丈量土地的工具, 土为意符。《说文》畺, 界也。从畕。三, 其界畫也。疆, 畺或从彊土。畺, 金文。疆, 俗。

fǔ 甫甲 金 古 篆

752B — just, only.

脯, 辅fǔ; 逋bū; 補=
补, 捕, 哺bǔ; 铺pū;
匍, 葡, 莆, 脯, 蒲pú;
浦, 埔, 圃pǔ; 铺pù.

A single seedling in a field 田tián. Later, the *seedling* was replaced by a phonetic 父fù.157, and 田tián was replaced by 用yòng.176. PLC, 圃pǔ: garden, plot, with 囗 wéi: enclosed area, as a radical.

甫即圃, 象田地里生长的小苗。

miáo

苗

82D7 — seedling; something resembling a young plant.

描, 瞄miáo; 喵miāo; 猫māo; 锚máo.

Two seedlings, the grass-radical 艸cǎo.40, in field 田tián.

象田地中小苗之形。

nóng

農 = 农 甲

8FB2 = 519C — agriculture; farmer; agrarian.

侬, 哝, 浓, 脓nóng.

Hands holding a *chen*-sickle. The 囟xìn.10 was later added as a phonetic element. In the modern form of this character, both the hands and the ancient phonetic element were merged into the unit 曲qū.195. ☞ 艸cǎo.40, 辰chén.73, 又yòu.17.

象手持辰镰从事农作之形。

rù

蓐 甲

84D0 — straw mat or mattress.

辱rǔ; 溽, 褥, 缛rù.

或体 耨 《说文》从木作 槈 或从金作 鎒

A farmer's hand holding a *chen*-sickle to weed. PLC, 薅hāo: to weed, and 耨nòu: weeding hoe, weeding.. ☞ 农nóng, 艸cǎo.40, 辰chén.73, 寸cùn.17

象手持辰镰除草之形，是薅、農的本字。

yì

藝 = 艺 甲 金

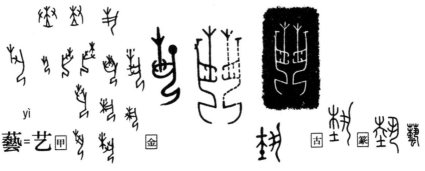

85DD=827A
— skill, art.
呓 yì.

A farme planting a seedling. The character is topped with a grass-radical. The lowr part of this character 云 yún.34 perhaps originated as the fanmer's foot and leg. The simplified form is a pictophone, see 乙 yǐ.95. ☞ 艸 cǎo.40, 热 rè.118.

象栽种植物形。本只作枛、埶，后加艸、云作蓺、藝。

fēng

4E30 — abundant; great; fine-looking; a surname.

邦，梆，帮 bāng；蚌 bàng；峰，烽，蜂，锋 fēng；逢，缝 féng；缝 fèng；蓬，篷 péng.

Packing the roots of a plant with soil. See below.

象用土包住植物根部之形。《说文》 夆 féng.5906, 悟也。从夂半声。半，篆文。丰 jiè.4E2F, 古芥字。

fēng

5C01 — to seal; to confer (a title, territory, etc.); feudalism.

幇=帮 bāng.

A hand planting a tree. The trees might have been planted to mark the boundary of a fief. ☞ 丰 fēng, 埶=艺 yì.75, 木 mù.38, 土 tǔ.74, 又 yòu.17 or 寸 cùn.17.

用手将树苗载入土中。邦封古同字。垗，古文封。

fèng

5949 — to give or present with respect; receive; esteem, revere; wait upon, attend.

俸 fèng: pay, salary; 捧 pěng: to extol, flatter; 棒 bàng.

Two hands holding a plant . 丰 fēng is also a phonetic element. The lower 手 shǒu.17. hand, was added later as a radical. PLC, 捧 pěng: to hold in both hands.
☞ 丰 fēng, 又 yòu.17 or 共 gòng.157, 手 shǒu.17.

双手持树苗形。《说文》奉，承也。从手从廾半声。烖，古文奉。从廾丰声。

以 甲 金 古 篆

4EE5 — to use; to take; according to; so as to.

似, 姒sì; 似shì.

A farmer using a spade or an ancient plow ☞ 厶sī, 人rén.1, 耜sì: plow. PLC.

象人用耒耜sì形。以字中厶即耜。

氏 甲 金 古 篆 参

6C0F — family name, surname.

舐shì; 祇qí; 纸, 抵zhǐ.

氏shì and 以yǐ are cognate characters. PLC. See above.

氏、以两字同源。或以为氏、氏、抵同源，以槌抵物。祇䝯酳齰四字同，人名，并见《訇鼎》。

利 甲 金 古 篆

5229 — shape; benefit; favourable.

犁, 梨, 蜊, 黎, 藜, 黧li; 俐, 莉, 痢, 猁li.

Ancient glyphs of 利lì show land being plowed to prepare for planting rice, and the dots represent the clods of dirt. However, the modern form of 利lì is a combination of 禾hé.44: rice and 刀dāo.85: knife, actually implying the harvest.

象以耒刺地种禾之形。古文字中的点象翻起的泥土。

井 甲 金 古 篆

4E95 — well.

阱jǐng: trap; 讲=講jiǎng; 进=進jìn.

Drawing of the frame of a well. The prehistoric oblong wells have been discovered in the Yellow River basin.

象井栏四木相交之形。中国人发明水井是在龙山文化早期，约公元前2800年。有了水井，先民就可以摆脱河湖的地理限制了。井、丼、邢=邢，并古姓氏。㓝，同鉡鈃鈃鈃瓶甄鏗。音形。长颈酒壶。

77

3. 2. 3—Harvest, Food Processing and Storage　农作物的收获加工与贮藏

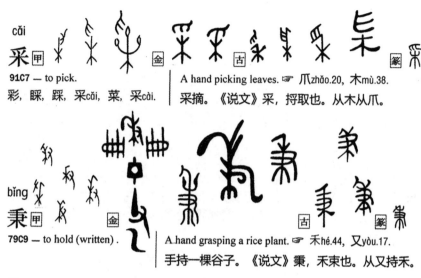

cǎi

采甲

91C7 — to pick.

彩，睬，踩，采cǎi，菜，采cài.

A hand picking leaves. ☞ 爪zhǎo.20, 木mù.38.

采摘。《说文》采，捋取也。从木从爪。

bǐng

秉甲

79C9 — to hold (written).

A hand grasping a rice plant. ☞ 禾hé.44, 又yòu.17.

手持一棵谷子。《说文》秉，禾束也。从又持禾。

jiān

兼金

517C — to combine, merge;
simultaneously, side by side; and.

鹣jiān; 廉, 籨=帘, 镰lián;
谦qiān; 歉qiàn; 嫌xián; 赚zhuàn.

A hand grasping two rice plants禾hé.44 at the same time.
☞ 秉bǐng.

手持两棵谷子。《说文》兼，并也。从又持秝。
兼持二禾，秉持一禾。廉qiān，谨。

lí

釐=厘甲

91D0=5398 — 1/100 or 1%;
a fraction.

嫠lí.

The upper element 犛lí indicates the threshing of wheat. 里lǐ is
a phonetic. ☞ 来lái.44, 攴pū: to beat lightly.

对谷物或小麦进行脱粒。

wǔ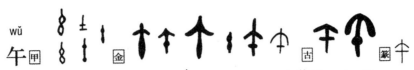

午甲 金 古 篆

5348 — the seventh of the twelve Earthly Branches; noon.

忤, 忤wǔ; 杵chǔ; 浒hǔ; 许, 浒xǔ.

A wooden pestle. PLC, 杵chǔ: pestle; with a wood-radical.

象木杵之形。忤篆文作牾。

jiù

臼古 篆

81FC — mortar, molar, joint.

舅, 舊=旧jiù.

A cutaway view of a mortar. 臼jiù is a radical. ☞ 舂chōng.80.

臿chā: pound the wheat, and its PLC 插chā: to insert.

象臼的剖视图。匷2096C=臿5336=柩。

yǎo

舀篆 参   金文稻

8200 — to ladle out.

蹈dǎo; 稻dào: rice; 韜图𦥑與图𦥑匷𦥑𦥑: 古器名, 鷂=駋, 馬行貌, 滔, 韜, 慆tāo.

舀 2695D=臼 shows a hand 手shǒu.17 taking the race cake from a mortar. PLC, 搯tāo: take out, with a hand-radical. ☞ 爪zhǎo.20, 臼jiù and 米mǐ.45.

象用手于臼中搯=掏物形。抗、𦥑、臼或体。

▶ **Pounding rice.**

杵臼图。(采自《中国科技史资料选编·农业机械》,257页,原书采自徐光启《农政全书》。)

chōng

春 甲 金 古

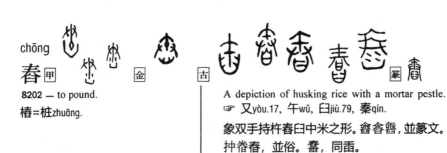

篆

8202 — to pound.

椿=桩zhuāng.

A depiction of husking rice with a mortar pestle.
☞ 又yòu.17, 午wǔ, 臼jiù.79, 秦qín.

象双手持杵舂臼中米之形。舂舂舂，並篆文。
抩卷舂，並俗。舂，同舀。

kāng

康 甲 金 古

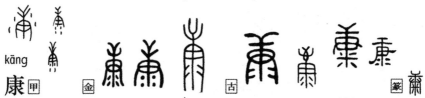

篆

5EB7 — health; a surname.

慷kāng.

Sifting flour from bran. PLC, 糠kāng: chaff.

象筛糠皮之形。糠糠糠糠，並古文。

qín

秦 甲 金 古

篆

79E6 — the *Qin* Dyansty,
B.C.221- B.C.207; a surname.

嗪qín; 蓁, 榛, 臻zhēn.

Pounding rice禾hé with pestle. PLC. ☞ 舂chōng.

双手持杵舂米形。秦秦秦秦，並古文秦。秦 guó，从三
秦，古文国字。

sǎn

散 甲 金 古

篆

6563 — to come loose;
scattered.

撒sā: to cast, let out,
撒sǎ: to scatter, sprinkle, spill;
霰xiàn; 散sàn: to disperse.

㪔=㪚 shows a hand holding a tool 攴 pū, used to peel off the
outer fibers of a hemp plant. ☞ 麻má, 攴 pū: to beat lightly.

攴击剥取麻类植物的表皮纤维。㪚，正作㪔，散本字。
散，正作㪚，或㪚字之讹。今通作散。

bīng

禀 甲 金 古 篆

7A1F — to be endowed with; to report to one's superior.
懔bǐng; 凛, 廪lǐn.

A barn. PLC, 廪lǐn: granary. ☞ 禾hé.44, 广guǎng.98: shed.
象谷仓之形。亩、禀、廪古同字,
声纽分属帮、来, 上古通。

▶ 禀的示意图。

sè

啬=啬 甲

55C7=556C — stingy; miserly.
墙, 蔷, 嫱, 樯qiáng; 穑sè.

金 古 篆

A wheat silo. PLC, 穑sè: reap, harvest, gather in, with a grain-radical 禾hé.44. ☞ 来lái.44: pictograph of wheat.
象麦仓之形。

bǐ

啚 甲 金 古 篆

555A
— ancient form of
鄙bǐ: small city, vulgar.

Perhaps the 囗wéi, top part of 啚bǐ, indicated the location of a granary.
啚, 从囗从亩, 鄙字初文, 表示都鄙界划图形。畐, 古文啚。
瘤, 肠中结病。屄属, 臀部。爐、皵, 俗燤字。圖=图, 从囗从啚, 版图之图。悥, 金文图谋字从心。鼺rùa, 喃字, 龟。
懔、啬、墙、鄙等汉字都与粮仓有关, 可能反映出收获以后大家的一些心态。

3.3 Domestication of Animals 驯化

The earliest animal to be domesticated by the early Chinese was probably the boar. The character 家 **jiā** (literally "home") may hint at the domestication process. In English, by comparison, the Latin root "domus" of domestication means "house". Perhaps, the modern use of 家 **jiā** came about as a result of the preliminary conditions which needed to be met before the domestication of animals could occur: the establishment of a durable shelter, the need for plenty of food, the use of fire and the development of hunting and agricultural skills.

中国古代青铜器铭文中有一种族徽图案(clan insignia),为一人双手牵马,胯下有猪形。这一图形可能反映了先民驯化动物的经历,也是"家"字的字源。考古研究证明,公元前6000年到5700年,黄河流域的先民已经开始驯养猪、狗和鸡;长江流域在公元前5000年也出现了狗,猪和水牛等家畜。马的驯化可能迟至青铜时代。"家"源于驯化正与英文中的情况相反,"驯化"(domestication)一词的拉丁词根"domus"意为"房子"。只有在人类有了永久性的聚居点,打猎和农业得到发展从而获得更多的猎物和多余的粮食,才有可能开始驯养动物。

jiā

家

5BB6 — home.
嫁: (of a woman) marry,
稼: to sow(grain), 稼jià.

豭2BBE6＝家jiā depicts a man riding on or otherwise controlling a boar. ☞ 大dà.3: , 宀mián, 豕shǐ.53.

人胯下有猪,表示驯化野猪。豭犳豭豭豭豭豭,古文家。

huàn

  甲骨文

金文圈，猪圈

豢 甲

8C62

— to feed, keep.

卷juǎn; 卷, 眷juǎn;
拳quán; 誊téng;
券quàn.

The glyphs show two hands 収=廾 gǒng catching a boar, note that the boar in the first pictograph is pregnant, since the baby boar is good for domestication. In later forms of this character, the rice 米mǐ.45 was added to indicate the meaning of 豢 huàn: to feed. The upper part 羑=䒑 juàn is also a useful picto-phonetic implying the hands or the action of hands.
☞ 子zǐ.26, 豕shǐ.53, 又yòu.17 and 舂chōng.80.

抓获野猪用来驯化。《说文》本从豕羑作豢。圂 hùn，厕也。

chù

篆豕 参㭬 椓 甲骨文刏

豖 甲

8C56 — castrated boar
(archaic).

豦zhǒng; 琢，啄，逐zhuó.

A castrated boar. PLC, 㭬 zhuó: to castrate, emasculate. 豦 as a componet has the meaning of beating. ☞ 豕shǐ.53.

象去势的野猪形。猪去势便于肥育。甲骨文有去势之刏字，卜辞记载：刏羌百……H.307、刏百羌 H.308。

xiù

篆臭

臭 甲

81ED — to castrate, emasculate;
beat.

臭chòu: ill-smelling; 臭 or 嗅xiù:
to smell, scent, sniff at; 溴xiù.

A combination of the pictographs of a nose 自zì.12 and a dog 犬quǎn.54, because the dog has a keen sence of smell.

自（鼻子）和犬的组合。先民已经认识到狗的嗅觉灵敏。肉腥臭篆作胜殠 ，鱼腥臭篆作鲑殠。

láo

牢 甲

7262 — prison, jail;
firm, fast, durable.

A corral for animals. 宀mián above 牛niú: ox, indicates an enclosure.

象兽栏之形。奥，篆文牢。囷宰馬，古文牢。牢，俗牢。

83

mù

牧甲

7267 — to tend.

Tending oxen. ☞ 牛niú, 攴 pū: to beat lightly.

牧牛。惄lí，同離，忧虑。

Rock painting · Tending sheep.

岩画·放牧图。内蒙狼山（自《世界美术史》第一卷225页）。

wéi

爲=为甲

7232=4E3A

— to do, act.

为wèi; 伪wěi.

A hand 又yòu.17 or 爪zhǎo.20 leading an elephant 象xiàng.52. PLC.

以手引象。䘏䍐䍐，古文。為，同爲。爲、为，俗。

chú

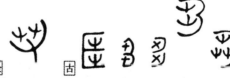

芻=刍甲

82BB=520D — to chew;
to cut grass; hay, fodder.

雏chú; 趋qū; 诌zhōu;
绉，皱zhòu; 邹，骑zōu.

Shows a hand 又yòu.17 gathering grass 艹cǎo.40 for animal.
☞ 反刍fǎnchú: to ruminate, cud.

象手取草形。《说文》芻，刈艸也。象包束艸之形。

dāo

刀 甲 金 古 篆 刀

5200 — knife.

忉, 氘, 叨dāo; 叨tāo; 刁diāo;
倒dǎo; 到, 倒dào; 钊, 招,
昭zhāo; 沼zhǎo; 召, 诏zhào.

Pictograph of an ancient bronze knife. ☞ 刃rèn, and 刂 also radical.

象青铜刀形。刅, 同从。刕lí, 姓。出蜀刀达
之后, 避难改为刕字。

rèn

刃 甲 古 篆 刃

5203 — blade.

刅, 纫, 認 = 认,
韧, 韌rèn; 忍rèn.

The dot in this character was derived from the blade of a knife to mark the cutting edge of the knife. ☞ 刀dāo.

刃字中的点源于表示刀刃部的线条, 或即以点指示刃
部。歰, 同涩。釰, 同刃。

▶ **Pottery fragments with pictures of knives.**
Shang period
陶文·刀

bā

八 甲 金 古 篆 八

516B — eight.

扒, 叭bā; 趴pā;
扒pá.

Derived from both the drawing of two separate things and the sound of breaking. PLC. See below.

八表示一物分成两部分, 也是借用了物体分裂开的声音。
肎, 从肉从八, 祭品之數。佾, 舞行列也, 一列八人。

fēn

分甲 〔oracle forms〕 金 〔bronze forms〕 古 〔old forms〕 篆 〔seal form〕

5206 — distinguish; separate; divide, share; a cent; a minute.

芬，吩，纷，酚 fēn；
汾，棼，豮 fén；粉 fěn；
分，份，忿，氛 fèn；
掰=擘 bāi；颁 bān；
扮 bàn；岔 chà；盼 pàn；
盆 pén；贫 pín。

A combination of 八 bā.85 and 刀 dāo.85: knife, means something having been cut and separated.

用刀剖物，一分为二。从分之字，多有分开、细小之意：米分则成粉，财分则贫穷，土分则坋塵矣。或有大意：颁，大頭。帉，大巾。粉，牂羊，高壮之羊。豮 hài，要也。

▶ **Inscriptions on some oracle bones with "八" and animals.**

甲骨文所见从八之字。

bàn

半 金 〔bronze〕 古 〔old〕 〔seal forms〕 篆

534A — half, semi-; in the middle.

判 pàn: to chop；伴，拌，绊 bàn。

A combination of 八 bā.85: a meaning element for cutting into separate parts, and 牛 niú.52: cow, probably a large object for share. PLC, 判 pàn: to chop, with a knife-radical 刂=刀 dāo.85.

八与牛的组合。八有剖分之意。

suì

豙 甲 〔oracle〕 古 〔old〕 〔seal forms〕 篆

34B8 — archaic form of 遂 suì: to satisfy; then.

遂 suì；隧，遂，邃，燧 suì。

A combination of 八 bā.85: a meaning element that indicates cutting into separate parts, and 豕 shǐ.53: boar. PLC.

☞ 隊=队 duì.69.

八与豕的组合，八有剖分之意。劉，音旋。

kè

刻 金 古 篆

523B — to carve, inscribe; a quarter of an hour; petty; harshly.

A combination of a boar 亥hài.54 and a knife 刀dāo.85, then 刻kè shows a boar being slaughtered.

用刀宰猪之意。捌22BB0埘2A8EB，二字生僻未详。蜊2B2C9，きさ，同蚶，日本字，赤貝の古名。

mǎo

卯 甲 金 古 篆

536F — mortise; roll call; the fourth of the twelve Earthly Branches.

聊liáo；柳liǔ；贸mào；泖，峁，昴，铆mǎo.

The incision made when slaughtering animals. PLC. ☞ 劉=刘liú: to kill, with 卯 as phonetic. In ancient times, the consonant *m* and *l* in Chinese language were not distinguished.

可能指屠宰牲畜的割口之形。或以为卯是卵字的初文，后加点以指示树干皱褶处藏有虫卵。非非非卝聊，並古文卯。

liú

留 金 古 篆

7559 — to remain, reserve, keep.

溜，熘liū；榴，瘤，镏，骝，馏liú；遛，镏，溜，馏liù.

Combination of 卯mǎo and 田tián: a symbol for hunting. ☞ 番fān.63 and 畜chù.65.

从田从卯。篆作畱。留畱甾，俗。䄂㽞，宿留。

jiě

解 甲 金 古 篆

89E3 — to separate; to solve.

蟹，懈，解，邂xiè.

Shows the horn 角jiǎo.55 of an ox 牛niú.52 was hold and the ox being butchered, later a knife 刀dāo.85 was introduced in the glyph to replace the hands.

甲骨文解字表示以手解牛角之形，后在字形中用刀代替了人手。

qí

奇 甲 古

5947 — strange, queer, rare; to surprise.

崎, 骑qí; 绮qǐ; 奇, 剞, 犄, 畸jī; 寄jì; 猗, 漪yī; 倚, 椅, 旖yǐ.

A man riding a horse. The lower part 可kě is a phonetic element. PLC, 骑qí: to ride cavalry: with the radical 马mǎ: horse. ☞ 大dà.3.

人骑马之形。

kè

克 甲 金 古 篆

514B — to restrain; to overcome; gram.

氪kè.

A cleaver with a handle for skinning animals, a flaying tool. PLC.

象剥皮工具形。传统的解释为象人肩形。兢jīng。嶃zhān。

pí

皮 甲 金 古 篆

76AE — skin; leather, hide; surface.

波, 菠, 玻bō; 跛, 簸bǒ; 簸bò; 披pī; 陂, 疲, 铍pí; 坡, 陂, 颇pō; 婆pó; 破pò.

A hand 又yòu.17 holding a flaying tool. ☞ 克kè.

手持剥皮工具。或用手剥皮形。皮为部件多有波动意。摲, 菣字俗讹。皴, 俗皱。

gé

革 甲 金 古 篆

9769 — leather, hide; to change.

A spread-out hide of a flayed animal. The animal's head and tail are still attached to the hide. It is a radical in characters referring to leather.

象一张摊开的带有动物头和尾的兽皮。

Chapter 4

CRAFTSMANSHIP 手工业

To some extent, the characters in this chapter reflect certain feats of craftsmanship achieved in China 3000 years ago. However, China did not maintain her glory in the emergence of modern science and technology. In Chinese history, monarchs and philosophers only emphasized the skills of governing. From the Spring and Autumn Period (770 — 476 BC), Chinese intellectuals had a habit of "talking tall" and took a casual attitude towards engineering and technology. They themselves lacked a system of logic and a spirit inclined towards practical experimentation. As a sharp contrast, a lot of craftsmen were illiterate. They could neither read nor write complicated characters. Therefore, sometimes Chinese inventions were repeated. China's failure to develop technologically was associated with its feudal customs and closed society.

这一章的汉字在一定程度上能够反映出中国三千多年前在工程技术方面所取得的成就。但是,中国的知识分子从春秋战国以来,只知坐而论道,缺乏逻辑体系和实践精神;而大批有实践经验的手工艺人往往目不识丁。汉字本身的复杂性也是造成这一状况的原因之一。加之历代帝王只知"治人"的"南面之术"而不重视科学知识,使得中国人没能为近代科学的产生做出她应有的贡献。

4.1 Silk and Weaving 丝绸与纺织

The cultivation of the silkworm and the weaving of silk originated in China. Silk is the main Chinese contribution to the world's material civilization, and sericulture is a featuristic of Chinese civilization.

The earliest existing fragments of silk gauze, which belong to the Liangzhu culture dated about 3300 — 2200 BC, were discovered in Zhejiang Province in 1958. The silk was identified as that produced by domesticated silkworms. In the Han Dynasty the fine and brilliant material was traded and eagerly sought by the Romans, and later by the Byzantines. Having acquired a taste for such dress, they imported the silk and coveted the secret. At that time, an extensive trade was established along the routes through Central Asia to the West. Silk was the product which gave its name to this trade route, though it was not the only item in the trade. The trade was organized by officials in the form of government-sponsored caravans and made safe by the Chinese armies.

BELT LOOM
腰带织机

中国是全世界最早饲养家蚕和缫丝制绢的国家，而且长期以来曾经是从事这种手工业的唯一的国家。丝绸是中国对于世界物质文化最大的一项贡献。

中国最早的丝织品开始出现于中国东南的良渚文化*中，经商代到战国则已相当发达。由于在汉代画像石上出现了不少反映纺织的内容，人们对汉代的纺织业有了较详细的了解，著名的丝绸之路也是在汉代开辟的。但这部分汉字所反映的一些纺织工艺则要早于汉代。

suǒ

索 甲   金   古   篆

7D22 — large rope; to search; a surname.

嗦suo.

Glyphs 糸=𢇁=索 suǒ show a braided rope. The threads are hung and steadied with a H-shaped fixture.

编绳索形。《说文》索，艸有茎叶，可作绳索。从米糸。

* 良渚文化是指中国长江下游地区的新石器时代文化，因浙江省杭州市余杭县良渚遗址而得名，主要分布于太湖地区，年代为公元前 3300 年至前 2200 年。

zhuān

專＝专[甲]

5C08＝4E13 — special.

砖zhuān; 转zhuǎn; 传, 转, 啭zhuàn; 传chuán; 團＝团, 抟tuán.

A spindle 叀 zhuān being turned by a hand 又yòu.17 or 寸cùn.17. PLC, 转zhuǎn: to turn, change, transform; 转zhuàn: to turn, revolve, rotate, with the radical of 车 chē.142.

用手旋转纺锤使三线捻成绳。𧄍㢉玄㙜玄，並古文專。

sāng

桑[甲]

6851 — mulberry.

嗓, 颡, 搡, 磉sǎng.

A mulberry tree with its leaves shown. Later, the *hands*, three 又yòu.17 in the treetop may represent picking the fresh leaves. Leaves from thirty full-grown trees are needed to produce 5 or 6 kilograms of silk, and of that probably only half can be used to make thread. ☞ 木mù, 采cǎi.

桑树形。㮼㮐㮛桒桒㮠，並古文桑。

W 91.8

◄ Gathering mulberry leaves. This motif occurs on a bronze vessel. Warring States Period（475－221 BC）.

战国铜器·采桑图。图中所绘桑树为经过人工改良的矮株的"地桑"或"鲁桑"。

shǔ

蜀[甲]

8700 — ancient name of Sichuan Province.

觸＝触chù; 躅, 独dú; 烛, 躅zhú; 屬＝属shǔ; 浊, 镯zhuó; 嘱, 瞩, 属zhǔ.

A silkworm with a big eye 目mù.11. The 虫chóng: worm-radical was a later addition. PLC.

象蚕之形。在五千多年前中国人已开始驯养家蚕并利用蚕丝进行纺织。一个蚕茧的丝纤维长度能达到八百至一千米，其中雄性的蚕平均能比雌性的多吐丝一百米左右。

jīng

巠 = 巠 _金

5DE0 = 22016 — warp, vertical textile.

劲jìn; 径, 茎, 经jīng; 颈, 刭jǐng; 劲, 径, 胫, 痉, 经jìng; 轻, 氢qīng; 烃tīng.

Glyphs show the organzine on a prehistoric belt or back-strap loom which was tied on one end around the weaver's waist and stretched at the other end by his or her feet. It is a common element in certain Chinese characters, indicating *straight* or *stretched*.

象史前的一种腰带织机，亦称腰机。这种织机通常由两根平行杆支承经纱，一根固定在织布者的腰带上，另一根由织布者双脚蹬开以绷紧经纱。

jǐ

幾 = 几 _金

5E7E = 51E0 — several, some; 几jī: almost.

叽, 饥, 玑, 讥, 机, 矶jī.

An ancient wood loom rigged with silk thread 丝sī. PLC, 機=机jī: machine; with a radical of wood 木mù. ☞ 人rén.1, 几jī.137.

象织机上装挂丝线形。

▶ **Reproduction of a wooden loom, Han Dynasty** (*after Wu*, *Cengde*. *p.* 29).
汉代织机复原图。

yǔ

予 _金

4E88 — to give, grant.

予, 预yù; 抒, 纾shū; 序xù; 野yě.

Shows a shuttle which flies back and forth on the loom. PLC, 杼zhù: shuttle, with a radical of wood 木mù.
予表示在织机上来回飞动的梭子。幻 huàn 𠃟，从反予。

mì

糸 甲 金 古 纟,古文糸 篆

7CF8 — fine silk.

絲＝丝: silk, mulberry silk, 噝, 鸶 sī.

A skein of silk. It is a radical as 糸 7CF9 = 纟 2EB0 for characters related to silk and weaving. Meanwhile, most words referring to color contain the silk-radical, an indication of the brilliance of the ancient material: 红 hóng: red, 绯 fēi: bright red, 绛 jiàng: crimson, 绿 lǜ: green, 紫 zǐ: purple.

束丝之形。从糸之字多与颜色有关。縹，浅青色。緗，浅黄色。縹緗，指书卷。古人习用浅青或浅黄色的丝帛作书囊书衣。萧统《文选·序》詞人才子，則名溢於縹囊；飛文染翰，則卷盈乎緗帙。

ěr

爾＝尔 甲 金 古 篆

723E＝5C14 — you; so (written).

迩 ěr; 弥 mí; 玺 xǐ; 你 nǐ.

A tool for spinning silk thread. PLC.

象一种络丝的工具形。

luàn

亂＝乱 金 古 篆

4E82＝4E71 — in a mess; disorder; arbitrary.

恋, 挛, 娈, 孪, 脔, 銮, 鸾 luán; 变 biàn; 恋 liàn; 蛮 mán; 弯, 湾 wān; 辭＝辞 cí.

The glyph 矞＝亂 shows two hands arranging the disheveled silk. ☞ 叟 biāo, 爪 zhuǎ.20, 又 yòu.17.

双手理丝形。乱字古代训治。緣、亂同源。

jiū

丩 甲 金 古 篆

4E29 — archaic character.

叫 jiào; 纠, 赳 jiū; 收 shōu: to gather, collect.

Tangled silk. 纠 jiū: to entangle.

象丝线纠绕形。𣄙 chōu, 目不从正。𦬖 jiū, 草之相丩者。疝, 腹中急。訆, 大呼。䚋, 高声。句字从丩。

4.2　Architecture　建筑

In China, the history of architecture can be traced back to two forms of dwellings——the cave-dwelling and the pile-dwelling. Remains of many prehistoric houses have been discovered; they are considered the prototypes of characteristic Chinese architecture.

中国的建筑史可能源于两种史前建筑形式——穴居和巢居。半地穴居址已有考古发现，它是由穴居发展而来的；而架空居住面的所谓"干栏式建筑"即巢居则比较难于留下什么遗迹。随着人类社会的发展，地面建筑逐渐成为建筑的主要形式，并发展为独具特色的中国建筑体系。

Neolithic wattle-and-daub dwellings, facing south and half-buried to avoid the icy winter winds. Banpo site.

半坡遗址建筑·半地穴居。

xué

穴 古

7A74 — a cave, cavern, grotto; a den; vital points recognized in acupuncture.

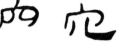

甲骨文突字

Drawing of a cave. The two dots indicate drops of water in the cave. It is also a radical with the meaning of cave or hole.

象洞穴形。两点指洞穴内的水滴。

shēn

深 金

7F59 — deep.

琛 chēn; 探 tàn: to delve into.

A hand 又 yòu.17 exploring the inside of a cave 穴 xuè. PLC.

象用手探试洞穴深浅之形。

yǐ

乙 甲

金　古　篆

4E59 — the second of the ten Heavenly Stems; second.

钇 yǐ, 藝=艺, 億=亿, 憶=忆 yì.

An ancient spade or billhook. It was borrowed to be used as one of the elements in the decimal counting cycle. ☞ 挖 wā: to dig; with a hand-radical 扌 shǒu.17 and the meaning component 穴 xué: cave.

或象挖土的工具形。《说文》解释为象草木生长受阻委曲上出之形。乁 4E41.yí, 流也。〈 21FE8.quǎn, 水小流也。或三字同。

gè

各 甲

金　古　篆

5404 — each, every, various.

铬 gè; 搁, 格, 胳 gē; 格, 阁 gé; 貉 hé; 咯 kǎ; 客, 恪 kè; 落 là; 烙, 落, 酪 lào; 咯 lo; 璐, 鹭, 露, 路, 赂 lù; 略 lüè; 洛, 烙, 落, 络, 骆 luò.

A combination of the symbol of a foot 止 zhǐ.22 and the cave-dwelling. 各 gè itseft implies a man entering the dwelling. PLC. ☞ 客 kè: guest, 出 chū.97, 复 fù.

以足向居穴表示落脚为客。古文或从彳作洛。《客家方言詩》四客詺 21AE5 鑫 21B1A 酒醉歸。

95

chū

出

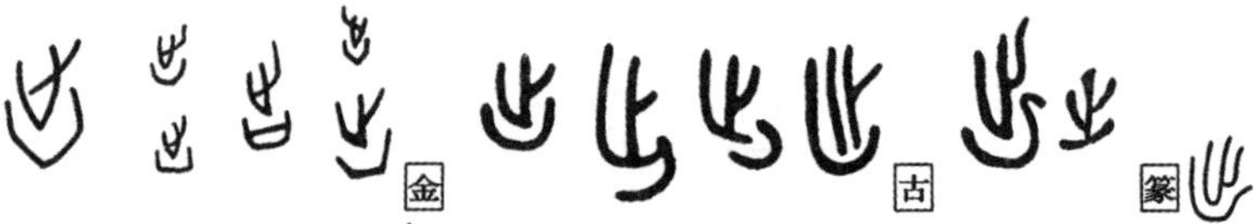

51FA — to go or come out; exceed; issue, put up; arise, happen; pay out; and 齣=出: a dramatic piece.

础=礎chǔ; 绌, 黜chù; 咄duō; 祟suì; 拙zhuō; 茁zhuó; 屈qū; 倔, 掘, 崛jué; 倔juè; 窟kū.

A combination of the symbol of a foot 止zhǐ.22 and the symbol of a cave–dwelling. 出chū implies a man leaving the dwelling. ☞ 各gè.95.

出字上为止下为古代居穴，以足背向穴居，表示自穴居外出。𡴶，古文供。

fù

阜

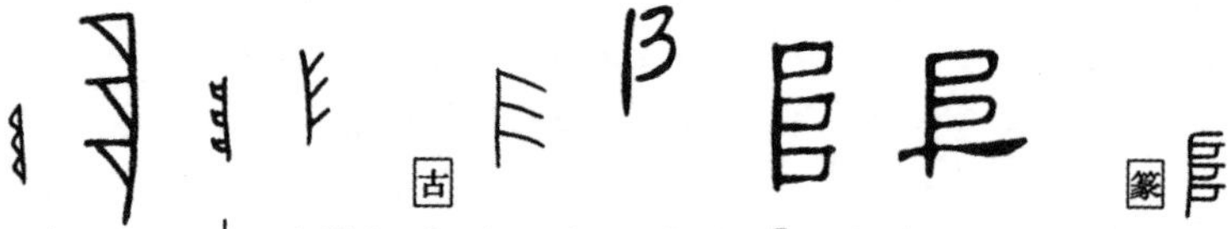

961C — mound; abundant.

埠bù.

A flight of stairs. It is a radical as 阝 referring moving up and down which appears on the left side of some Chinese characters such as 降jiàng.30. See 邑yì below.

象峭崖有阪階之形。《说文》𠂤，大陸山無石者。象形。𨺅，古文。又𨼦，同𨺅。

yì

邑

9091 — town, city.

悒, 挹yì; 扈, 滬=沪hù.

The settlement of early man. It is a radical as 阝 referring settlement or city which appears on the right side of some Chinese characters such as 都 dū: capital, metropolis. See 阜fù.96 above.

先人聚居之所。𨙨，反邑为苑。𨛜=𨝌，同巷。

yōng

邕

9095 — harmonious, peaceful; a city's name.

癰=痈yōng.

A settlement near a river. ☞ 川chuān: river, 邑yì.96: city.

近水而居。

liáng

良 甲 金 古 篆

826F — good, fine.

粮liáng; 跟liàng; 狼, 锒, 琅, 郎, 廊, 螂láng; 朗lǎng; 浪làng; 娘niáng; 酿=釀niàng.

The foundation and porches of a prehistoric dwelling. PLC, 廊láng: veranda. ☞ 广guǎng.

象半地穴居址。一说良象河流上架的桥梁形。㐭，篆文。㐭，俗㐭。昌眉饀箟，並古文良。

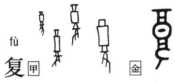

fù

复 甲 金 古 篆 復

590D — to turn round, turn over; duplicate; compound, complex; answer; again.

復=复, 腹, 鰒, 蝮, 覆fù; 愎bì; 履lǚ.

A footpring 止zhǐ.22 and the prehistoric dwelling 良liáng. It represented a man leaving the building.

人出入半地穴居室。《说文》复，行故道也。復，往來也。覆，地室也。複，重衣貌。

liù

六 甲 金 古 篆

516D — six.

陆=陆lù, liù.

A prehistoric house. The first glyph shape * may be a drawing of a pile-dwelling. A common radical in characters related to the idea of dwellings, 宀 mián, derived from these ancient pictographs.

史前地面建筑。甲骨文第一个字形或指干栏式建筑。

Neolithic roundhouses, Banpo site.
半坡遗址圆形房子。

97

yǎn

5E7F — shed, ridge of a roof.

廣=广: wide; to expand,
犷guǎng; 矿, 邝, 圹kuàng.

A shed attached to a house.
PLC, 扩kuò: to enlarge. ☞ 六liù.97.

象扩建的棚屋。庵ān 字初文。

xiàng

向甲 金 古 篆

5411 — direction.
饷, 响=響xiǎng; 垧, 晌shǎng.

The window of a building.

房子的窗形。

shàng

掌, 古玺文

5C1A — still; to esteem, value;
a surname.

赏shǎng; 绱shàng; 裳shang;
常, 嫦, 償=偿, 嘗=尝, 倘
裳cháng; 敞, 廠=厂chǎng; 撑
瞠chēng; 當=当, 裆, 铛dāng;
黨=党, 谠, 挡dǎng; 棠, 堂,
膛, 镗, 螳táng; 倘, 淌, 躺,
镗, 鹔, 傥tǎng; 趟tàng;
掌zhǎng.

Vapor or smoke issuing out from the window of a dwelling.
PLC. ☞ 八bā.85, 向xiàng, 敞chǎng: to open.

尚表示由窗口向上散气。或敞字初文。

▶ **Neolithic cave-dwelling, Banpo site.**
半坡遗址建筑·地穴居。

98

yú

余 甲  金 古 篆

4F59 — I (written) .

餘=余yú; 除, 蜍chú; 荼, 塗, 酴, 途tú; 徐xú; 叙, 漵xù.

A shed with one center pole. PLC. ☞ 舍shě: shed, hut; compare the lower square element with those of 高gāo and 仓cāng.100.

中间有柱的栅舍。馀，金文叙字。

gāo

高 甲 金 古 篆

9AD8 — tall, high; of a high level or degree; a surname.

篙, 膏gāo; 藁, 镐, 缟, 搞, 稿gǎo; 嵩sōng; 敲qiāo.

A tall building. ☞ 京jīng, 享xiǎng.100.

象台观高貌。冂表示高台。

qiáo

乔=乔 金 古 篆 参

55AC=4E54 — tall; to disguise; a surname.

侨, 荞, 桥qiáo.

Derives from 高gāo: high building, by adding some strokes on the top of the building. ☞ 高gāo.

乔是高的加划衍生字。从乔之字多有高、长之意。挢，举手。蹻，举足。镐，高足鼎。鷮，长尾雉。骄，马高六尺。趫，善缘木之人。

jīng

京 甲  金 古 篆

4EAC — the capital of a country.

惊, 鲸jīng; 景, 憬jǐng; 凉liáng; 凉, 谅, 晾liàng; 掠lüè; 影yǐng.

A palatial structure. ☞ 高gāo.

象宫殿高貌。

99

Reproduction of a palace, Western Zhou Dynasty (*after Mao, Peiqi*). 西周宫殿建筑复原图（陕西岐山凤雏村）。

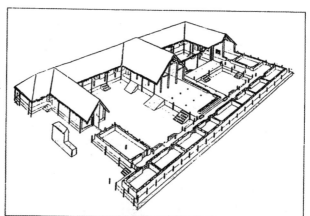

xiǎng 享 甲

4EAB — to enjoy.
淳, 醇, 鹑chún; 敦, 墩dūn; 燉 = 炖dùn; 谆zhūn.

亯＝章＝官＝享 shows a tower built over a city gate, or a temple built on the high platform. PLC, 鄣＝郭＝章＝章＝郭guō: the outer wall of a city, with the city-radical 邑yì.96. ☞ 廓kuò: outline.

官象高台上的享堂建筑。章＝郭象四面建有城楼的城堡。

wǎ 瓦 古

74E6 — tile, slate; watt.
瓦wà: to tile.

Two roof tiles. It is a radical for earthenware. ☞ 户hù.

两片屋瓦俯仰相承。一说象旋转的纺塼（古称瓦）形。

cāng 倉＝仓 甲

5009＝4ED3 — storehouse, barn, granary.
伧, 沧, 苍, 舱cāng; 疮, 创chuāng; 创, 怆chuàng; 枪, 抢, 呛qiāng; 抢qiǎng; 呛, 炝, 跄qiàng.

A simple house with a door, 户hù.135, and a stone step. Here, the upper 스 jí represents the roof of the storehouse.

只有一扇门的仓廪形。

guō

29AD6 — outer wall or surrounding area of a city; frame; rim; a surname.

墎 guō; 槨 guǒ; 廓，鞹 kuò.

亯=亯=章=章=郭 guō shows a city or palace with four gate towers. It was a radical, and later the character was replaced by 郭 guō. ☞ 享 xiǎng.

象四面建筑有城楼的城堡。城亯字后世作郭。

yè

業=业

696D=4E1A — career, line of business or industry; achievement.

A pillar, particularly pillars for musical instrument shelf. PLC.

古代悬挂乐器木架上的支柱。鐷、鐷，金文业。鐷29443=鐷29444，乐也。

duì

對=对

5C0D=5BF9 — to set, adjust; right, correct; an answer, reply; mutual, face.

懟=怼=懟=懟 duì.

A hand erecting a pillar on the land. ☞ 业 yè, 土 tǔ.74, 又 yòu.17 or 寸 cùn.

象在地上用手树立起柱子。古文字从土作對，或从士作對。對，讹字。

The following four characters illustrate an ancient method of building walls by stamping earth between wooden frames.

　　下面四字可能反映了一种远古的建筑方法——版筑法。版筑法就是在拟筑的城墙内外两侧壁和向前延伸的一个横头处用横列木板堵成长方形板槽，然后在木板槽内逐层填土夯实。继之提高堵板，逐步加高和伸延以夯筑出墙体。这种建筑方法可能要早于商代中期，是由更为古老的夯筑法发展而来的。

基_甲 金 古 篆

57FA — foundation; basic, cardinal.
椇 = 棋 qí.

A bin 其qí.136 and earth 土tǔ.74. It implies earth being filled in a trench and tamped into form for wall foundition. 其qí is a phonetic as well.

用土筐向地面上挖出的槽中填土，再经夯实形成墙壁基础。

zhuàng

壯=壮_金 古 篆

58EF= 58EE— strong, robust; to strengthen.
莊=庄, 裝zhuāng.

Earth being filled into the wooden frames to be compacted into a silid wall. ☞ 裝zhuāng: to fill in, 爿pàn: board.

（用土筐）向板槽中装土。玄裝zàng。奘zhuāng 汉，壮汉。

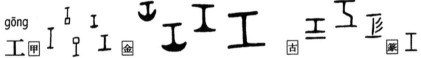

gōng

工_甲 金 古 篆

5DE5 — labour, work; skill; be good at.
攻，红，功gōng；汞gōng；贡gòng；扛，肛，缸gāng；杠gàng；红，虹hóng；讧hòng；江，豇jiāng；扛káng；项xiàng.

A wood tamper, or mallet.
夯杵。《说文》玒zhǎn，极巧视之也。屦，转也，今作展。裘=襄zhàn，丹縠衣，红细绸缎衣。汸23C85同江。盉，或同舌。䡇，同軖。

gōng

巩_金 古 篆

5DE9 — to consolidate.
恐kǒng；跫qióng；築=筑zhù: to build.

A man pounding the earth with a tamper 工gōng which is also a phonetic.
人手持夯杵。《说文》鞏，擕也。巩=巩，抱也。鞏=巩，以韦束也。鞏同巩。今简化字鞏作巩。

4.3 Pottery Making and Metallurgy 陶冶

4.3.1—Pottery Making 制陶

▶ Reproduction of two Neolithic
kilns, Banpo site.
半坡遗址陶窑复原图。

After the glaciers of the Ice Age retreated, clay and pottery-making surfaced. Thus, pottery is often identified with the Neolithic culture in China. Certain potsherds dating back as far as 10,000 years ago have been found in Guangxi Province.

陶器的出现是人类从旧石器时代进入到新石器时代的重要标志。中国有着悠久的制陶历史。在中国广西出土过距今约一万年的陶片,这是目前已知有关中国制陶史的最早记录。

táo

匋 金

530B — ancient form of
陶 táo: pottery.
淘,陶,萄 táo;掏 tāo.

A potter, 人 rén.1 or 勹 bāo, pounding clay in a container with a pestle.
勹 bāo is also a phonetic. ☞ 人 rén.1, 午 wǔ. 79 and 缶 fǒu.

象陶工持杵捣泥形。

fǒu

缶 甲 金

7F36 — an amphora-
like jar.
窑 yáo: kiln.

The pestle and the container in 匋 táo. It is radical for earthenware.
陶字中的杵与容器。鈢,金文缶。炻=炰=臬 fǒu,烧制陶器。
花是扬州种,瓶是汝州窑。

gōng

公 甲 金

516C—public; male (animal); a surname.
蚣 gōng;忪,松,淞,菘 sōng;讼,颂 sòng;忪 zhōng;翁,嗡,蓊 wēng;滚 gǔn.

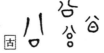

An earthen jar. PLC, 瓮 wèng: urn. ☞ 八 bā. 85.
象瓮口之形。从八或表示公平分物之意。《说文》公,平分也。从八从厶。厶,古文私。
厸 20AEC, 同厸 221B6, 古文幽。

4. 3. 2—Metallurgy   冶金

In view of the Chinese bronze culture, the characters derived from metallurgy are limited. The reason may be that bronze-casting was a special technique used for making weapons and ritual vessels which were imperative for governing. Common people could not duplicate the process of metallurgy.

"国之大事,在祀与戎"。在中国的商周时代,青铜主要用来制造维护国家统治的工具——祭器与兵器,一般人不易了解青铜冶炼与铸造方面的技术。因此,反映原始冶金技术的文字出现较迟,数量也有限。

Chinese bronze vessels.

中国青铜器。

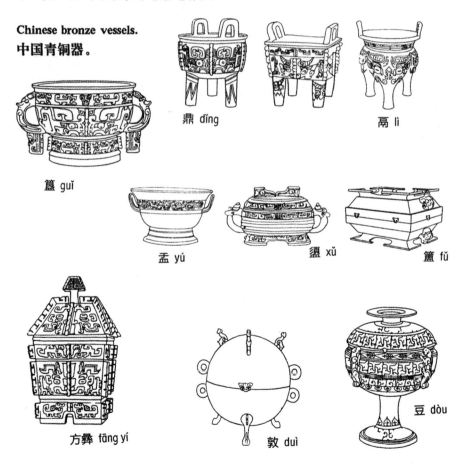

鼎 dǐng

鬲 lì

簋 guǐ

盂 yú

盨 xǔ

簠 fǔ

方彝 fāng yí

敦 duì

豆 dòu

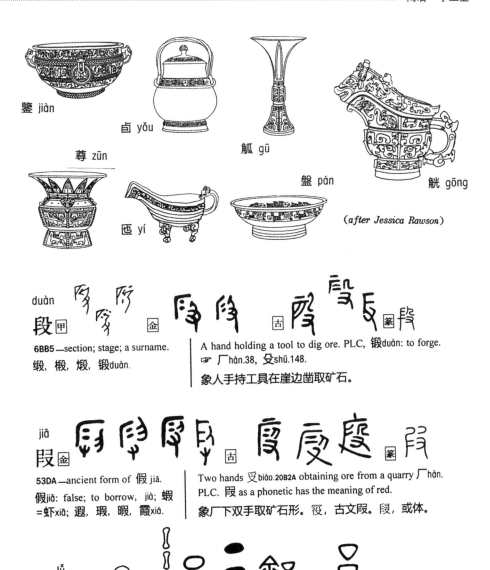

鑒 jiàn

卣 yǒu

尊 zūn

觚 gū

匜 yí

盤 pán

觥 gōng

(after Jessica Rawson)

duàn

段 甲 金 古 篆

6BB5 —section; stage; a surname.

缎, 椴, 煅, 锻 duàn.

A hand holding a tool to dig ore. PLC, 锻 duàn: to forge.
☞ 厂 hàn.38, 殳 shū.148.

象人手持工具在崖边凿取矿石。

jiǎ

叚 金 古 篆

53DA —ancient form of 假 jiǎ.

假 jiǎ: false; to borrow, jià; 蝦
=虾 xiā; 遐, 瑕, 暇, 霞 xiá.

Two hands 殳 biào.20B2A obtaining ore from a quarry 厂 hàn.
PLC. 叚 as a phonetic has the meaning of red.

象厂下双手取矿石形。 㱮, 古文叚。 叚, 或体。

lǚ

吕=呂 甲 金 古 篆

5442=5415 —surname.

閭 lǘ; 铝: aluminum, 郘
梠 lǚ; 莒, 筥 jǔ.

Two bronze ingots. PLC, 鋁=鑢 lǜ: metal ingots (ancient).
☞ 金 jīn.106.

象两块圆饼状的铜锭形。

jīn

金 [金]

91D1 — gold; bronze.

鍇 ǎn; 淦 gàn; 锦 jīn;
钦 qīn; 捦 qín; 趛 yǐn;
銜 xián; 鑫 xīn.

Shwos a mould for casting an ax 王 wáng.158, and taking the top part of 今 jīn.162 as phonetic, two dot 呂 lǚ.106 stands for bronze. It's a radical more often on the left as 釒 or 钅 than at the bottom like 金.

象青铜箭头。鉹 9342.piān 鈌，鉌鐐。鑫 28C3B，宝、玉二音。

fán

凡 [甲]

51E1 — commonplace, ordinary; this mortal world, the earth; every, any, all.

矾=礬，钒 fán；帆 fān；犯，梵 fàn.

A mould with four carrying bars. PLC.
☞ 范 fàn: model, pattern, limits.

凡象铸金属件的范模。传统的解释为象盘形。

Iron casting, rubbing from a stone relief showing a round bellows and iron forging. Han Dynasty, excavated from a tomb in Shandong Province (*after Wu, Cengde. p. 25*).

汉画像石·冶铁图。山东滕县宏道院出土。

tóng

同 [甲]

540C — same, alike, similar; to be the same as; together; and.

垌，茼，峒，桐，酮，铜 tóng；筒 tǒng；
侗，垌，恫，峒，洞，胴，硐 dòng.

A combination of 凡 fán: mould, and 口 kǒu.13, symbol for utensils, thus the meaning of 同 tóng derives from the idea "same castings". ☞ 興=兴 xīng.107.

同字从口从凡。凡系铸范，以范模会同意。

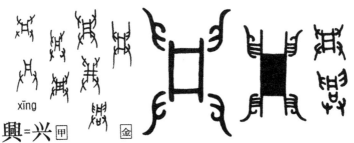

xīng

兴＝兴 [甲] [金] [篆]

8208＝5174 — to get up, rise; to prosper, prevail; to promote.

兴＝兴＝嬹 xìng: happy.

Shows hands carrying a moulding box. ☞ 同tóng，舁yù.19.

四手抬起范模。䵝wèng.269C5，燃烧。䵞2053B 音政。

---

yě

冶 [金]

51B6 — to smelt (metal).

[古] [篆]

Depicts the melting of bronze ingots 吕 lǚ.106.. ☞ 火huǒ，台yí.

古文冶从刀从火从吕从口，以火销吕，镕铸兵器。

---

zé

则＝则 [金]

5247＝5219 — criterion; rule; to imitate(written); however.

侧，测，恻，厕cè；铡zhá.

[古] [篆]

The glyph 刞 with two 鼎dǐng.123 or it simplified form 贝bèi.47, and 刀dāo.85: knife, which means to copy a pattern of a vessel for carving the model for moulding and casting of a new one.

按照一件鼎仿制雕刻另一件鼎的铸范。刞、剬，古文则。

---

zhù

铸＝铸 [甲] [金]

[古] [篆]

9444＝94F8 — to cast, to mint.

The ancient glyph for casting are delicate and complicate; and the modern 铸zhù is a pictophone with the metallurgy-radical and 寿shòu.29.
☞ 金jīn.106，又yòu.17，火huǒ.117.

初文作鼗250D8，象浇铸之形。后铸字改为形声。釙，金文铸。

4.4 Woodworking and Lacquer 木工与漆艺

4.4.1—Woodworking 木工

xiāng

相 甲 　　　　　　 金 　　　　　　 古 　　　　 篆 相

76F8 — observe, look at; watch for; a surname; mutually; together.

厢, 湘, 箱xiāng; 想xiǎng; 霜,孀shuāng.

To look at a tree 木mù.38 and judge its worth or curvature ☞ 目mù.11, 相xiàng: looks, to look at and judge.

察看木料。甲骨文或作果。眪猩猩，並俗。

jīn

斤 甲 　　　　 金 　　　　 古 　　　　 篆 斤

65A4 — *jīn*, a unit of weight = ½kg.

近jìn, 祈, 圻, 蕲, 颀qí; 芹qín; 欣, 忻, 昕xīn; 斫zhuó.

An ax with a crooked handle. PLC, 斧fǔ: ax; with the pictophonetic element. ☞ 父fù, 两liǎng.

一种曲柄斧的象形。斫zhì，椹櫍，砧板。

◀ **Adze on a clay vessel from Dawenkou, Neolithic period**

山东大汶口出土陶文·斤

kě

可 甲 　　　　 金 　　　　 古 　　　　 篆 可

53EF — may, can; to approve.

岢, 坷kǒ; 坷, 苛, 珂, 柯, 疴, 钶, 牁, 轲kē; 可kè; 阿, 锕ā; 啊ā, á, ǎ, à; 阿, 屙, 婀ē; 呵hē; 何, 河, 荷hé; 哥, 歌gē.

Drawing shows the handle of an ax, and a square which was used to differentiate this pictograph from other ancient words such as 乃nǎi, PLC, 柯kē; ax-handle; with a wood-radical. ☞ 斤jīn, 木mù.

象斤斧曲柄。哥20FB3. gē，大道君名。《上清大洞真經》其聖曰哥，其真曰靈。兆能知之，乃开金門。

析 甲 金 古 篆

6790 — to divide, separate; to analyse, dissect, resolve.

淅, 晰, 皙 xī.

To cut a tree. ☞ 木 mù.38: tree, 斤 jīn.108: ax.

用斤斧砍伐树木。

折 甲 金 古 篆

6298 — to break, snap; to suffer the loss of; to convert into.

哲, 蜇 zhé; 淅 zhè; 折 shé; 逝, 誓 shì.

To cut down a tree. Here, the hand radical was incorrectly derived from the broken trunk. ☞ 析 xī.

以斤砍断树木。篆文作断 3ABF，从斤断艸。古文作 𣂚 230AB 𣂪 230B9 𣂤 2309F。

直 甲 金 古 篆

76F4 — straight; vertical; just, upright; to straighten; direct; continuously.

值, 植, 殖 zhí; 置 zhì; 矗 chù; 德 dé: virtue, morals; 聽＝听 tīng.

Ancient forms of 直 zhí portray an eye gazing at a straight line or rule. ☞ 目 mù.11, 相 xiāng.

以目视测一直物形，或象目视悬锤以取直之形。悳 60B3. dé，篆文德。从直从心。悳 3941，古文德。

丁 甲 金 古 篆

4E01 — small cubes; man, population; the fourth of the ten Heavenly stems.

仃, 叮, 玎, 盯, 町, 钉, 疔, 耵 dīng; 酊 dǐng; 酊, 顶 dǐng; 订, 钉 dìng; 打 dǎ, dà; 灯＝燈 dēng; 汀, 厅＝廳 tīng; 亭, 停, 葶, 婷 tíng; 町 tǐng or dīng.

A nail. PLC, 钉 dīng: nail, tack; with a 金 jīn.106 or 钅 metal-radical.

象钉形。《说文》成，就也。从戊丁声。篆文作成 2F8B2。打，篆文杍。𠄌 daemq，古壮字，同袞，矮。汀 dumz，湿。

109

piàn 丿

片 甲 乀 甲骨文或象一片龟甲之形 篆 片 参 䉓 簰 《中山王方壶》载之箣箣。载之简策

7247 — a flat, thin piece. 版 bǎn.

Shows a chopped wood. It is the right-hand part of 木 mù.38: tree. ☞ 木 mù, 爿 pán.

象析木形。牉 zhé.3E1E，版也。簰 2C555，从竹斯聲。亦作 箣 25BA5，古文策。

méi 林 杈

枚 甲 金 古 篆 糌 参 肯

679A — stem; piece of stick used as mouth gag; a countable piece; a surname.

To plane or cut a piece of wood with a tool. ☞ 木 mù, 父 fù. 用工具修整树干。

yú HА

俞=俞 甲 金 古 肦 肦 冎 畚 舟 篆 俞

516A= 4FDE — a surname.

渝，愉，揄，逾，瑜，榆，觎，蝓，窬，嵛 yú；谕，喻，愈 yù；鮨，输 shū；偷 tōu.

To carve a canoe 舟 zhōu.141 with a chisel. PLC. 刳木制造独木舟。《说文》俞，空中木为舟也。从亼从舟从巜。巜，水也。从俞之字或有空、传输之意。

jǔ 榘 矩 巨

矩 金 古 巨 矩 榘 篆 矩

77E9 — carpenter's square; rule, regulation.

A carpenter using a ruler. The 矢 shǐ: arrow, was a modification of the similar 夫 fū: man. See below ☞ 夫 fū. 人手持矩形。《说文》本作巨。榘，同矩。榒梐，梁榘，规矩，木工工具。鉅 jù，秬本字。鉅鬯，黑黍香酒。

jù 工

巨 金 工 古 巨 巨 正 丂 篆 巨

5DE8 — huge.

苣，炬，距 jù；拒 jù；渠 qú；櫃=柜 guì.

The hand and the ruler from the character 矩 jǔ, see above. PLC. 矩字中的尺矩形。𢀜 22013，古文巨。

4. 4. 2—Lacquerwork 漆艺

The lacquer tree is a kind of Oriental tree. Its sap, lacquer, can be used to make lacquerware. The history of lacquerwork in China goes back to the earliest legends of Chinese history. The art was taken to Japan from China via Korea in the middle of the 6th century. During the same period, the lacquer tree was also introduced to Japan. European craftsmen in the 18th and 19th centuries also copied the technique of making lacquerware.

Lacquer itself, in its natural state, is a thick, syrupy whitish or grayish sap that turns dark brown or black when oxidized. The sap must undergo special preparation before it is ready to be used. First it is purified, then it is stirred until liquefied. Afterwards it is heated and stored in an airtight container until required for use. The base to which lacquer is applied is usually wood, sometimes animal skins or gunny cloth. In order to become as hard as possible, lacquer must "dry" in a damp atmosphere with plenty of moisture. This requirement led to the development of special techniques for hardening lacquerware.

Like oil painting and sculpture, lacquer painting is one form of art in China. The different colors of lacquer are mixed by the addition of different substances, such as cinnabar for red. Greens, dull yellow, brown, black, and purple are other possible colors. Gold, silver, engraving, carving, and inlay have all been used to create decorative effects of extreme richness. Both Chinese and Japanese craftmen favor shell inlays such as mother-of-pearl and egg-shells. Jade, ivory, porcelain and coral inlays are also used. The lacquer itself is a very good adhesive.

Like poison ivy, natural lacquer is highly irritating to the skin, but the finished product has no harmful effects.

同丝绸的发明一样,漆艺是中国人对世界物质文明的又一项重要贡献。

生漆是从漆树割取的天然液汁,主要由漆酚、漆酶、树胶质及水分构成。用它作涂料或制作漆器,不仅光彩照人,而且具有耐潮、耐高温、耐腐蚀等特殊功能。中国人使用漆的历史可上溯到新石器时代。浙江余姚河姆渡文化(公元前 5000 年)出土有一件据认为是涂有朱红色漆的木碗;山西襄汾陶寺龙山文化(公元前 2000 年左右)遗址中也出土一批外表涂料为漆类物的木器。自商周到秦汉漆与漆器制作技术得到很大发展,应用非常广泛。商代的漆器中已经出现漆绘雕花和镶嵌等工艺。春秋时代人们已经重视漆树的栽培。据史书记载,战国时期的庄子,曾经在蒙地当过漆园吏。《史记·滑稽列传》中还有关于利用"阴室"在潮湿环境下使漆易于干固的记载。在汉代中国的漆树和漆器制作技术就已经流传到亚洲一些国家。西方人多认为漆器制作源于日本,实际上,漆艺和漆树是在公元六世纪中叶经朝鲜传到日本的,在十八至十九世纪欧洲人也掌握了这门技术。

　　漆器的胎一般使用木、皮、麻布等材料。天然的漆在使用前要经过过滤和氧化处理。用多种矿物性和植物性染料可调制出各种颜色的漆。由于漆本身就是很好的粘合剂（中国有成语"如胶似漆"），而且多层涂层厚度和硬度都非常适于镶嵌和雕刻，同时镶嵌还能补充漆色的不足，如用蛋壳镶嵌可替代不易调制出的白色漆，因此利用漆制作工艺或美术作品有很强的表现力。在中国，同油画和雕塑一样，漆画被认为是艺术形式之一。

　　生漆有毒性。干漆可入药，有破瘀的功效。古人曾错误地认为干漆是中药中的延年上品。

七甲　金　古　篆　或体作

4E03
—seven.
柒 qī; 叱 chì.

Depicts the cross incision or crosscut made in a tree for tapping the lacquer. PLC. ☞ 汁zhī: juice, 切 qiē, and 十shí.193.

象漆树上取漆的切口形，柒是七的大写。漆画名家乔十光，十光即漆光也。柒，源自漆字草写。乇 3402，日本俗喜字。齔=齓 chèn，孩童换牙。

切甲　篆

5207 — to cut, slice, incise.
沏qī; 砌qì; 切, 窃=竊qiè; 彻=徹chè.

A combination of 七qī: cross incision, and a knife 刀dāo: knife.

切从七从刀。

漆=漆古　篆　泰　漆　参　甲骨文膝字

6F06=6F06
—lacquer; paint.
膝xī, qī.

A lacquer tree with the lacquer sap (the dots) flowing down. The left liquid-radical is a later addition. ☞ 木mù, 水shuǐ.

象漆汁從漆树中流下。《说文》漆，木汁。可以髹xiū,4C0D 物。漆，水。出右扶风杜陵岐山，东入渭。麭pào.3BE1，漆垸 huán 已，復黍之。古漆字系一条河流的名字，根据记载在古代有多至四条河流名叫漆水，可能随着古人的迁徙，漆水之名也在搬家。

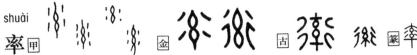

shuài

7387 — rate, proportion ratio.

率，蟀shuài；摔shuāi.

Put natural lacquer in a cloth sack, then wring out, making the lacquer purified. ☞ 系mì.93, 水shuǐ, 又yòu.17.

将生漆倒入布袋进行绞拧，滤去杂质。或曰象大索之形，点系麻枲之余。缞 7E42＝绋28134.lǜ，井索。率先篆作達先。

4.5　Making Wine　酿酒

Unlike Europe's method of making wine, early Chinese used wine leaven and grain to make "rice wine". The Chinese method is called the "amylomyces process".

In 1949, two Shang Dynasty brewery sites were found at *Erligang* in Henan Province, and *Taixi* Village, *Gaocheng* County, Hebei Province. However, the earliest wine found in China belongs to the Warring States Period, dated about 2000 years ago. In 1974, two kinds of wine were found in the Prince of Zhongshan's tomb in Hebei Province. One was green and transparent, the other was dark green. When excavated, both pots of wine were tightly sealed with rust. But on opening the pots, a fragrance of wine filled the room. Scientists believe that this wine was made by fermentation of yeast.

"清酤之美,始于耒耜"。中国人在农业起源时期已经开始酿酒了,也就是说中国人用霉菌酿酒已有六、七千年的历史。中国古代的酒是用酒曲和谷物发酵而酿成的。这种酿酒的方法为"淀粉霉法",它与西方的酿酒方法是不同的。

Bronze wine cups, Zhou period.
青铜酒杯。

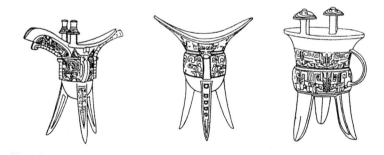

qūn

56F7 — barn.
麇qún; 菌jūn:
fungus, bacterium.

Grain stored in a sealed container or barn. ☞ 禾hé: rice.

圆形的粮仓，封存谷物。先民曾受到发霉发芽的谷物所产生的天然酒曲的启发，从而发明出酿酒的方法。《说文》困，廪之圜者。

yǒu

9149 — the tenth of the twelve Earthly Branches.
酒jiǔ.

A wine jug. PLC, 酒jiǔ: wine. 酉yǒu is a radical for characters associated with wine and fermenting.

象尖底酒罐形。酋，未详。喃字。

chàng

9B2F — a sacrificial wine.
鬯=郁yù; 斝=爵 jué.

A kettle containing wine leaven. ☞ 皀 jí.126.

象盛放有发酵醪的容器。鬯也指酿酒用的香草。

qiú

914B — chief of a tribe; chieftain.
遒 qiú; 猶=犹，蝤，
猷yóu.

A wine jug with a perforated lid that is filtering the sediment from wine leaven. PLC. ☞ 酉yǒu.

酉上置一容器，内盛发酵醪。后省为两点，多解释为酒香。

yóu

由 篆

7531 — cause, reason; due to; by through; to obey; from.

笛，迪dí；郵＝邮，油，铀，柚，蚰yóu；柚，釉，鼬yòu；抽chōu；轴，妯zhóu；宙，胄，轴zhòu；袖，岫xiù.

A filtering sack. PLC. 由yóu is an element with the meaning of *hole* or *perforated* by its extended meaning of *filtering* in certain derivatives.

象滤酒的囊形。

tán

覃金 古 篆

8983 — deep (written).

潭，谭tán；覃qín: a surname；蕈xùn.

A wine vessel with a cover. PLC. 罈tán: jar.

酒坛有封盖。《說文》𣋺2A277，長味也。从𣥂231AA 鹹省聲。《詩》曰：實覃實吁。𣋼2A259古文覃。𣋺2A25E篆文覃省。

zūn

尊甲 金 篆

5C0A — to respect, revere, venerate; venerable, honorable; a title of respect; an ancient wine vessel.

To toast. ☞ 酋qiú，又yòu.17 or 寸cùn.

双手捧酒尊敬酒。尊篆作𤔲2235C，从収20B1E，在酋部。篆作𤔲，误。隫2CBDA从阜从𤔲，古文尊。从阜表示进献。

diàn

奠甲 金 古 篆

5960 — to establish, settle; make offerings to the spirits of the dead.

鄭＝郑zhèng；鄭zhí；掭zhì.

Shows the offering of a wine jug. The lower stroke or 丌4E0C.jī indicates the base. ☞ 酋qiú.

象置酒尊于荐上。《说文·丌部》奠，下其丌也。

jué

爵 甲 金

7235 — an ancient wine vessel with three legs and a loop handle; the rand of nobility, peerage.

嚼, 爝 jué, jiào; 嚼 jiáo.

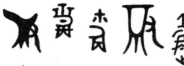

篆

Shows a hand holding a *Jue*.
☞ 皀 jí.126, 鬯 chàng.

手持饮酒爵形。篆作鬴鱟爵爵。

➡ 觴仲鼎：爵中（唐仲）作旅鼎。

fú

畐 甲　畗 金　　　　古　　　篆　　参 福 福 富 富

7550 — full (archaic).

逼 bī; 匐, 幅, 福, 蝠,
辐 fú; 副, 富: rich.fù.

A wine jar. PLC. ☞ 福 fú: good fortune, 酉 yǒu.

象瓵瓮酒满形。畐, 古文福。畕=畕=副。高丽人俗字用
卜代畐：补=福，下=富。畗字无头，表示富贵没有尽头。

lù

录=录 甲　　　金　　　　　古　　　篆

5F54=5F55 — collection; record; to copy; to employ.

渌, 逯, 绿, 禄, 碌 lù; 绿 lǜ;
碌 liù.

A hanging sack used for filtering lacquer, wine or other kind of liquid. The lower element is 水 shuǐ.36: water.

酒从挂起来过滤 lù 酒的袋中滤出。

Chapter 5

LIVELIHOOD 日常生活

5.1 The Use of Fire 火的使用

Some charred animal bones, the remnants of an early Chinese repast, were found in Xihoudu, a Paleolithic site dated 1,800,000 years ago. This is the earliest evidence of the use of fire by man on earth.

在中国已知最早的旧石器时代遗存——西侯度文化*中发现有被火烧过的兽骨，目前这是在世界范围内最早的人类用火遗迹。这一发现也大大提前了人类用火的历史。

huǒ

火 甲 古 篆 参 炎 炎

706B — fire; anger, temper; internal heat, one of the six causes of disease by traditional medicine.

伙，钬huǒ；灰huī；炎yán；淡，啖，氮dàn；秋qiū；痰，谈tán；毯tǎn；剡yǎn，shàn。

A flame. There are three forms of the fire-radical in many Chinese characters: one is on the left side of a character; the others are lower radicals written as a flattened 火 or 灬 huǒ as four dots.

象火焰形。燚 71DA = 焱 = 烶 yì，火焰貌。囙俗因。灬 biāo，烈火。亦同灬，燒，太平天国造火字。

fén

焚 甲 金 篆

711A — to burn.

A forest on fire. ☞ 林lín: forest, 火huǒ.117: fire.

焚烧树林，用以驱兽围猎或开辟农田。燓=焚。

* 中国华北地区旧石器时代早期文化，发现于山西省芮城县西侯度村附近，其年代初步测定为距今180万年。

117

liáo

寮 甲

5C1E — archaic form of 燎 liáo: burn.

潦liáo; 撩liáo; 療=疗, 遼=辽, 僚,
寮, 撩, 鷯, 嘹, 獠, 燎, 繚liáo;
潦, 瞭=了, 燎liáo; 瞭=了, 镣liáo.

金   篆 褰   参 燓 燎

A bonfire. The upper dots in this character
represent sparks, and the bottom 小 xiǎo derives
from 火 huǒ: fire. ☞ 木 mù, 燎 liǎo: to singe.

象一堆篝火之形。寮篆作褰。柴燎、庭燎字
篆作褰。燔燎字篆作䙡。

---

rè

熱=热 甲

71B1=70ED — hot.

篆 爇

A man holding a torch. PLC. In spite of pictorial similarity, this
character looks sililar to 藝=艺 yì.75 which is descended from the
drawing of a man planting. ☞ 执 zhí.169, 爇 ruò: ignite.

象人手持火把之形。爇=爇, 燒也。从火蓺聲。

---

sǒu

叟 甲

53DF — old man.

溲, 搜, 艘, 馊, 飕 sōu; 嫂 sǎo;
瘦 shòu.

古 㝜   篆 㝜

A hand holding a torch to search a house. PLC, 搜 sōu: to
search; with a hand-radical. ☞ 又 yòu.17.

象人手持火把在屋内搜索之形。叟篆作㝜。

---

shù

庶 甲

5EB6 — multitudinous; so
as to.

遮 zhē; 蔗, 鷓 zhè; 摭 zhí.

金   古   篆 庶

A pebble 石 shí.175 being heated over fire 火 huǒ.117, then putting in
a pot to heat water for cooking. PLC. ☞ 者 zhě.125.

庶表示以火燒石, 用以煮食。

huī

灰 固 篆

7070 — ash; gray.

恢, 诙 huī; 盔 kuī; 炭; charcoal,
碳: carbon tàn; 羹 tāng.

Something being picked up from a fire 火 huǒ.117. The semantic link would have been "ash". ☞ 又 yòu.17: hand.

从火中取物，会灰炭意。炗，篆。灰，俗。

lú

盧＝卢 甲 金 古 篆

76E7＝5362 — a surname.

庐, 芦, 炉, 胪, 舻,
轳, 颅, 鸬, 鲈 lú; 驴 lú.

An ancient stove. The upper part, 虍 hū: tiger's head, is a phonetic. PLC, 爐＝炉 lú: stove, furnace; with a fire radical. ☞ 虎 hǔ.51, 皿 mǐn.188, 火 huǒ.117.

象古代火炉之形。矑＝胪 lú，目中黑子，篆作盧。揚雄《甘泉賦》玉女無所，眺其清盧。

▶ A wattle-and-daub house with an earthenware stove in its centre. Neolithic period.

河南龙山文化 11 号木骨垛泥墙白灰面圆形房（采自《中国大百科全书．考古学》，204 页）。

guāng

光 甲 金 古 篆

5149 — light, ray; brightness, lustre, glory, honour; glossy, polished; bare, naked; only, merely; used up.

胱 guāng; 栦 guàng; 觥 gōng; 恍, 晃,
幌 huǎng; 晃 huàng.

A combination of 火 huǒ.117: fire, and 人 rén.1 or 卩 jié.9: a kneeling figure.

光从火在人上。爄 204C9，户政俗光。烑 2D02C，同煌。《龍龕》爌煌俗烑或作晄晃二今，胡廣反。光明暉晄也。

chì

赤 甲   金   古   篆

8D64 — red; loyal; bare.

哧chī; 赫hè; 赭zhě.

A combination of 大dà.3: a standing man, and 火huǒ.117: fire.

赤从大从火。 、 ，古文。篆作 ＝交。

rán

然 金   古   篆

7136 — right, correct; so; however.

燃, 嘫, 絲rán; 傛răn; 撚niăn.

A dog being roasted over fire 火huǒ.117. PLC, 燃rán: ignite. ☞ 犬quăn, 肉ròu.128.

象烧烤犬之形。篆作燃。

jiāo

焦 金   古   篆 或省作

7126 — burnt, scorched; coke; a surname.

礁, 蕉, 鷦jiāo; 嘹jiào; 憔, 谯, 瞧, 樵qiáo; 藮zhàn.

A bird 隹zhuī.56: being roasted over fire 火huǒ.117.

象烧烤鸟之形。 ＝熊、焦，古文。爨＝燋，篆文。

gāo

羔 甲   金   古   篆

7F94 — lamb, kid, fawn.

糕gāo: cake, pudding; 羹gēng: a thick soup.

A lamb 羊yáng.53 being roasted over fire 火huǒ.117. PLC.

象烧烤羊之形。羔、羖，并同羔。羔＝美，篆文。

120

qīn

亲＝親

4EB2＝89AA — blood relation, relative; parent; marriage; close, intimate; to kiss.

櫬＝梫; 襯＝衬chèn; 新, 薪xīn.

辛xīn.168, the phonetic, and 木mù.38: tree, then the pictophone 亲＝亲 indicates firewood. 新 xīn: new, with an ax 斤jīn.108, and 薪xīn: firewood, PLC of 新 xīn. 亲＝亲＝榛 zhēn: hazelnut, and 亲 today is the simplified form of 親 qīn.

亲从木辛声，表示柴薪。新、親从亲聲。憖＝親，親愛。嫀＝親，親屬。新、親並金文親。中山王鼎：妥邦難新。鄰邦難親。

shù

束

675F — to bind, tie; control, restrain; bundle, bunch, sheaf; a surname.

敕chì; 辣là; 嫩nèn; 悚, 竦sǒng; 速, 棘, 涑, 萩, 簌sù.

A bundle of firewood. ☞ 木mù.38.

象一捆柴禾之形。
金文棗、鼒、𩛰从束，並族徽字。𩛰，或讀束泉，亦族徽。

➡ 束泉爵

kùn

困

56F0 — to be stranded, be hard pressed; to surround, pin down.

悃, 捆, 梱, 阃kǔn; 睏＝困kùn.

Firewood corded up. PLC, 捆kǔn: to tie, bundle up, bundle. ☞ 木mù.

困表示捆扎木柴。从困之字多有约束义。梱＝閫＝阃，门槛；綑＝捆；悃，志纯一；睏，闭目。

121

5.2 Cooking and Eating 饮食

dòu

豆甲 金 古 篆

8C46 — an ancient stemmed bowl; bean, legume.

逗: funny; 痘dòu; 登dēng; 短duǎn; 頭=头tóu.

A vessel, consisting of a tall base stem supporting a bowl or platter. 荳=豆dòu: bean.

食器。古人席地而坐，故就食用高足的豆。

夜里千条路，早起卖豆腐。

豆 dòu

sháo

勺甲 金 古 篆 参 与

52FA — spoon, scoop.

芍sháo; 豹bào; 的 7684. dè; 的, 菂dì, 钓diào; 妁shuò; 约 7EA6. yāo, yuē; 药=藥yào; 哟yō, yo; 灼, 酌zhuó.

A ladle with something (the dot) in it. ☞ 斗dǒu.

象勺中盛物（一点）形。勺又音zhuó。斟酌篆作𣂈勺。一勺为与。與，黨與。賜與篆作𦎍勺。

dǒu

斗甲 金 古 篆

6597 — *dou*, a unit of dry measure for grain, or one decalitre; the Big Dipper.

抖 dǒu; 蚪dǒu; 斛, 槲hú; 戽hù; 科, 蝌kē; 魁kuí; 料liào: to expect.

A vessel with a long handle. The stroke on the handle indicates that this character was borrowed as a unit of measurement.

象有柄的容器。

shēng

升甲 金 古 篆

5347 — *sheng*, a unit of dry measure for grain; litre; to rise, hoist, ascend; to promote.

Meting out rice with a *dou* measure. PLC. ☞ 斗dǒu.

用斗量米。抍 zhěng，上举也。昇，日上也。俗升字。昇字没有简化，但篆文作升。

dǐng

鼎 [甲] [金] [古] [篆]

9F0E — an ancient cooking vessel with two loop handles and three or four legs, a tripod.

Pictograph. In certain characters, 贝bèi is the simplified form of 鼎dǐng, such as 员yuán below, and 贞zhēn.184.

象形。四足的鼎称为方鼎。

yuán

員＝员 [甲] [金] [古] [篆]

54E1＝5458 — member of staff.

圆＝圆yuán；损sǔn；员，郧yún；陨，殒yǔn；员yùn。

The glyph 口kǒu.13 indicates the round lip of a tripod. PLC, 圆 yuán: round, a circle. ☞ 鼎dǐng: tripod.

鼎的标准型为圆形，三足两耳。鼎字上面的口，指示圆鼎的上口沿，以会圆意。

●痽勺铭文
敤（微）白（伯）痽乍（作）勺

◀ **Rubbing of inscriptions on a bronze spoon, West Zhou Dynasty.**

西周青铜勺铭文。一九七六年出土于陕西省扶风县（采自陈全方《周原与周文化》）。

123

hú

壺 = 壶 [甲]

58FA = 58F6 — kettle.

薀薽 = 壹壹 = 氤氲 yīnyūn.

An earthenware kettle.

象壶形。白菜青盐糙米饭，瓦壶天水菊花茶。

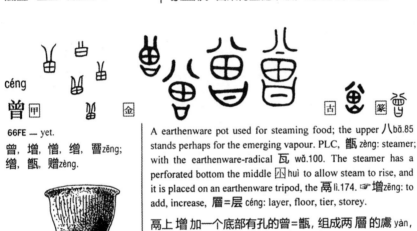

céng

曾 [甲]

66FE — yet.

曾，增，憎，缯，罾 zēng;
缯，甑，赠 zèng.

膚 yàn

A earthenware pot used for steaming food; the upper 八 bā.85 stands perhaps for the emerging vapour. PLC, 甑 zèng: steamer; with the earthenware-radical 瓦 wǎ.100. The steamer has a perforated bottom the middle 囦 huì to allow steam to rise, and it is placed on an earthenware tripod, the 鬲 lì.174. ☞ 增 zēng: to add, increase, 層 = 层 céng: layer, floor, tier, storey.

鬲上增加一个底部有孔的曾 = 甑，组成两层的膚 yàn，即蒸 zhēng 锅。曾字上面的八表示蒸气。

huì

會 = 会 [甲]

6703 = 4F1A — to meet together; association; meeting; can, will.

荟，烩，绘 huì; 刽，桧 guì; 会，侩，狯，脍，郐，哙，浍 kuài.

A lid placed on a steamer. 囦 huì: bamboo grid is in the middle, and for a phonetic as well. PLC, 鐀 = 铪 guó: pot. ☞ 曾 céng, 合 hé.125.

会字表示在锅上加盖。囦在會、黑等字中是声符。

hé

合

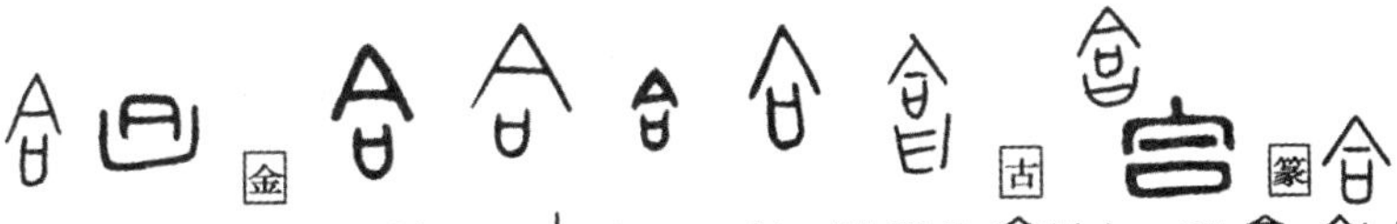
甲
金
古
篆

5408 — cover, close; to join, combine; whole; proper.

盒，颌hé; 鸽gē; 蛤，搿，阁gé; 合gě; 给gěi，jǐ; 哈，铪hā; 蛤há; 洽，恰qià; 拾shí; 答，搭，嗒，褡dā; 答，荅dá.

A case with a lid. PLC, 盒 hé: box. ☞ 會=会huì.

器盖相合，盒字初文。或曰上下两口相向，会对答意，是答的本字。

jiāng

將=将

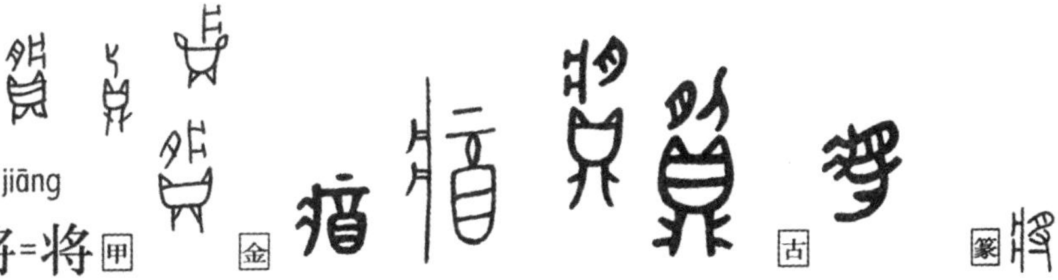
甲
金
古
篆

5C07=5C06 — to take, bring; with, by means of.

漿=浆jiāng; 奖，桨，蒋jiǎng; 酱，将jiàng; 锵qiāng.

A piece of pork being put on a chopping block 爿 pán.110: board. PLC. ☞ 鼎dǐng.123, 刀dāo.85, 肉ròu.128, 寸cùn.17, 片piàn.110.

用手将肉置在几俎上。𤖫287FB，古文酱。鬺shāng，煮。

zhě

者

甲
金
古
篆
参

8005 — this; person who does (something); functions like "-er"; a surname.

赭，锗zhě; 躇chú; 储，楮chǔ; 都dōu; 睹，堵，赌dǔ; 都，嘟dū; 奢shē; 署，暑，曙，薯shǔ; 屠tú; 绪xù; 猪，诸，槠，潴，豬zhū; 渚，煮zhǔ; 著，箸zhù.

Shows food being put into a pot. The kind of food is not clear. The lower 甘gān.13 derives from the drawing of the pot. PLC, 煮zhǔ: to boil, cook: with 灬 706C a lower fire-radical. ☞ 火huǒ.117: fire.

者是煮的本字，象将食物投放到锅中形。着是著的变体字。

xiāng

香 甲 金

 古 篆

9999 —fragrant; appetizing; popular; perfume or spice; incense.

馥fù: fragrance; 馨xīn: strong and pervasive fragrance.

Shows rice 禾hé.44, or 黍shǔ: millet in its ancient glyph shape 香, being put into a pot. It's a radical as well. ☞ 者zhě.125.

将禾放入锅内。《说文》香2A3FD，芳也。从黍从甘。

薰29862=香2984C=馩29850. xiāng，大香。馨99AB=馨 xīn，香气远闻。

jí

皂 甲 金

 篆  乡

7680 —delicious.

簋guǐ; 即jí; 既jì; 食shí; 卿=卿 qīng; 皂, 鄉=乡 xiāng.

A bowl containing food. PLC, 簋guǐ: a round-mouthed food vessel with two or four loop handles. ☞ 豆dòu.122, 皿mǐn.188, 匕bǐ.7.

象碗（豆）中有饭之形。皂 xiāng，或作皀24F3F宫3FDD，古文香。

jù

具 甲 金

古 篆

5177 —implement, utensil; to provide; to possess; ability; a unit of things.

俱, 颶, 惧=懼jù.

Shours hands holding up a cooking vessel for guests. ☞ 鼎dǐng，共gòng.157.

象双手持鼎以款待。

dēng

登 甲 金

古 篆

767B — to ascent; to record.

燈=灯，噔，蹬dēng; 凳，鄧=邓，瞪，澄，嶝，磴，鐙dèng; 橙，澄chéng; 證=证zhèng.

The upper two footprints in the ancient glyph 登dēng represented moving forward or presenting. Thus, 登dēng showed two hands holding a *dou*-bowl to present an offering to the God or their ancestors. Later, the hands were omitted. 豆dòu.122 is also a phonetic. ☞ 共gòng.157, 止zhǐ.22.

登表示双手捧豆升阶以敬神。

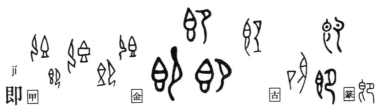

jí

即 甲 金 古 篆

5373 — to approach, reach, be near; to undertake; at present; prompted by the occasion.

唧jī; 鲫jì; 節=节jié; 栉zhì.

A man preparing for dinner. PLC. ☞ 皀jí, 卩jié.

象人就簋而食。

shí

食 甲 金 古 篆 饮

98DF — to eat; food, meal; feed; edible; eclipse.

飾=饰shì.

食shí shows mouth eating the food from a bowl. The top A is from the open mouth, and the dots around the bowl and food 皀jí.127 represent saliva. 食 or simplified 饣 is a radical for food or eating.

象人张嘴吃饭。飾=饰shì 从食得声。

shú

朮 甲 金 古 篆 秫

672E — archaic form of 秫shú; a surname.

術=术: skill, technique, 述shù; 秫shú; 怵chù; 术zhú.

Sticky food, the dot, adhering to a hand. PLC, 秫shú: glutinous sorghum. ☞ 又yòu.17, 禾hé.

粘nián 秫米粘zhān 手之状。

jì

既 甲 金 古 篆

65E2 — already; since; now that; both... (and) ...

暨jì; 溉, 概gài; 慨kǎi.

Depicts a man having enjoyed his dinner. PLC. ☞ 皀jí, 即jí.

食既, 象人吃完饭调头欲走之状。

qīng

卿 [甲] [金] [古] [篆] 卿

537F — minister (ancient).
饗=飨 xiǎng; 鄉=乡 xiāng.

Two people eating together. PLC, 饗=飨 xiǎng: to provide dinner for, entertain. ☞ 即 jí.127.

两人对坐于簋前相向而享食。卿即飨，二字同源。

lǔ

鹵=卤 [甲] [金] [古] [篆] 卤

9E75=5364
— bittern.

A bag containing salt. The four dots are grains of salt. It's a radical for primordial chemistry. PLC, 鹽=盐 yán: salt; 監=监 jiān is a phonetic. 鹹=咸 xián: salty.

象盐袋之形。

ròu

肉 [甲] [古] [篆]

8089 — meat, flesh;
pulp.
臛 qué.

肉 ròu is usually supposed to be a drawing of a piece of meat. However, it may derive from the mouth and fangs of a carnivorous animal such as 能 néng.50, pictograph of b bear. It's an useful radical, written as 月 yuè, referring to the human's body.

象肉块形。《说文》肉，胾肉。胾 zì，大臠。臠 luán，膞也。
一曰切肉也。宍宑肉宊宋宨並古文肉。

yǒu

有 [甲] [金] [古] [篆]

6709 — to have, possess; to exist.
肴 yáo; 淆 xiáo; 铕 yǒu; 侑，宥，
囿，有 yòu; 贿 huì.

A hand 又 yòu.17 holding a piece of meat 肉 ròu. The top 又 yòu is also a phonetic. ☞ 牛 niú.52.

象手持有一块肉形。甲骨文有字由牛字省变而来。

5.3 Clothes and Ornament 衣饰

biǎo

表   襁襲 古文 篆作 表

8868 — surface, outside; exterior; to show, to express; list.

裱, 婊, 錶=表biǎo.

A fur coat with the pelt on the outside. ☞ 毛máo.11: hair, fur, 衣yī.25: clothes.

从衣从毛。古人兽皮为衣，皮里毛外。

shuāi

衰 金

8870
— to decline, wane.

蓑suō.

A straw raincoat. PLC, 蓑suō: straw or palm-bark raincoat.
☞ 衣yī, 草cǎo.

人穿蓑衣形。褒衾䍅𧝓𧝇，並
古文。俗又从疒从死作痕衋。

▶ 蓑笠。

笠

suō
蓑

zhà

乍 甲   金   古   篆

4E4D — for the first time; abruptly.

咋, 炸, 痄, 诈, 榨, 柞zhà; 砟zhǎ;
咋zǎ; 怎zěn; 窄zhǎi; 作zuō; 作, 昨
筰zuó; 作, 祚, 柞, 酢, 胙, 阼zuò.

Stitching the neckband of an ancient garment. PLC, 作zuò: to make. ☞ 衣yī.

乍表示缝制衣领。一说乍象刀砍木，是柞字
初文。除草曰芟，除木曰柞。

jīn

巾 甲 ... 金 ... 古 ... 篆 ... 参 ... 佩

5DFE — a piece of cloth (as used for a towel, scarf, kerchief, etc.).

佩pèi: to wear, admire.

A scarf. It is a radical for cloth.

佩巾形。市，遮羞布。《说文》市，韠也。上古衣，蔽前而已，市以象之。《子犯編鐘》王賜子軷輅車三駟、衣裳、帶市、巿。《獄簋》王或賜（又賜）獄佈。巿、佈，並同佩。

bù

布 金 ... 古 ... 篆 ...

5E03 — cloth; to arrange.

怖bù.

布bù was made up of 巾jīn and the phonetic 父fù.157, which was then transformed into 𠂇=又yòu.17.

形声字。声符"父"后被"又"所替代。

bó

帛 甲 ... 金 ... 古 ... 篆 ...

5E1B — silks.

锦jǐn; 棉, 绵mián.

A pictophone. ☞ 白bái.18, 巾jīn.

形声字，从巾白声。

bì

敝 甲 ... 古 ... 篆 ...

655D — worn-out, shabby; my (written).

幣=巿，蔽bì; 憋，鱉biē; 蹩bié; 撤，瞥piē; 撇piě; 弊，斃=毙bì.

A hand holding a duster to brush dust (the four dots) off a piece of ragged clothing. ☞ 巾jīn, 父fù.

手持木棍掸去巾上的尘土。

mào

冒 金 ... 篆 ...

5192 — to send out; to risk; rashly; a surname.

帽, 瑁mào.

A person wearing a headgear with that leaves the eye 目mù.11, uncovered. PLC, 帽mào: hat; with a radical 巾jīn. ☞ 冑zhòu. 149.

象人头上戴有帽子，眼睛露在外面。

cān

参=参金

53C3 — to pay one's respects to (a superior, etc.); to take part in.

骖cān; 惨cǎn; 掺chān; 参shēn, 人参rénshēn: ginseng; 渗shèn; 参cēn, 参差, cēn cī; 参=叁 sān.

A person wearing a beautiful head ornaments or perhaps a man standing under the Ardia, three Stars Mansion.
☞ 星xīng.32, 大dà.3, 彡shān.197.

象人头上有参宿三星。杜甫《赠卫八处士》人生不相见，动如参与商。

xiǎn

顯=显金

986F=663E— to show, display; apparent, obvious, noticeable.

濕=湿shī; 隰xí.

Hair arranged in braids. ☞ 页yè.10, 日rì: sun, 丝sī.

象人在阳光下检查头上的发辫。《说文》顯，頭明飾也。㬎，衆微杪也。从日中視絲。古文以爲顯字。

ruò

若甲

82E5 — like, seem, as if; if.

偌, 箬ruò; 匿nì; 喏, 诺, 锘nuò; 若, 惹rě.

Shows a person putting his hair in order with his hands. PLC.
☞ 毛máo.11, 又yòu.17, 卩jié.

象人双手理顺头发形。

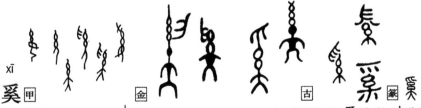

xī

奚甲

595A — why; a surname.

溪, 蹊, 騱xī; 鷄=鸡爪; 蹊qī.

A person wearing a queue or a pigtail. PLC. ☞ 爪zhǎo.20, 大dà.3.

象人手编辫子。古代奚是一个辫发的族称。

yù

7389

— jade; (of a woman) beautiful.

宝=寶bǎo: treasure; 玨=珏 jué: two joined pieces of jade.

䐗=䐡yù，人之身精气不散乱为宝。图21228，玉字的轮廓字。

玉·许慎《说文解字》

A string of jade beads. The dot was a late addition in order to distinguish 玉yù from 王wáng.

The manufacture of jade object began in China's Neolithic period. Jade is rather loosely understood by the Chinese to include both nephrite and jadeite as well as other hard stones. More important than such distinctions are the objects carved from those hard stones. These objects are intrinsically valuable and metaphorically equated with human virtues because of their hardness, durability, rarity, and beauty. ☞ 玉 2EA9 as radical.

象贯穿起来的一串玉饰。玊、玉，古文玉。

玉，石之美者。中国的制玉历史始于新石器时代。玉石艺术是中国文化的一个组成部分，它是中国人对石器时代先民制造石器工具的一种升华。玉石的品种众多，其稀有程度也有非常大的差异，因此中国人对玉石没有严格的定义。对中国人来讲更为重要的是玉石的雕刻，以及通过陈设和佩戴玉制品所反映出的人的品质和精神。

古代中国人所称的玉，用近代矿物学来分类，可分为两大类：一是软玉（nephrite），一类是硬玉（jadeite），也就是翡翠。一般所说的玉都属闪石类（amphibole group），颜色白的和透闪石（tremolite）相近，颜色绿的和阳起石（actinolite）相近。透闪石的理想成分为 $Ca_2Mg_5Si_8O_{22}(OH)_2$ 阳起石的理想成分为 $Ca_2(Mg, Fe^{2+})_5Si_8O_{22}(OH)_2$，均属单斜晶系。翡翠今属辉石类（pyroxene group），一般又分为两种：红的是翡，绿的是翠。翡是含锰的青辉石（violan），色红紫带青，往往和翠（jadeite）共生，而且也是同属，所以合称翡翠。翡翠的理想成分为 $NaAlSi_2O_6$，属单斜晶系，主要产于缅甸。

péng

朋 甲 金

670B — friend.

棚, 硼, 鹏 péng;
崩, 绷, 嘣 bēng;
绷, 蹦 bèng.

A string of cowry shells. Cowry shell was used as both money and jewelry in early Chinese civilization. The form of this element 月 yuè derives from 贝 bèi: cowry. PLC.

以贝为饰。北京周口店山顶洞人遗址发现有顶部磨出洞的贝。《说文》无朋字。篆文朋 羂 是鳳字。《说文》鳳, 鵩, 古文鳳, 象形。鳳飛, 羣鳥從以萬數, 故以爲朋黨字。朋黨字当篆作倗攎 偂儳。

pú

羮 甲

749E — uncut jade.

璞 金 撲 戮 剻 古 羮 篆

醭 bú; 撲=扑, 噗 pū; 僕=仆, 镤 pú; 樸=朴, 蹼 pú.

The of 璞 pú shows a jade hunter on a mountain digging jade and putting it in his basket ☞ 玉 yù, 父 fù, 山 shān.

甲骨文璞象人在山上采集玉石。金文剻、戮并同撲。

quán

全 金 全 古 全 篆

5168 — to keep intact; to complete; whole, entire; entirely; a surname.

荃, 痊, 诠, 铨, 醛, 筌 quán; 拴, 栓 shuān.

A man placed over a piece of jade, or with jade placed between his legs, indicating his ownership of the piece. PLC. ☞ 大 dà.3, 玉 yù.

象人胯下有玉形。《说文》全, 完也。从入从工。全, 篆文全从玉, 纯玉曰全。䘏, 古文全。

lòng

弄 甲 金 篆

5F04 — to do; play; play with.

俫, 恽, 衖 lòng.

Admiring a jade 玉 yù held in hands. ☞ 廾=収 gǒng: two hands, to carry.

双手赏玩玉形。《说文》筭, 长六寸。计历数者。从竹从弄。言常弄乃不误也。䡔䡔, 㖿字, 生死。

chuàn

串【金】 【篆】串

4E32 — string; to string together.
患 huàn; 窜＝竄 cuàn.

A string of two (jade) beads.
象串起来的两个玉珠之形。闌，古文關。

guài

夬【甲】 【金】 【古】 【篆】夬

592C — a term in *The Book of Changes*《易經》.
决，抉，诀，鈌 jué; 快，筷，块
＝塊 kuài; 袂 mèi; 缺，炔 quē.

史＝叏＝夬 shows two hands holding a jade ring. PLC, 玦 jué: penannular jade ring, 缺 quē: lack; be incomplete.
象人双手持玦之形。玦为环状而有缺口的玉璧。或指射箭时套在手指上的扳指。

huáng

黄＝黃【甲】 【金】 【古】 【篆】黄

9EC3＝9EC4 — yellow, sallow; decadent, obscene, pornographic.
蟥，璜，磺，簧 huáng; 横 héng; 横 hèng.

A person wearing a jade pendant and cheerfully opening his mouth upward. PLC, 璜 huáng: semi-annular jade pendant. ☞ 大 dà.3.
象人佩戴环形玉饰。

dài

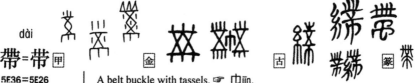

帶＝带【甲】 【金】 【古】 【篆】帶

5E36＝5E26
— belt, band; take, to bring; to lead.
婦，滞 zhì.

A belt buckle with tassels. ☞ 巾 jīn.
象衣服钩带相连之形。带字上部为钩带的变形，下面内巾相叠，为装饰用下垂的须子。緤，金文带。㡯，同帗。篕，喃字，籧。饜，同幯，喃字，下面，底下。蒂婦，亦作殢滞，歐，嬌，刁。
元·宋方壶《一枝花·蚊蟲》聚朋黨成羣隊，逞輕狂撒蒂婦。

5.4　Habitation　居住

汉瓦当。

家

關

hù

户

6236 — family; (bank) account.

沪=滬, 护=護, 戽, 扈hù; 妒dù; 雇gù.

A door. 户 6237, simplified form used in main land China, and 戸 6238 in Japan.

《说文》户, 护也。半门曰户, 象形。冻, 古文户, 从木。

mén

門=门

9580=95E8 — door; gate; way to do sth; knack; a surname.

扪, 钔mén; 们men; 闷mēn, 焖mèn, 闩shuān: bolt, latch.

Double doors or a gate. It is a radical. ☞ 户hù.

象形。民国 12 年刻本《崀新两县续补合志·卷一·方言》门之关，横者曰闩，竖者曰閂。字当作枨 chéng, 亦作撑 chēng。又《客家方言詩》九扇門楣尸弖開。

kāi

開=开

958B=5F00 — to open; make a opening; come loose; start, operate.

锎kāi.

Two hands removing the large bolt from a gate. ☞ 廾=収 gǒng.

象双手打开门闩形。開闢閞，古文。開闓閞，俗开。

qǐ

啟=启

555F=542F — to open; to start, initiate.

綮qìng; 肇zhào.

A hand opening a door. ☞ 户hù, 口kǒu.13, 攵pù: to beat lightly.

启表示用手开启门户。《说文》啟, 教也。启, 開也。则啟蒙字篆作啟, 開啟字篆作启。

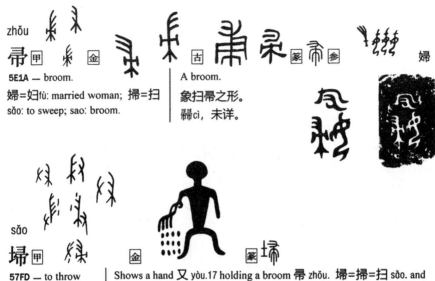

zhǒu

帚 甲　金

5E1A — broom.

婦=妇fù: married woman; 掃=扫
sǎo: to sweep; sao: broom.

A broom.

象扫帚之形。
帚cì，未详。

婦

sǎo

埽 甲　金 篆

57FD — to throw
away，discard;
to abandon.

浸jìn; 侵qīn; 寝qīn.

Shows a hand 又 yòu.17 holding a broom 帚 zhǒu. 埽=掃=扫 sǎo. and
土tǔ.74: dust, or 手 shǒu.17: hand, was added as radicals. 塂=墐jìn:
ground, land, is archaic today, but the component 蔓qīn is an useful
phonetic. 寝qīn: sleep, to sweep the bed off with the broom.

手持扫帚扫除尘土之形。

qí

其 甲　金 古 篆

5176 — his (her, its, their); he
(she, it they); that; such.

萁，淇，骐，琪，棋，祺，蜞，
綦，麒qí; 期，欺qī; 箕，基jī.

A bin or dustpan; the lower element 丌 is a phonetic. PLC,
箕jī: dustpan, with a bamboo radical. ☞ 基jī.102.

象簸箕之形。丌，古文。

răn

冉 金　　古 篆

5189 — slowly; something soft
and drooping.

髯，蚺rán; 苒răn.

A bamboo broom. PLC.

象竹编器形。《说文》冄，毛冄冄也。

xūn

熏 [金]

718F — to smoke, fumigate.

薰: sweet grass, fragrance,
曛, 醺 xūn; 熏 xùn.

A bunch of savory in bag, perfume satchel. ☞ 黑 hēi: black,
火 huǒ: fire.

囊中香料。纁 xūn, 浅绛色。瑻, 或同纁。薰, 鼓鸣。
黦 xùn, 物被熏色。镶, 金色渲染。

jī

几 [古] [篆]

51E0 — a small table.

饥, 肌 jī, 麂 jī.

A small table. ☞ 幾 jī.92.

象几案形。处=处、尻=居、凭等字从几。

pán

爿 [甲] [篆]

723F — a flat,
thin piece.

A wooden bed. It is a radical for plank-like object. PLC. ☞ 片 piàn.110.

象牀形。牀形竖立是由于刻写的方便。

◀ 榻·[宋]槐荫消夏图。

ān

安 [甲] [金] [古] [篆]

5B89 — safe; settled, calm; to
install; a surname.

按, 桉, 氨, 鞍 ān; 铵 ǎn; 按,
案, 胺 àn; 鴳 yàn; 晏, 宴 yàn.

Shows a woman kneeling in a room. The rules of decency
required that proper women spent most of their lives
sequestered at home. ☞ 六 liù.97 or 宀 mián, 女 nǚ.27.

女子在房中，表示安详悠闲。安，俗安。敦煌·S.133
《春秋左传杜注》百姓绝望，社稷无主，将安用之？

137

yīn
因 甲

56E0 — cause, reason; because of; in accordance with.

茵, 姻, 氤, 铟 yīn; 恩, 葱 ēn; 咽, 烟, 胭 yān; 咽 yàn, yè.

A woven mat. The character 大 dà.3: in 因 yīn derives from the woven pattern. PLC, 茵 yīn: mattress; with a grass-radical. Or it shows the person 大 getting dressed.

象席形。或以为人在衣中。《说文》因，就也。从口大。囙回囟靁，并俗因。

sù
宿 甲

5BBF — to lodge for the night, stay over night; long-standing, veteran (written); a surname.

缩 suō; 宿 xiǔ; 宿 xiù; 蓿 xu.

痛=宿 sù shows a man sleeping in a room. The element 囟=囟 tiǎn or 百 bǎi derives from the drawing of a mat. 宿舍 sù shè: dormitory. 一宿 yì xiǔ: one night; 星宿 xīng xiù: constellation, stars; 苜蓿 mù xu: alfalfa. ☞ 六 liù.97, 人 rén.1, 因 yīn.

象人在屋内坐卧于席上。痛，本字。宿，俗。

xiū
休 甲

4F11 — to rest; to stop.

咻, 庥, 㺢, 鵂, 髹 xiū.

A person resting against a tree. ☞ 人 rén.1, 木 mù.

象人倚树休息之形。

mèng
夢=梦 甲

5922=68A6 — to dream.

薨 hōng;
懜, 甍 méng;
懵 měng.

A man and his bed. The bed 爿 pán.137 indicates the location where dreams occur. The man is pointing to his eye; perhaps he is giving a glowing account of the tempting or tormenting dream he just had. The upper part, the dreamer's dancing eyebrow, may also derive from 眉 méi: eyebrow, as a phonetic, and the bottom 夕 xī.33: night, is a meaning element added later.

甲骨文象人在夜里做梦，醒来以手指目，讲述梦境之情形。《说文》夢训不明，夢寐字篆作寱。

138

jiān

監=监[甲]

76E3=76D1 — to supervise; prison.
监，艦=舰，鑒=鉴，槛 jiàn；
槛 kǎn；蓝，篮，褴 lán；滥 làn；
鹽=盐 yán.

A man seeing, 见 jiàn.12, a water-filled vessel 皿 mǐn.188 as a mirror. PLC, 鑒=鑑=鉴 jiàn: mirror; with a metal-radical 金 jīn.106. Mirrors were made of bronze.
象人俯身向盘中水面照看状。

yíng

盈[甲]

76C8 — to be full of, be filled with; have a surplus of.
楹 yíng.

Portrays a man standing in a big vessel to take a bath.
☞ 人 rén.1，又 yòu.17 or 止 zhǐ.22，皿 mǐn.188.
象人在盆中洗澡形。《说文》盈，满器也。从皿、夃。夃 gǔ，即股字初文，大腿。

niào

尿[甲]

5C3F — urine; pee, urinate.
脲 niào，尿素.

Shows a person passing water. PLC. ☞ 人 rén.1，尸 shī.36，水 shuǐ.36.
象人小解形。亦作溺。㞙、屎，篆文。尾尿屙屁溺溺，并同尿。㐱 zhěn，亦作鬒，头发稠密。

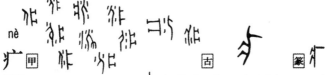

nè

疒[甲]

7592
— rely on (archaic).

A diaphoretic patient lying on a bed. It is a radical for characters related to disease. ☞ 爿 pán.137，人 rén.1.
象病人卧床发汗之形。牀，篆文。疒，同疒。

139

wèi

尉

5C09 — an officer, a military rank.

蔚，慰wèi；熨yùn.

Shows a patient being cauterized by burning moxa, moxibustion. PLC, 熨yùn: to iron (clothes); with another *fire*, 火huǒ.117, as a lower radical. ☞ 尸shī.30, 寸cùn.17.

尉字可能反映了古代的艾灸疗法。

yīn

殷

6BB7 — name of dynasty; thriving.

A patient undergoing acupuncture treatment. PLC. ☞ 㐆=㐆yī mirror image of 身shēn.4, 殳shū.148.

象病人接受砭针治疗。

5.5 Interrelationship 交往

huà

化

5316 — to change; culture; chemistry.

花，化huā；讹é；货huò: commodity；靴xuē: boots.

Shows two, one positive one down, coming and going. ☞ 人rén.1.

象一正一倒两人形，表示人们来往变化交易。

dé

寻

3775 — the ancient form of 得dé: to get.

得，锝dé：得děi.

A hand holding a cowry shell, which was used as money. 旦dàn is a simplified form of 贝bèi. ☞ 又yòu.17 or 寸cùn.17.

手抓贝。貣寻罖尉曼貣寻得得得尉淂鞭，或古或俗，并得字。

mǎi

買 = 买 甲 ☐ 金

8CB7 = 4E70 — to buy, purchase.

賣 = 卖 mài: to sell; 觌 dí; 窦, 读 dòu; 渎, 犊, 牍, 读, 黩 dú; 赎 shú: to redeem; 续 xù.

A cowry shell being dredged up with a net. ☞ 网 wǎng, 贝 bèi.

买表示网获宝贝之形。

guàn

貫 = 贯 金 ☐ 古 ☐ 篆 ☐

8CAB = 8D2F — a string of 1000 copper coin; pass through, pierce; a surname.

惯, 掼 guàn; 實 = 实 shí.

String of cowry shells. ☞ 贝 bèi.

象串起的两个贝形。

xíng

行 甲 ☐ 金 ☐ 古 ☐ 篆 ☐

884C — to go; to travel; to do; behaviour, conduct; all right.

行, 绗 háng; 珩, 衡, 桁 héng.

Diagram of a crossroad. Both 行 xíng and the left - hand part 彳 chì are radicals implying motion.

十字路口形。《客家方言詩》十行彳亍問秀才。

---

chuò

辵 = 辶 篆 ☐

8FB5 = 8FB6 — archaic character.

A combination of 彳 chì and 止 zhǐ.22: footprint. It is a radical for movement or motion.

彳与止的组合。

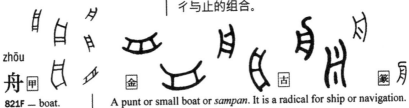

zhōu

舟 甲 ☐ 金 ☐ 古 ☐ 篆 ☐

821F — boat.

A punt or small boat or *sampan*. It is a radical for ship or navigation.

舟船形。艬 bàng, 同艕, 並舟。舑 tān, 俗艃, 葱艕, 藜芦。

yōu

攸甲 金 古 篆

6538 — passing to, toward; past.
悠yōu; 修xiū; 倏shū; 條=条tiáo.

Shows a man rowing with an oar. ☞ 人rén.1, 攴pū.
象人持桨划水形，表示行水悠远。

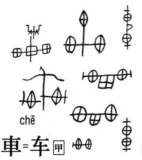

chē

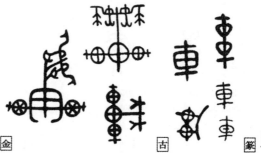

車=车甲 金 古 篆

8ECA=8F66 — chariot; vehicle.
轟=轰hōng; 擊=击jī; 车jū;
库kù; 阵zhèn.

The multidimensional perspective of an ancient chariot with spokes, shaft and yokes, and then 車 chē is a top view of the chariot's box with an axle and two wheels, two strokes on the axle. In *Shang* and *Zhou* Dynasties, the chariot was a symbol of the might of both kings and lords. It was also used as a practical weapon in warfare.

古代两轮战车的散点透视图形。戟戴轗伟伻，并同车。轆283FF.kē，或同磕。郫，同车，姓氏。轃yìn，俗轃，车名。蕯鑫xiē zhē，做事轩昂太过。

Rubbing of bricks, the Han Dynasty.
汉代画像砖。

è
厄=厄 甲 丯 金 夃 古 夬 曱 冄 篆 厄 厄 厄

6239=5384
—adversity.

扼: to grip, clutch,
苊，呝，軛=軛è.

The yoke of a chariot. PLC, 軛è: yoke; with a chariot-radical 车chē.142.

象軛形。《说文》厄，科厄，木節也。厄，隘也。后厄、厄二字
通用。呝=呝，鸡叫声。桅=軛。啟歀=歁歀，笑语。

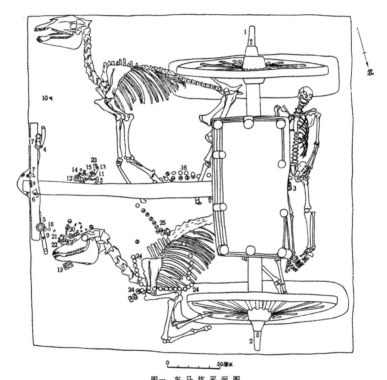

图一 车马坑平面图

1、2．喜 3．踵饰 4、5．軛饰 6、7．兽面形衡饰 9、10．铜鼻 11、19．铜镳 12、21．特大铜泡
13、20．小兽面形铜饰 14．锥形铜饰（另一件包括在22内） 8、15—18、22—25．铜泡

Plan of a late Shang dynasty chariot burial excavated at Xiaomintun, Anyang.
安阳孝民屯商代车马坑平面图（采自《考古》1972/4，p.25）。

liǎng

兩 = 两 [金] [古] [篆] 兩

5169 = 4E24 — two; *liang,* a unit of weight, 50 gram.

俩, 魎liǎng; 俩liǎ; 辆liàng.

网=两liǎng shows the shaft, cross bar and two yokes of a chariot. Two horses were yoked to the chariot. The shaft and cross bar of a chariot could be used as a pair of scales by the ancient merchants in their trades; therefore 两liǎng, *liang* was borrowed to represent a unit of weight. PLC, 辆: liàng: a classifier for vehicles, 车chē.142 and 厄è.143.

两字源于车辕与衡的象形, 中间的"从"表示车衡上的两个轭。買, 同贵。冕, 同魎。飔飔, 同魍魎。悦悯, 悦悯之谓。觞,同纟。觞觞觞觞, 三三两两。铢觞, 铢两。翈, 喃字, 从羽两聲。翱翔。

Chariot

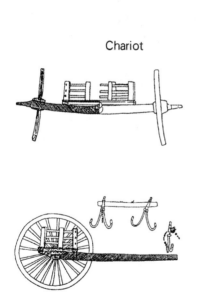

Shang Dynasty

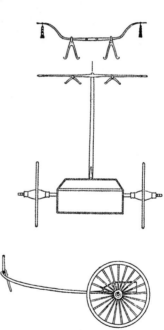

West Zhou Dynasty

The yokes of chariots.
车衡。

Chapter 6

THE EMERGENCE OF WAR   战争的出现

6.1   Weaponry and the Military   兵器与军事力量

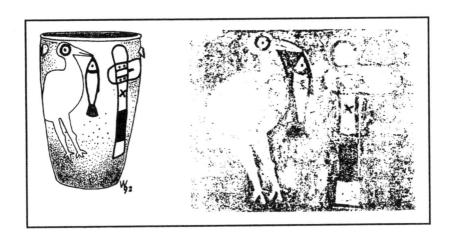

A Neolithic clay vessel with the design of a stork holding a fish in its mouth. Both the stork and the fish are totems, symbols for two clans. The stone ax on the design alludes that this vessel was a victory souvenir for the winner, the stork-clan, fighting against the fish-clan.

彩陶缸·鹳衔鲢鱼石斧。河南临汝出土，仰韶文化庙底沟型。

这件彩绘陶缸是用来装殓某个部落首长的。画面高三十七厘米，宽四十四厘米，由棕白两色构成。彩画中的白鹳与鲢鱼含有部落图腾的意味。捆扎在木棍上的石斧和白鹳衔鲢鱼的造形，记录了白鹳氏族战胜鲢鱼氏族的历史事件。

6. 1. 1—Armory　军械库

gē

戈 甲　金　古　篆　参

6208 — dagger-ax; a surname.

划=劃huá: to scratch; 戟jǐ: halberd; 戕: kill, 戗qiāng: to clash; 找 zhǎo: to look for.

A bronze dagger-ax or *ge*-halberd with a long shaft and tang. The upper dot of this character derives from the upper curved end of the shaft instead of the halberd's spike. The stroke on the shaft's butt indicates the finial. The *Ge* was a principal weapon of the *Shang* and *Zhou* Dynasties as well as a radical. ☞ 菱 jiān.163.

格斗兵器。戈的使用与发展历经商周两代，直到公元三世纪，它是上古时期一种主要的实战兵器。盏、鈬，并金文戈。金文戜2BF03、蒿2CDC1，同蒿，族徽。

yuè

戉 甲　金　古　篆

6209 — battle-ax.
戉=钺=鈬; 越yuè.

A bronze ax with a curved blade.

一种用于劈砍战斗的曲刃战斧。斧鈬之鈬篆作戉。戜，古文越。兏2BD50，同瑼zhuán。金文有戜2BBF7 字，《戜觚》戜。又羘2BE17，从奴戉聲。《羘羊觯》羘羊。成2BBE2，从大戉聲。或讀伐。《成父乙觯》成父乙。并族徽。

wù

戊 甲　金　古　篆

620A — the fifth of the ten Heavenly Stems.
茂mào.

A bronze ax. This character was later borrowed to represent one element of the decimal cycle. PLC. ☞ 戉yuè, 戌xū, 戍 shù.

平刃战斧。

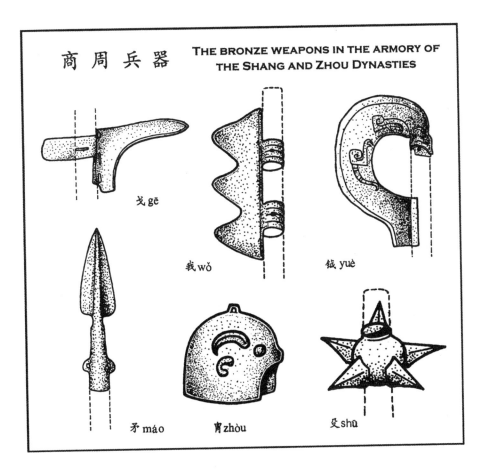

商周兵器

THE BRONZE WEAPONS IN THE ARMORY OF THE SHANG AND ZHOU DYNASTIES

戈 gē

我 wǒ

钺 yuè

矛 máo

胄 zhòu

殳 shū

xū

戌 甲　　金　　古 戌 戓 戌

620C — the eleventh of the twelve Earthly Branches

威 wēi; 滅＝灭 miè: to kill, extinguish.

Drawing of a battle-ax with a long shaft. PLC.
☞ 戊 wù, 戍 shù.161, 戎 róng.161.

战斧。

147

wǒ

6211 — I, myself.

俄, 哦, 娥, 蛾, 鹅, 莪,
峨é; 饿è; 哦ó, ò; 硪wò;
義＝乂yì.

戋22990 shows a saw-ax with a wave-like or zigzag blade and a tubular socket attaching it to the shaft. PLC. ☞ 戈 gē.

一种古代刃部呈锯齿形兵器的象形，后假借作第一人称代词。戋𢦓成𢦻𢦒靠𣪠杖狱，或古或俗，並同我。

máo

矛

77DB — spear, lance, pike.

茅, 蟊máo; 袤, 瞀, 懋mào.

Sketch of a tasseled bronze lance.

长柄格斗刺兵器。我鉾𢦏桙杵矜锊韴鸐戟，或古或俗，並同矛。《燕王𧊒矛》郾王𧊒作巨攻鋚。𨱋，同鉚，亦作鋣，即矛。

shū

殳

6BB3 — mace

股gǔ; 没méi; 沒, 殁mò; 芟shān;
设shè; 投, 骰tóu; 役, 疫yì.

Shows a hand holding a mace - a club with a heavy head of stone or bronze. ☞ 父 fù.157, 攴 pū: to beat lightly.

手持殳形。殳或作杸，用以砸击的车战兵器。殳，从又几声。几shū，鸟短羽。攴，从又卜声。

dùn

盾

148

76FE — shield. 遁dùn; 循xún.

Shows a man holding an oval shield. The small cross indicates the handle of the shield. In the *Shang* and *Zhou* Dynasties, most shields were made of animal skin strengthened by a coat of lacquer.

人手持盾牌形。櫓，大盾。𩋡，俗鞱。[illegible]sài，塞。𨧴=錟，槍。

zhòu

冑 金 古 篆

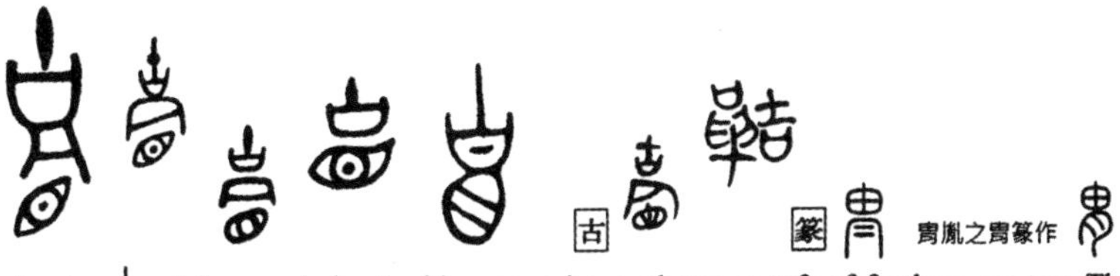

冑胤之冑篆作

5191 — helmet; descendants.

A bronze helmet with a panache, a plume or tuft of feathers, on top. The lower 月yuè was incorrectly derived from 目mù.11: eye. ☞ 冒mào.

象人头戴头盔，眼睛露在外面的样子。冑 5191，甲冑。《说文》冑字在冃部，《康熙字典》在冂部。冑或从革，作鞸、軸、轉。胄 80C4，胄胤。《说文》、《康熙字典》胄字並在肉部。因读音相同，字形太过相似，今二字不分，並入月部。

jiè

介 甲 金 古 篆

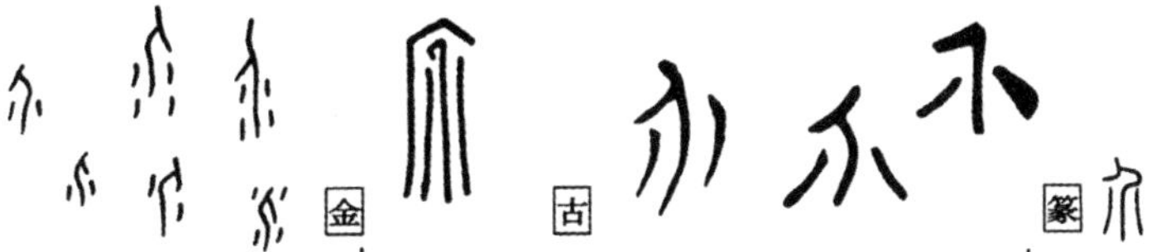

4ECB — armor, shell; to be between; to take seriously.

价，芥，疥，界，骱jiè; 芥gài; 价=價jià; 阶=階jiē.

Shows a soldier girding on his armor. ☞ 人rén.1.

人身着片状盔甲形。乔，俗𢍁，古文共字。

bì

必 甲 金 古 篆

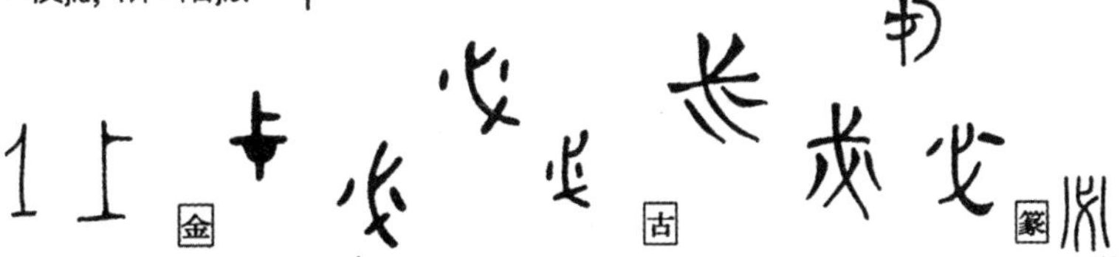

5FC5 — must, certainly.

秘，飶，泌，䟆bì; 宓，嘧，蜜，泌，秘，谧mì; 瑟sè.

The shaft of the ge - halberd without the blade. PLC, 柲 bi4: shaft of ancient weapons. The two dots on the sides are either later additions for decoration's sake, or an ancient phonetic element 八bā.85. ☞ 戈gē.

象戈矛等兵器的柲柄形。

6. 1. 2—Archery 弓箭术

Rock Painting • Bowman
岩画 • 弓箭手

Rock Painting (*after Gai* (1) *fig.* 49).

gōng

弓甲 金•

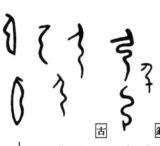

古 篆ʅ 参

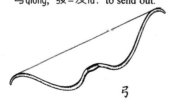

弓

5F13 — bow; bent, crooked.
躬gōng: to bow; 窮＝穷；
穹qióng; 發＝发fā: to send out.

A reflexed composite bow (before being strung). Reflexion places the limbs of a bow under greater tension when the bow is strung, storing more power than straight bows do. The combination of extended draw length and short limbs enables the composite bow to shoot an arrow faster and farther than can a wooden straight bow of equal draw weight. See below.

复合回复弓的象形。ʅ2D6A5，草书弓字。弜，俗州。霧，俗靈。

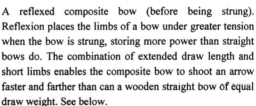

150

jiàng

弪 甲 金 篆

5F1C

— strong, powerful; double;
multiple.

弪 = 弢 = 弻 bì: to assist;
弱 ruò: weak, feeble;
粥 zhōu; 鬻 yù;
强 jiàng, 倔强: stubborn.

Ancient China's bowmakers used adhesives derived from hide
and fish's swim bladders to glue animal sinew to the backs of
their bows, they also painted thick layers of lacquer on the bow
backs. Both the sinew and the lacquer have high tensile strength.
Other materials such as horn were sometimes glued to the bellies
of wood or bamboo reflexed bows to reinforce the compressive
loads. ☞ 弓 gōng.

中国古代的工匠用把动物筋腱粘在弓背上的，或在弓
背上涂上多层大漆的方法来制造强背复合弓。弢、
弻，古文弪。

rù

入 甲 金 古 篆

5165

— to enter, take in.

汆 cuān: quick-boil;
仚 = 仙 xiān: immortal.

Represents an arrowhead. PLC.

入表示箭头。《说文》从𠆢 liǎng，
二入也。两从此。
𠆢 liǎng，未详。伙，同供。

▶ **Bone arrowheads from
Banpo, the Neolithic**

骨制箭头·半坡遗址出土

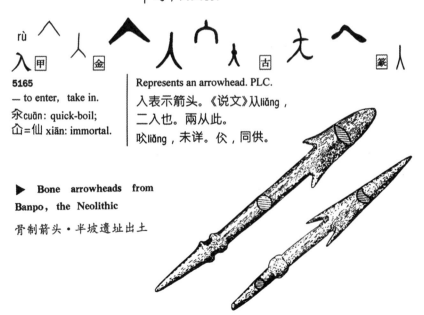

shǐ

77E2 — arrow; to vow, swear. 知zhī.

An arrow with its arrowhead and nock. The short stroke on the arrow shaft was used to differentiate 矢shǐ from the ancient forms such as 大dà.3 and 交jiāo.8.

象箭形。

yín

5BC5 — the third of the twelve Earthly Branches. 夤yín; 演yǎn.

寅yín and 矢shǐ: arrow are cognate characters. When 寅yín was borrowed to use in the duodecimal cycle, a square symbol was added on the shaft.

寅矢同源分化。

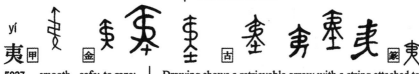

yí

5937 — smooth, safe; to raze; to exterminate. 姨, 痍, 胰, 咦yí.

Drawing shows a retrievable arrow with a string attached to it. PLC. ☞ 矢shǐ, 弋yì, 弋射: shoot a retrievable arrow.

象古代射鸟用的一种拴有丝绳便于回收的箭。

彈, 夷字繁文。

Detail of a bronze jar from the Zhou period. See the whole design on page 60.
弋射。

shè

射 甲 金 古 篆

5C04 — to shoot, emit; inject; to aim at.
麝shè; 榭，谢xiè.

Glyph show an arrow being shot. Later, the bow 弓gōng and arrow were replaced with the element 身shēn. ☞ 又yòu or 寸cùn.17.
手引弓箭形。后"身"代替弓箭。猤，古文射从倒矢。躲，篆文。作射，重文。麝香，麝香。鮮牪：喃字，射箭。

zhì

至 甲 金 古 篆

81F3 — to come to, reach, attain; so far.
侄zhí; 桎，致，窒，蛭，轾，郅，膣zhì; 室shì; 倒dǎo, dào.

Shows an arrow 矢shǐ hitting its target, or the ground.
象矢中靶或矢远来落地之形。

hóu

侯 甲 金 古 篆

4FAF — a shooting target; a marquis, a rand of nobility; a surname.
喉，猴，篌，瘊hóu; 侯hòu.

厌=矦=侯 hóu shows an arrow flying to a shooting target. Later, the form of target is changed, a man-radical being substituted for the left side. ☞ 矢shǐ, 厂hàn.
象矢射侯（箭靶）之形。

bèi

备=备 甲 金 古 篆

5099=5907 — to prepare, provide.
惫bèi.

蔔=蒈=備 shows arrows being placed in a frame. PLC.
箭置盛矢架中，后造箙字专指盛矢器。

bì

畀 [甲]

7540 — to bestow.
箅，痹bì；鼻bí.

畀＝畁 shows an arrow with a flat arrowhead. PLC, 錍 pī: flattened arrowhead. ☞ 矢 shǐ.

带有扁平箭头的箭形。錍，箭镞，广长薄镰。亦作鈚鈚鎞。

hán

函 [甲] [金]   [古] [篆]

51FD — a case, shield; letter.
涵hán: to contain; 菡hàn.

Derives from a drawing of a quiver for arrows. ☞ 矢 shǐ.

箭囊。备射之时所用为箙，矢之括与筈之半露在外。藏矢所用为函，全矢皆纳其中。圅，篆文。

fú

弗 [甲] 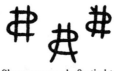 [金] [古] [篆]

5F17 — not.
佛，怫，拂，绋，氟fú；
沸，狒，费，镄fèi；佛fó.

Shows arrow shafts tied together to avoid warping. The "rope" is written as a 弓 gōng. PLC.

将燥矫取直的箭杆急浸冷水后用绳捆在一起，干燥定型。

zhī

知 [甲] [金] [篆]

77E5 — to know, be aware of; knowledge.
蜘zhī，智zhì，痴chī，踟chí.

A combination of 矢 shǐ.152: arrow and 口 kǒu.13, a symbol for the sound of a flying arrow. PLC.

从矢从口，表示射箭时的声音。矤、矤，古文知。

jí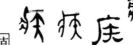

疾 [甲] [金] [古] [篆]

75BE — disease, sickness;
to abhor; fast, quick.
蒺，嫉jí.

A man being shot with an arrow. ☞ 矢 shǐ, 大 dà.3, 疒 chuáng.

人腋下中疾矢。矢伤人则疾矣。痳痳痳廿疾，并古文疾。誺，语急。悈悈瘝，并同痳。遬，同疾，迅疾。

6.1.3—Flag　旗帜

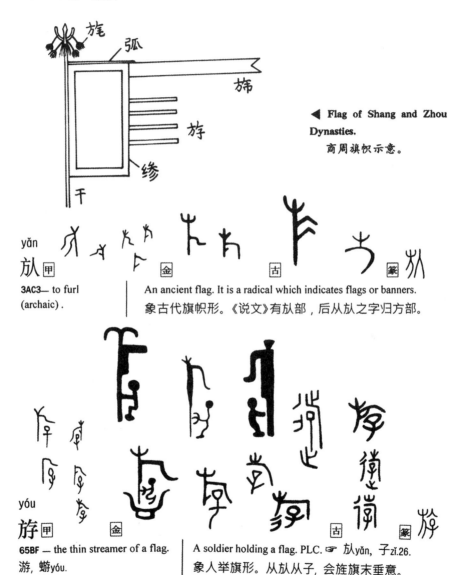

◀ Flag of Shang and Zhou Dynasties.
商周旗帜示意。

yǎn

㫃甲　　金　　古　　篆

3AC3— to furl (archaic).

An ancient flag. It is a radical which indicates flags or banners.
象古代旗帜形。《说文》有㫃部，后从㫃之字归方部。

yóu

斿甲　　金　　古　　篆

65BF — the thin streamer of a flag.
游，蝣yóu.

A soldier holding a flag. PLC. ☞ 㫃yǎn，子zǐ.26.
象人举旗形。从㫃从子，会旌旗末垂意。

155

lǚ

旅 甲 金 古 篆

65C5 — to travel; brigade; troops.

膂 = 膐lǚ: backbone.

Soldiers massing under the colors. ☞ 放yǎn.155，人rén.1.

旅，古文旅，表示众人聚集在战旗之下。炊、衣，亦古文旅。榔lǚ，同栌，松别种。劳，俗膂字。䮫，同骏，驿传所用之马。𥳇，同筥，圆形竹筐。盨，从皿旅声。读若鲁。商晚期族徽。又《睡虎地秦墓竹简·为吏之道》段门逆闾，赘婿后父。段门逆闾，读若监门御旅。

xuán

旋 甲 金 古 篆

65CB — to return, come back; circle.

漩，璇xuán; 旋xuàn.

Represents fighters returning (from battle) with flying colors. ☞ 放yǎn.155，止zhǐ.22.

旗帜与足趾的组合，表示举旗凯旋而归。《睡虎地秦墓竹简》旋通係颈。旋通，读若繯通，即上吊的绳套。

zú

族 甲 金 古 篆

650F — clan; race; a class of things with common features.

镞zú; 簇cù; 嗾sǒu.

A combination of a flag and an arrow, which indicates the gathering of a clan to do battle. ☞ 放yǎn.155，矢shǐ.152.

旗帜与矢的组合，表示族众集合于族旗之下。鏃，俗镞。

6. 2　Nation and Warfare　国家与战争

fù

父 甲 金 古 篆

7236 — father.

父, 釜, 澄, 斧fǔ;
爸bà: pa; 爹diē: father;
爺=爷yé: grandpa.

A hand holding a celt or stone ax. PLC, 斧fǔ: ax.
☞ 斤jīn.108, 又yòu.17.

手持石斧形。

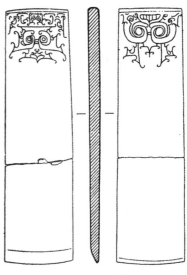

图二　石　锛 (1/2)

▶ A design on a ritual jade ax. Neolithic Period, Longshan culture, late third millennium BC. Excavated at *Rizhao Liangchengzhen* in Shandong Province.

玉斧及其阴刻纹样。山东日照两城镇出土,龙山文化。长18.0,上宽4.5,厚0.85,下宽4.9,厚0.6(cm)。（采自《考古》1972/4. p. 57, fig. 2）。

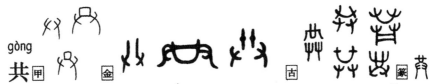

gòng

共 甲 金 古 篆

5171
— together; common; total; to share.
供, 恭gōng; 拱gǒng; 供gòng; 哄,
烘hōng; 洪hóng; 哄hǒng; 哄hòng.

Shows two hands making an offering. PLC. 供gòng: to lay offerings. ☞ 又yòu.17, 廾=収gǒng: action of two hands.

双手捧物进供。舜, 古文。

◀ An inscription 共 gòng on a potsherd. Late Henan Longshan culture, 2000 BC. Excavated at *Dengfeng*, Henan Province. This inscription may indicate that this earthenware vessel was a peace offering.

陶文・共。

jūn

君 甲   金   古   篆

541B — king.

裙，郡 jùn；窘 jiǒng；
裙，群 qún.

A hand holding a stick or mace and issuing orders. It was thought that a monarch must possess both the mace and the magic flute, a symbol of persuasive power, to maintain his rule. ☞ 父 fù.157，口 kǒu.13: mouth.

手持权杖发号施令。君，同王。璺 24AA1，俗争。二君争玉会意。

wáng

王 甲   金   古   篆

738B — king; a surname.

汪 wāng；往，枉 wǎng；旺 wàng；
逛 guàng；狂，诳 kuáng.

A bronze ax head which was used as a symbol of power.

象青铜战斧之形。瑝，俗相。圛 2D371，俗兵。

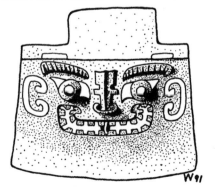

▶ A bronze ax head, Shang.
商代青铜大钺。

huáng

皇 金 古 篆

7687 — emperor, sovereign.

凰, 隍, 惶, 徨, 煌, 蝗,
篁, 鳇 huáng.

皇 is a combination of a crown and 王 wáng.158: a symbol of power.

皇字上象皇冠，王为意符。䤵，繁文。篆作皇，讹。

chén

臣 甲 金 古 篆

81E3 — official under a feudal ruler, subject; to acknowledge; allegiance to.

Shows the eye of a bowing person. ☞ 目 mù.11, 见 jiàn.12, 监 jiān, and 卧 wò: to lie.

臣表示人低头弯腰时侧目而视形。𦣻，同臣。

huò

或 甲 金 古 篆

6216 — or; probably; someone.

惑 huò; 域, 閾, 蜮 yù; 國=国, 掴, 帼, 馘 guó.

A combination of 戈 gē.146: dagger-ax, 口 kǒu.13: a symbol of a city, and 一 yī for territory or land. The weapon is needed to protect the territory. PLC, 域 yù: territory; with a soil-radical 土 tǔ; 國=国 guó: notion, country. ☞ 咸 xián.163.

或中的"口"象城邑形，戈表示守城。甲骨文或国同字。

wéi

韋=韦 甲 金 古 篆

97CB=97E6 — leather, a surname.

帏, 违, 围: to enclose, 涠 wéi; 伟, 苇, 纬, 玮, 炜 wěi; 卫=卫 wèi; 韩 hán; 讳 huì; 韧 rèn.

𧾷 2C18F=韋=韦 shows feet 止 zhǐ.22 surrounding a square, a symbol which indicates the settlement or city, while the footprints represent a patrol. It's a radical as well. PLC, 圍=围 wéi: to enclose, and 衛=卫 wèi: to defend, protect; with the radical 行 xíng, implying action.

城邑四周有足迹，会巡逻护卫意。𧦝，俗䜌 wèi，言不信。

zhèng

正 甲 金 古 篆

6B63 — right, correct; proper, main; to rectify; just, exactly.
怔, 征, 症, 正zhèng; 证, 政, 症zhèng; 惩＝懲chěng.

A footprint 止zhǐ.22 pointing to a city or settlement, intending to invade the city. Later, the small square, symbol for the city, was replaced by a single stroke. PLC, 征zhèng: to invade, invasion; with a radical 彳 chì indicating movement.

正字从止，一横源于城邑的象形，征本字，表示征伐城邑。以口象郭郭，则𫞒2C18F 读若圍；𫞐2C190 读若征，占领中；𫭋2BB4B 读若定，已占领；并金文族徽。

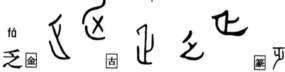

fá

乏 金 古 篆

4E4F — exhausted; tired, weary; lack.
砭biān; 贬biān; 泛fàn; 眨zhǎ.

Derives from the mirror image of 正zhèng. PLC.
反正为乏。乏字为正字镜像。

zāi

𢦐＝戈 甲 金 古 篆

22992＝2298F
— calamity; wound (archaic).
载, 哉zāi; 载zǎi, zài; 裁cái; 截jié; 戴dài.

An enemy's scalp with hair 毛máo.11 on a *ge*-halberd 戈gē.146 to express defiance. The content of this character recalls the practice of scalping enemies also practiced by some North Amorican Indians during wartime. 才cái.40 was introduced into the character as a replacement for the scalp as well as for a phonetic. ☞ 灾zāi: calamity.

将带有毛发的头皮系在戈上用来向敌方挑战。美洲印第安人也有剥取敌人头皮作为战利品的风俗。

bīng

兵 甲 金 古 篆

5175 — military; soldier.

乒乓 pīng pāng; 宾=賓, 傧, 滨,
缤, 槟, 镔bīn; 摈, 殡, 膑, 髌,
鬓bìn; 槟bīng.

Two hands holding an ax. ☞ 斤jīn.108, 廾 gǒng.

《说文》兵, 械也。从収持斤, 并力之貌。俀
剓𠂤𠈃𠈼𠈽𠈿𠈾𠈗𠈼, 或古或俗, 並同兵。

jiè
戒 甲 金 古 篆

6212 — to guard against; to
exhort, warn; to give up.

诫jiè: to admonish; 械xiè.

Two hands holding a ge-halberd. ☞ 戈 gē, 又yòu.17.
双手持戈警戒之形。

shù
戍 甲 金 戉 古 篆

620D — garrison; to
guard a frontier.

A combination of a man and a ge-halberd. ☞ 人rén.1, 戈gē.146, 幾.92.
金文戉2A945戉2BEE8, 象人持戈而立, 表示戍守。蔑、幾从戍。

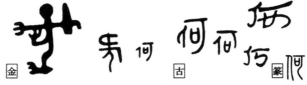

hé
何 甲 金 古 篆

4F55 — what, how,
why; a surname.

荷hé, hè.

A man carrying a ge-halberd. The small square is used only to occupy the
space under the halberd. 可kě is also a phonetic. PLC, 荷hè: to carry,
burden. ☞ 人rén.1, 戈gē.146.

人荷戈形, 荷字初文。古文何字形中, 戈或亦为声符,《说
文》何从可声。𩨧sao, 何。𩨧sao, 星星。並喃字。

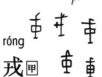

róng
戎 甲 金 戉 古 篆

620E — military
affairs; a surname.

绒róng; 贼zéi.

A ge-halberd and a shield. ☞ 戈gē.146, 盾dùn.148.

象兵士手持戈盾之形。戔2BEF8 从二戎相对, 讀若鞁bèi, 古
文誖。戉2BEF3, 讀若戎。並商晚期族徽。

Fighting on a bridge. Rubbing of a frieze from the lintel of a tomb gate. Eastern Han Dynasty, Shandong Province.　胡汉两军桥上激战图。山东沂南画像石墓墓门门额拓片，东汉。（选自《中国大百科·考古学》，607页。）

jīn

今 甲 金 古 篆

4ECA — today.

衿jīn; 妗jìn; 岑，涔cén;
钤，黔qián; 衾qīn; 芩，琴qín;
贪tān; 阴=阴，荫yīn; 吟yín.

An ancient bell. The outline of a bell is A shaped 亼 jí: calling together, and the short stroke on the bottom of the pictograph indicates the clapper tongue of the bell. PLC. See below.

今象古代的铃形。假借。亽2B746 亼4ED2，並俗今。

lìng

令 甲 金 古 篆

4EE4 — to order, command; law.

拎līn; 伶，苓，呤，囹，铃，玲，瓴，
聆，蛉，羚，翎，零，龄líng; 嶺=岭，
领lǐng; 冷lěng.

A man sitting or kneeling under a bell-symbol 今jīn.
☞ 卩 jié.9, 命mìng: order, and 铃líng: bell.

人跪铃下受命。龡líng.20350 令狐合文。俗作
孤21988。

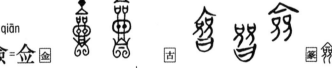

qiān

僉=佥 金 古 篆

50C9=4F65 — unanimous.

签qiān; 佥，拴，检，脸jiǎn;
剑jiàn; 敛，脸，裣liǎn; 殓，
潋liàn; 险xiǎn; 验yàn.

Shows people gathering to discuss military affairs after hearing the sound 口kǒu.13 of a bell 今jīn. ☞ 令líng,人rén.1.

众人听到铃声聚集之意。僉20472=鈐2B8DB，古文
佥。鑾，俗壑。

wǔ

武 甲 金 古 篆

6B66 — military, martial; a surname.
鹉wǔ; 斌bīn; 赋fù.

A *ge*-halberd 戈gē and a footprint 止zhǐ.22, a symbol of movement.

武从戈从止，表示动武。珷、珷，并俗武。正3C50，缺笔避讳字。

cán

戋=戈 甲 金 古 篆

6214=620B — small, tiny, fragmentary.
笺jiān; 贱, 践: to tampel, 溅, 饯jiàn; 残cán; 钱qián; 浅qiān; 线xiàn; 盏zhǎn; 栈zhàn.

Two *ge*-halberds in fighting position. PLC.
☞ 戈gē, 戋=残=残cán: to injure, ferocious.
从二戈相向。从戋之字多有残、少之意。

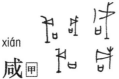

xián

咸 甲 金 古 篆

54B8 — all; a surname.
鹹=咸xián, 感gǎn, 喊hǎn, 憾hàn; 减, 碱jiǎn; 缄jiān; 箴zhēn.

A combination of 戌xū: a battle-ax and 口kǒu.13 mouth. PLC. ☞ 戌xū, 口kǒu.13, 喊hǎn: to shout.
从戌从口，会以斧钺杀戮之意。

nì

屰 甲 金 古 篆

5C70 — archaic form of 逆nì: contrary; to go against; inverse.
逆nì; 朔, 蒴, 搠, 槊shuò; 塑, 溯sù; 嗍suō.

An inverted man who, perhaps, was defeated on the battlefield. ☞ 大dà.3.
象倒人形。

fá

伐 甲 金 古 篆

4F10 — to fell, cut down; to send a punitive expedition.
筏, 阀fá.

An enemy being killed by a ge-halberd. ☞ 人rén.1, 戈gē.146.
以戈击杀人。𠂤，从𠂤从一。伐省文。商晚期族徽。

6. 3 To the Victor Go the Spoils 俘获与暴行

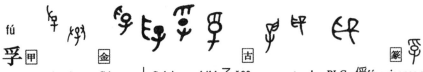

fú

孚 甲　金　古　篆

5B5A — to inspire confidence; to trust.

俘, 浮, 莩, 桴, 蜉, fú; 孵fū; 荸, 殍piǎo.

Seizing a child 子zǐ.26: son as a trophy. PLC, 俘fú: prisoner of war. ☞ 爪zhǎo.20: claw, 乳rǔ: breast-feed, milk.

俘获儿童。戜，或作戜。戜伐，戜伐。见《齊鼎》。

qǔ

取 甲　金　古　篆

53D6 — to take, get, obtain; to aim for.

娶qǔ: to marry a woman; 趣qù; 陬, 鲰, 诹zōu; 聚jù; 骤zhòu; 最, 蕞zuì; 撮cuō.

A hand holding the left ear of a war prisoner. In ancient times, the left ears of war prisoners and corpses were lopped off as testimony to military exploits. ☞ 耳ěr, 又yòu.17, 馘guó: a prisoner of war with his left ear cut off.

手持耳。古割取敌人左耳以计数献功。蕞，同聚。

yìn

印 甲　金　古　篆　参　抑

5370 — to print; a seal; mark, print.

昂áng; 仰yáng; 抑yì; 迎yíng.

A prisoner of war being held down by a hand. PLC, 抑yì: to bend (head), concede; with a handradical. Compare . ☞ 爪zhǎo: claw, 子zǐ.26: son.

以手俘获儿童形。《说文》归，按也。从反印。抑，俗从手。

jí

及 甲　金　古　篆

53CA — reach, come up to; in time for.

汲, 岌, 笈, 级, 极=極jí; 圾jī; 吸xī.

A hand catching a person or enemy. ☞ 人rén.1, 又yòu.17.

象手追逮人形。《说文》及，逮也。从又从人。乁，古文及。《秦刻石》及如此。弓，亦古文及。遪，亦古文及。孂gǒp，喃字。从二及聲。合，并。

jiā

夾=夹

593E=5939 — to press from both sides; to clip; to mingle.

浃jiā; 夹, 荚, 蛱, 颊, 郏, 铗jiá; 夹gā; 惬, 箧qiè; 侠, 峡, 狭xiá; 瘗yì.

Two small people, servants or prisoners, being held under a big person's arms. PLC, 挟 xié: to hold sth. under one's arm; coerce. ☞ 大dà.3: , 人rén.1.

二人夹辅一人形。夾3692. shǎn，盗窃怀物。陕从夾。

bìng

并

5E76 — side by side; and; to combine, merge.

摒bìng; 并bīng; 饼, 屏bǐng; 迸bèng; 碰pèng: to touch meet; 胼, 骈pián; 姘, 拼pīn; 屏; 瓶píng.

Shows two prisoners of war, their legs being tied together with sticks. ☞ 人rén.1.

将两战俘的腿绑连在一起并行。并，相从。竝=並，从二人併立。

qiú

囚

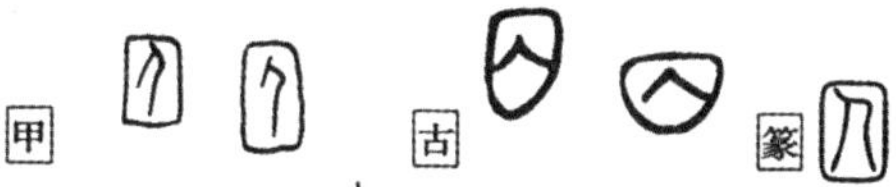

56DA — to imprison; convict.

怮, 泅qiú.

A prisoner in jail. ☞ 人rén.1.

人在口中，会囚禁意。𡇒21236, 同𤳳，古文雷。怮，虑。

kòu

寇

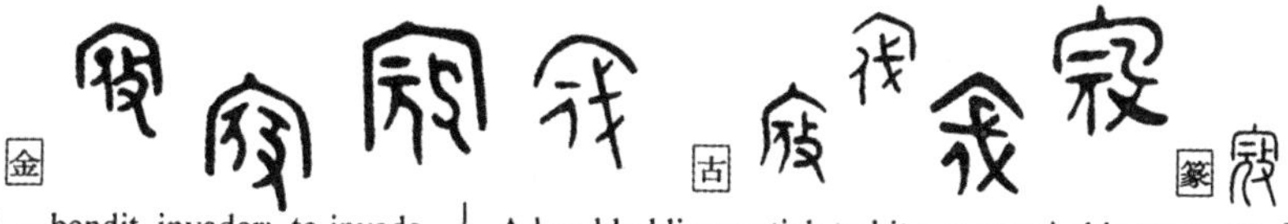

5BC7 — bandit, invader; to invade.

蔻kòu.

A hand holding a stick to hit a person in his room. ☞ 六liù or 宀mián, 元yuán, 父fù or 殳shū.

象持棒进屋击人之形。

yāng

央

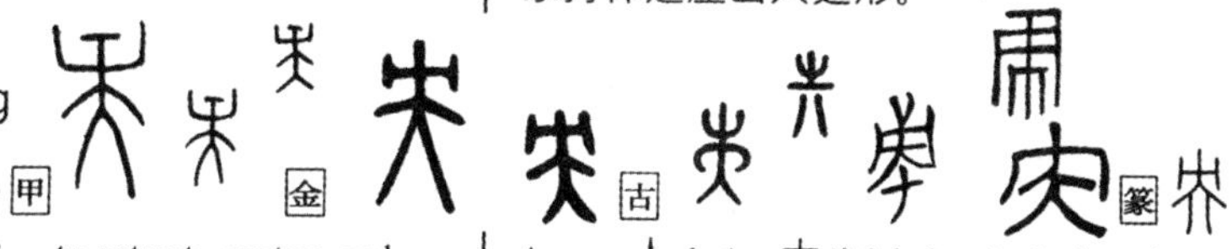

592E — to entreat; centre; end.

殃, 秧, 鸯yāng; 怏yàng; 盎àng; 英, 瑛yīng; 映yìng.

A man 人rén.1or 大dà.3 being locked up in a cangue or pillory. PLC, 殃yāng: misfortune. ☞ 人rén.1, 歹dǎi.

戴枷的人形。

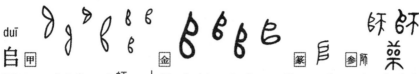

duī

自 甲

200A4 — archaic form of 師 =
师 shī: troops, army; division.
帥 = 帅 shuài: commander; 狮 shī,
筛 shāi; 蛳 sī; 追 duī, zhuī.

May depict a pair of testes. The prevalent explanation is that this character is drawing of buttocks. As a symbol used in Chinese paleography, 自 duī indicates certain military affairs such as an establishment, garrison, or force station.

象睪丸之形。在古文字中作为一种军事有关的符号。

xuē

辥 甲

859B — archaic form of 孽 =
孽 niè: evil, sin.
薜 = 薛 xuē; 孽, 蘖 niè.

辥 shows the testes 自 duī of a prisoner of war being cut off by a 辛 xīn.168, a *xin*-sword, an ancient torture instrument.

用刀割取敌方俘虏睪丸。

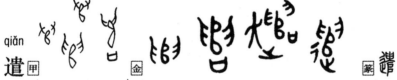

qiǎn

遣 甲

9063 — to send, dispatch;
to dispel, expel.
譴 = 谴, 缱 qiǎn.

𨙸 qiǎn shows two hands placing a pair of testes 自 duī (on an altar). Later 辶 chuò.141 was introduced as a sign for the verb 遣.

双手持自（进献）。𨙸，遣字初文。趞，金文谴。

guān

官 甲

5B98 — officer; official,
public; organ.
倌, 棺 guān; 管, 馆 guǎn;
逭 huàn; 菅 jiān; 绾 wǎn.

Combination of 六 liù or 宀 mián: hut, and 自 duī. a symbol for military affairs. PLC, 馆 guǎn: accommodation, inn.

从宀从自，表示军旅途中止息之馆舍。宀𠂤，古文。官，篆文。

166

xiàn

縣=县 金

7E23 = 53BF
— county.

悬xuán; 纍dào.

The head of an enemy hung tied on a tree. Here, the eye, 目mù.11, represents the head 首shǒu.11. It was an ancient form of revenge to display an enemy's head on a tree, exposing it to public view as a warning or provocation. PLC. 懸=悬xuán: to hang, suspend in midair. ☞ 系xì: to tied, 木mù.

县即悬字初文，表示枭xiāo首示众。

jǐn

堇 甲 金 古 篆

5807 — only.

僅=仅，瑾，谨，馑jǐn；觐jìn；勤qín；鄞yín；艱=艰jiān；漢=汉hàn；難=难nán, nàn；滩，摊，瘫tān；嘆=叹tàn.

A prisoner of war being tied up and then burnt, as an offering to bring rain. PLC. ☞ 大dà.3:，火huǒ.

从莫从火，堇表示焚人牲。从堇之字，多有艱難意，引申又有细小意。

màn

曼 甲 金 古 篆

66FC — prolonged; graceful.

漫，慢，蔓，幔，澷màn；蔓，谩，馒，鳗mán.

嫚 shows two hands holding an eye 目mù.11 open, and 冃=冒mào is a phonetic introduced later. PLC.

初文作嫚，象以双手张目之形。后从冃声。

zāng

臧 甲 金 古 篆

81E7 — good, right.

臧=赃zāng，臟=脏，藏zàng；藏cáng.

A ge-halberd jabbing into an enemy's eye. The left part 爿pán is an ancient phonetic element. PLC. ☞ 目mù.11, 臣chén.159, 戈gē.

以戈伤目。臧字从戈从臣，会臧获之意，故训善。

mín

民

6C11
— people; folk; civilian.
泯, 抿 mǐn; 眠 mián.

An eye being stabbed by a needle. In the glyphs, the eyeball has been removed from the eye socket. PLC. ☞ 目 mù.11.

用针刺瞎眼睛而致盲。上古刺盲俘虏之一目以为奴隶。

xīn

辛 甲

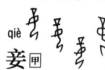   

8F9B — suffering;
laborious; pungent.
锌 xīn; 莘 shēn; 宰 zǎi:
to slaughter, butcher;
滓, 梓 zǐ; 新 xīn; 亲 qīn.

辛 41C2.qiān or 辛 xīn shows a torture instrument, perhaps a kind of sword. It's a symbol to indicate someone guilty, see below.

辛或辛象古代刑具形。《说文》辡 biàn, 罪人相与讼也。则必有一是非，因之为辩论，亦作辩；为辡别，亦作辨。

qiè

妾 甲

59BE — concubine.
接 jiē; 嬖 shà.

A *xin*-sword. resting on a woman's head. ☞ 辛 xīn, 女 nǔ.27.

《说文》妾，有罪女子，给事之得接於君者。从辛从女。《春秋》云：女为人妾。妾，不娉也。

tóng

童 甲

7AE5 — child; virgin; a surname.
僮, 潼, 瞳 tóng, 憧, 艟 chōng;
鐘＝钟 zhōng; 僮, 撞, 幢 zhuàng.

A man's eye being gouged out with a *xin*-sword. 東＝东 dōng was a phonetic. Later, the 目 mù.11: eye, and 东 were merged in 立 lì: a simplified form of 辛 xīn. PLC.

用辛（刑具）刺目。

niè

幸＝幸 甲

168

3694=5E78—handcuff.
悻 xìng; 圉 yǔ: jail;
prison; 報=报 bào.

古代腕械之形。《说文》卒 niè，所以惊人也。从大从羊。
按，俗作卒幸。夆 委 xìng，吉而免凶也。从夲从夭。夭，死
之事。故死謂之不委。按，俗作夲。卒、委今並作幸。幸
免字篆作委。

zhí

執=执 甲 金 古 篆

57F7=6267 — hold in the hand;
carry cut, execute.
縶 zhí; 挚, 贽, 鸷 zhì; 势 shì;
褻 xiè; 蛰 zhé.

A man being led away in handcuffs 幸 niè.
戴手铐的人形。墊嚇，金文执讯。

pì

辟 甲 金 古 篆

8F9F — punishment; law; capital.
辟, 避, 壁, 襞, 臂, 璧 bì; 擘 bò; 臂 bèi;
劈, 噼, 霹 pī; 劈, 擗, 癖 pǐ; 僻, 譬 pì.

A prisoner being tortured with a *xin*-sword. ☞
尸 shī, 口 kǒu.13, 辛 xīn.
用辛刀施肉刑。

xíng

荆=刑 金 古 篆 參

34DD=5211
— punishment.
型 xíng; 荆 jīng.

Crisscross incisions made by a knife 刀 dāo. 井 jīng is a phonetic as well.
《说文》荆，罚罪也。从井从刀。又刑，到也。从刀幵 qiān 聲。
按，刑篆作㓝，是刑字之讹。今刑、荆並作刑。

The following characters come from an ancient practice—marriage by capture.
下列汉字可能反映了古代抢婚制的风俗。

wēi

威 甲 金 古 篆

5A01 — impressive
strength; by force.
葳, 崴 wēi.

A woman kneeling beneath an ax. The woman is threatened by force.
☞ 戌 xū.147: a battle-ax, 女 nǚ.27: woman.
女人在斧下受威慑之形，会刑威意。

169

nú
奴 金 古 甲骨文 篆

5974 — slave.
驽 nú：努，驽 nǔ：怒 nù；
呶 náo；帑 tǎng.

A woman being captured by a hand. ☞ 女 nǔ.27, 又 yòu.17.
以手抓女之形。仗、仅，古文奴。

tuǒ
妥 甲 金 古 篆

59A5 — settled, ready; prope.
馁 něi；荽 suī；绥 suí.

A woman being pressed down by a hand. ☞ 爪 zhǎo.20: claw.
以手抑女之形。燊、叟，妥二音。或妥繁文。

mǐn
敏 甲 金 篆

654F — nimble, agile.
鳖 mǐn，繁 fán.

A hand capturing a woman. 每 měi.180 is also a phonetic. PLC.
掠夺长发的妇女之形。从攴每声，训敏疾。

qī
妻 甲 金 古 篆

59BB — wife.
凄，萋 qī.

A hand 又 yòu.17 seizing a woman's long hair. ☞ 女 nǔ.27.
以手抓住妇女长发，强抱为妻。妻妻妻妻妻妻，古文妻。

lóu
婁=娄 甲 金 古 篆

5A41=5A04—empty;
a surname.
偻，喽，楼，蝼，耧，
髅 lóu；嵝，篓 lǒu.

A woman being captured by two hands. PLC. ☞ 要 yòu.8, 搂 lōu: to hold up; 搂 lóu: to hold in one's arms, bug, embrace.
双手抓女之形。《说文》娄，空也。从母中女，空之意也。按，母中女，即表示母生女。因女性复生女性，从婁之字或有不绝、重叠之意，如：数、楼、屡。䁖 lòu，贪财。娄训空，重男轻女思想的体现，抱怨生育未获男孩。

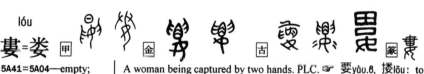

𝕮𝖍𝖆𝖕𝖙𝖊𝖗 7

FROM CULT TO CULTURE   从神化到文化

7.1   Primitive Art   原始艺术

According to archeological discoveries, early Chinese, like today's aborigines, eagerly sought communication with God. They pried out their teeth, tattooed themselves and danced with masks for God's blessing, as well as for fun. Rituals were performed for their magic efficacy in totem feasts, hunting and harvesting. Primitive art existed in their dances, music, crafts, rituals and magic. The characters in this section help to show us the shrouded marvels of Chinese Neolithic culture and art. Later, in the Chinese Bronze Age, these rituals were replaced by the complicated ceremonies of sacrifice.

通过考古发掘展现在现代人面前的中国原始艺术是丰富多彩的,然而蕴藏在汉字中的史前中国人的艺术,他们的技艺与舞蹈,他们的各式各样的仪式与巫术使人感受到的却是史前中国人的艺术冲动和同神灵交往的强烈愿望。

7.1.1—Neolithic Pottery Culture
史前陶艺

▶ The Banpo human face design and fish design.
半坡人面鱼纹展开图。
(采自《西安半坡》,
180页。)

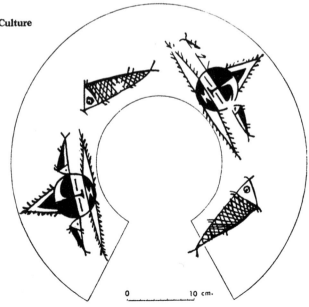

0   10 cm.

Use of pottery is a feature of Neolithic society. The following characters reveal the Neolithic pottery culture of China, including the famous Yangshao painted pottery culture and some typically Chinese clay vessels.

wū

巫甲   十   王   王   十   ⊞金   田古   巫   晉   巫   巫篆

5DEB — shaman; sorcery; wizard.
诬wū; 靈=灵 líng: spirit;
噬, 筮 shì.

▼ **Painted pottery ritual vessels with face motifs, Yangshao culture. Excavated at Banpo near Xi'an.**

人面鱼纹彩陶盆，西安半坡出土。

This character derives from the character for 五 wǔ: five.

The painted pottery at the site of a large Neolithic village at *Banpo* near *Xi'an* was one of the main focuses of attention in 1953 and 1959 when that settlement site, dated around 5000 BC, was excavated. Some ritual potteries were found with painted patterns in various motifs. The composite designs of human faces and fish are the most intriguing among those motifs. The face designs appear on the inner walls of pottery basins which have curving rims. The designs have some subtle differences; however, the mouths are identical. The mouth's outline is in the form of a prehistoric 区 wǔ. Since wizards prefer to simulate the sound of wind and call for rain. When early Chinese designed this face and called it *Wu*, the character 巫 wū, had not been created, so the number five 区 was borrowed to indicate the wizard. The 区 placed on the mouth seems to be uttering: I am the sorcerer to command the wind and rain. Later, the ancient form of 五 wǔ was rotated 45 degrees, giving rise to the character 巫 wū.

筮 shì: divination, with the top radical 竹 zhú: bamboo. Bamboo slips are tools in divination for noted oracles.

上古之人敬风畏雨。巫师做法，习惯模仿风声，以呼风唤雨，则巫源于五。半坡出土的彩陶中有一种人面鱼纹图，其中人嘴的轮廓为五字的古字形，即借五为巫，指明所画为当时的巫师的面孔。毉=醫=医、巫并为上古时期高级智力劳动者。

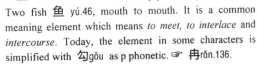

gòu

冓甲

5193

— archaic form of 構=构gòu; to compose.

沟, 篝, 鞲gōu;

构, 购, 媾: coition, coitus,

遘gòu;

講=讲jiǎng: to speak.

Two fish 鱼 yú.46, mouth to mouth. It is a common meaning element which means *to meet, to interlace* and *intercourse*. Today, the element in some characters is simplified with 勾gōu as p phonetic. ☞ 冉rǎn.136.

The double fish design portrays another feature of the painted pottery culture. The fish appeared in face motifs containing 巫wū. Many articles of painted pottery with double fish designs were discovered at some Neolithic sites near rivers. The location of these settlements probably accounts for the popularity of the motifs about fish. These pottery vessels with decorative patterns are more appropriate to ceremonial use than everyday use. It has been suggested that the double fish motif is a symbol for the vulva, and the fish is a prehistoric cult object for efficacy. In the Chinese symbology, the fish represents woman, because it bears a large number of eggs in its body.

象嘴对嘴的两条鱼形，在中国彩陶艺术中有一种双鱼的图案被认为是表现女阴;彩陶人面鱼纹中也有双鱼的形象。史前可能用崇拜多子的鱼的方式祈求女子多产。一说象两个竹编器对接，见冉.136。

◀ Double fish design on painted pottery vessel. It may be the emblem of a vulva. Yangshao culture.

鱼蛙纹盆。仰韶文化。

173

9B32 — *li*-cauldron.

鬲, 隔, 嗝, 膈, 镉gé;
融róng;
獻＝献xiàn.

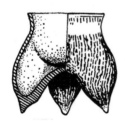

A prehistoric earthenware pot with three hollow legs. 鬲 lì is a radical as well. ☞ 豆 dòu.

In Chinese prehistoric art, it is hard to find a Stone Age idol like the Venus of Willendorf, a fertility image with the breasts and buttocks accentuated. However, prehistoric Chinese also wondered about the woman's reproductive organs. There is evidence of both implicit and explicit interest in sex — 鬲 lì: a prehistoric pottery tripod with bulbous or breast-shaped hollow legs. The *li*-cauldron is a Chinese earthenware pot. This kind of vessel has been unearthed from many sites in China. Because of its large heating surface, the *li*-cauldron was a good tool for cooking. It is also an embryonic form of the famous bronze tripod. The reader can liken it to the Venus of Willendorf. Both of them are steatopygous, but the *li* is more exaggerated and abstract. You may also feel that the potter's veiled feelings lurk within the cauldron, whose shape may perhaps reveal traces of a once matriarchal society.

鬲是中国特有的新石器时代陶器，在鬲的基础上发展出一种以中空乳房状三足为基本特征的陶器系列。如果我们把鬲与欧洲石器时代的"维纳斯"偶象比较，会发现鬲是一种既实用，同时也更抽象、更夸张的，具有表现力的原始人体艺术品，在这种陶器中或许蕴藏有史前女性崇拜的秘密。又《正字通》鬴，俗鬲字。

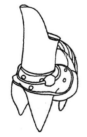

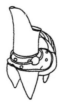

7. 1. 2—What Song the Chinese Sang
史前音乐

▶ *Above.* Chipped chime-stone.
Longshan culture, the Neolithic.
The stone is almost a meter hight.

打制大石磬。山西襄汾陶寺遗
址出土，龙山文化。

Below. Chime-stone with the tiger
motif engraved on the both sides,
Shang Dynasty.

虎纹石磬，商代。

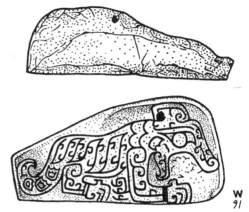

W
91

shí

石 甲 金 古 籀

77F3 —stone.

泵 bèng; 宕 dàng; 硕 shuò;
拓 tà, tuò; 祏 tuō, 拓,
跖 zhí; 磔 zhé; 斫 zhuó。

A chime stone. 口 kǒu.13 stands for the sound of the percussion
instrument. It's a radical for stone or ore. ☞ 厂 hàn.38, 岩 yán: rock.

象磬形。砳 lè, 二石相击声。磈 sǒi, 字喃, 碎石。矗=磊 lěi。
巌=邑=岩 yán。

qìng

磬 甲 籀

78EC — *qinq*-bell, chime stone.

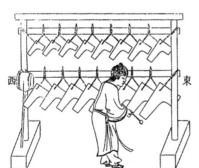

西 東

殸 qìng shows a suspended *qinq*-bell or chime stone
声=声 shēng being struck with a mallet held by a
hand. 殸 qìng itself is a phonetic too, such as 謦 qìng:
chat; 磬=殸 qìng; 聲=声 shēng: sound; 馨 xīn:
softly fragrant. ☞ 石 shí, 殳 shū: mace.

象手持槌击磬之形。《说文》磬，樂石也。从
石殸。象縣虡之形。殳，擊之也。古者毋句氏
作磬。殸，籀文省。硜，古文从巠。

◀ 击磬。

175

yòng

用 甲

7528 — use, apply; need;
expenses.

佣yòng; 佣=傭, 痈=癰,
拥=擁yōng.

A prehistoric bell or tube made from bamboo. PLC, 桶tǒng: a
section of thick bamboo, tube. See below.

象打通竹节的竹筒（桶）形，竹筒可用来敲击发声。

yǒng

甬 金

752C — a bronze bell.

俑，勇，愿，涌，蛹，踊=踴yǒng；
诵sòng；通tōng；桶，捅tǒng；痛tòng.

Bamboo bell with a ring on the handle to suspend it by.

象甬钟之形。《说文》归马hàn 又部，现归用部。

▶ **Rubbing of a stone from
a tomb, Han Dynasty.**

汉画像石·击甬钟。

nán

南 甲

5357 — south.

喃，楠nán；腩nǎn；献=獻xiàn.

An ancient suspended percussion instrument. PLC.

象一种悬挂的打击乐器。殻，讀若殻=殻què。

què

殻 甲

3C7F — archaic form of 殻=壳ké: shell.

殻gòu；穀=谷，穀gǔ；殻=殻=殻=殻
=壳ké，qiào；愨=愨què.

A hand holding a mallet to strike a percussion
instrument. PLC. ☞ 南nán, 殳shū: mace.

象手持槌击打乐器之形。

zhù

壴甲 金 古 篆

58F4 — archaic character.

澍, 樹=树shù; 厨, 橱, 蹰chú.

A *jian*-drum, an ancient ritual instrument. The drum was mounted on a long pole and decorated with a kind of plume.

象建鼓形。系一种直立从两侧击打的鼓，下有支架，并有木桩穿过鼓身，木柱上带有大量装饰。

Jian-drum. **Rubbing of a stone and two bricks, Han Dynasty.** 汉代画像石、砖·击建鼓。

gǔ

鼓甲 金 古 篆

9F13 — drum.

膌, 瞽gǔ.

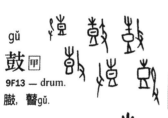

A hand holding a drumstick to beat the *jian*-drum.

象手持鼓槌击鼓之形。

xǐ

喜甲 金 古 篆

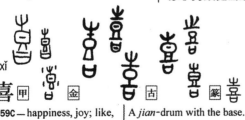

559C — happiness, joy; like, be fond of; happy, pleased; concerning weddings.

禧xǐ; 嘻, 嬉, 熹xǐ.

A *jian*-drum with the base.

象建鼓和基座之形。喜=
喜=囍2BB14=囍21155, 同喜。

▶ **Bronze drum, Shang.**
商代青铜鼓。

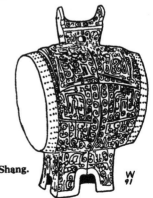

177

péng

彭 甲　金　古　篆

5F6D — a surname.

澎péng; 澎，膨，蟛péng.

Indicates the sound of a drum. PLC.

从壴彡，表示鼓声。

yuè

龠 甲　金　篆

9FA0 — an ancient short flute.

瀹，鑰=钥yuè; 钥yào;

籥=吁yù; 龢龤=和谐héxié.

An ancient panpipe. The upper element, could be the mouth playing the panpipe.

象排箫形。其音龢龤。

▶ **Bone flute. Peiligang culture, the Neolithic. Length 22.2cm.**

骨笛。裴李岗文化，新石器时代，河南舞阳贾湖遗址出土。该骨笛是同遗址出土十六支骨笛中最完整无裂纹的一支，并有测音研究报告。

yuè

樂=乐 甲　金　古　篆

6A02 = 4E50 — music.

樂=乐lè; cheerful; 栎，砾lì; 烁，铄shuò; 藥=药yào.

Two strings fastened to a plank, an attempt to represent a stringed instrument. The upper middle 白bái.18, glyph of a thumb, was added later as a meaning element. ☞ 丝sī: silk, 木mù: wood.

象古代的弦乐器。

qín

琴 古　金　篆　蓁

7434 — a seven-stringed plucked instrument in some ways similar to the zither; a general name for certain musical instruments.

An ancient zither. The lower part 今jīn.162 is a phonetic added later. ☞ 琵琶pípā: a plucked string instrument with a fretted fingerboard; 瑟sè: a long stringed instrument, originally with five or ten strings, later 25 stings.

象古琴形。金、今为声符。瑟瑟瑟瑟瑟瑟瑟瑟瑟瑟瑟瑟瑟瑟瑟瑟瑟瑟瑟，或古或俗，並同琴。

7. 1. 3—The Body in Art　　史前人体艺术

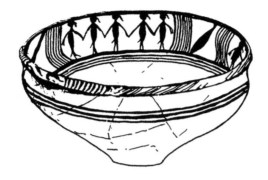

A 5000-year-old pottery bowl from Qinghai Province. It is painted with a ring of 15 dancers, adorned in headdresses and sashes and stepping in unison.

舞蹈彩盆。青海大通出土。

wén

文 甲　　　　　　　　金　　　　　　　　古　　　　　　　篆

6587 — writing, character, script; language; literary, composition; culture; civilian; gentle.

雯 wén; 紊 wěn; 坟=墳 fén; 吝 lìn.

A person with a tattoo on his chest. PLC, 纹 wén: weins, grain. ☞ 文身 wénshēn: tattoo, 蚊 wén: mosquito.

有文身图案的人形。㸚=文，商代族徽。焱=文，姓氏。

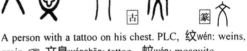

wú

無=无 甲　　　　　　　金　　　　　　　古　　　　　篆

7121=65E0 — nothing; not have; not.

芜 wù; 妩, 怃, 庑 wǔ; 抚 fǔ.

A dance with props, perhaps holding ox tails. PLC, 橆=舞 wǔ: to dance; the lower part of 舞 wǔ derives from the dancer's feet. ☞ 大 dà.3.

象手持物而舞的人形。金文有訶遮一辞，读若歌舞。鄦=鄦=鄦=䣞=鄦，金文许国专名。许，姜姓古国，故地在河南许昌。

yì

異 = 异 甲

7570 = 5F02 — strange, different, spooky.

戴dài; 羿=粪fèn.

A dancer with a mask. PLC, 戴dài: to wear, respect. ☞ 冀jì, 鬼guǐ.

戴面具跳舞的人形。羿羿，古文。《说文》异，举也。从廾目声。朱俊声《说文通训定声》异，段借为異。

jì

冀 甲 金

5180 — to hope, look forward to.

A dancer wearing a mask and horn ornaments. PLC. ☞ 異=异yì.

从北異声，象人戴面具角饰而舞，有所祈冀之意。骥jì，千里马。

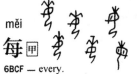 

měi

每 甲

6BCF — every.

海hǎi; 悔huǐ; 晦，诲huì; 莓，梅，酶，霉méi; 侮wǔ; 毓yù.

A woman in headdress. PLC. ☞ 母mǔ, 美měi.

象发饰盛美的女子。媄，篆文美。

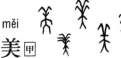

měi

美 甲

7F8E — beauty; beautiful.

媄: beautiful, 镁měi.

A man in headdress, a chief of a tribe. PLC. ☞ 每měi, 大dà.3.

象发饰盛美的男子。陕=嵨，地名；浼，湖名；蓂，草名；躾，习礼，教养；羪、羮，户政字。并音美。

hēi

黑 甲

9ED1 — black.

嘿hēi; 墨，默mò.

The dots on the dancer's face stand for the tattoo. Tattooing the face was for fun, and had become a punishiment in ancient China. The lower parts transformed into a fire-radical. Burns are often black. ☞ 舞wǔ, 大dà.3:, 火huǒ.117.

象歌舞者面部有纹身图形。面部刺青后世称为墨刑。《说文》从囧。

lín

舛 金  篆

7CA6 — archaic of 磷 lín: phosphor; phosphorus; phosphorescent light; will-o'-the-wisp.

憐＝怜 lián；鄰＝邻，遴，嶙，瞵，辚，麟，鳞 lín；膦 lín.

A pictograph of a dancer holding props in his hands. Later, this character represented a ghost dancing between grave mounds with a jack-o'-lantern. ☞ 舞 wǔ, 黑 hēi, 火 huǒ.

象舞蹈的人形。此字又用于指"鬼火"。篆文作舛。古文作替。金文有右矞一辞，读右邻，官名。

guǐ

鬼 甲 金 古 篆

9B3C — ghost, spook.

瑰 guī；槐 huái；魂 hún；塊＝块 kuài；魁 kuí；傀 kuǐ；愧 kuì；魄 pò；嵬 wéi；隗 wěi, kuí；醜＝丑 chǒu；蒐 sōu.

A figure with a mask and a tail ornament. See above.

戴面具和尾饰的人形。趣味对联：骑奇马，张长弓，琴瑟琵琶八大王，王王居上，单戈能戦；袭龙衣，伪为人，魑魅魍魉四小鬼，鬼鬼在边，合手就舒。

wèi

畏 甲 金 古 篆

754F — fear; awe.

喂 wèi；偎，隈 wēi；猥 wěi.

A *ghost* dancing with a stick.　PLC. ☞ 鬼 guǐ, 长 cháng.28.

象鬼持杖而舞，可畏之象。

《變文·秋胡小說》偎汝新婦，九年孤眠獨宿。

偎，俗愧。敦煌·S.133

The following characters may be related to the harvest dances. Early Chinese danced with rice headdresses, just like the festival of Saturnalia, and here 禾 hé: rice is a common element.

nián

年 甲  金 古 篆

5E74 — year; the times; condition of harvest.

A man wearing a rice headdress performing a dance to celebrate the harvest. ☞ 人 rén.1, 千 qiān.193.

人头顶禾谷，表示谷物丰收。姩，美女。秊，喃字。秊名：成名。

jì

季 甲 金 古 篆

5B63 — season; the fourth or youngest among brothers.
悸jì.

A combination of 禾hé: rice, and 子zǐ: child. PLC.

从子从禾，会幼禾意。古文或作秄。伯仲叔季排行，季为同辈中最小者。渼，水名。琫，玉名。鲚，鱼名，尖喙细鳞。瘁＝悸，气不定，病中恐。

wěi

委 甲 金 古 篆

59D4 — end (written); to appoint, send.
诿，萎，巍，逶wēi；诿，痿，萎wěi；魏wèi；矮ǎi；倭wō.

A combination of 禾hé: rice, and 女nǔ.27: woman. PLC.
☞ 禾hé, 女nǔ.27.

甲骨文从女从禾作妳，禾谷成熟，垂穗委曲之貌。古文字或从啬从凵、从匚，亦释作委，表示收储谷物。

xiù

秀 古 篆

79C0 — delicate, frail and beautiful; to flower.
绣，锈xiù；透tòu；莠yǒu；诱yòu.

A combination of 禾hé: rice and 引yǐn: draw, lead, stretch. 乃nǎi.27 is the graphemes wrong form of 引yǐn. ☞ 禾hé, 弓gōng.150.

从禾从引，会禾苗抽穗意。"乃"是"引"字之讹。趏＝透，跳也。偈僵，亦作偈偮，即宿留异文。秂、锈，户政俗字。

jì

稷 甲 禝 稷 金 禝 稷 禝

7A37 — the good of cereals; panicled millet.
稷＝稷，稷jì；谡sù.

禝jì: cereal Godness, praying before rice. ☞ 兄xiōng.188, 鬼guǐ.

象人在禾前祈祷之形。禝古文从女从鬼省作娞，谷神之谓也。后女形讹变。禝jì，俗字。男作女曰娞。娞奸，鸡奸。

182

7. 2　Divination and Sacrificial Offerings　占卜与祭祀

7. 2. 1—Divination　占卜

Superstition was extensive in ancient China, so that the early Chinese held frequent divining ceremonies. They consulted oracles about everything from the timing of sacrifices and military compaigns to pleas for rain and cures for disease.

The main materials used in divination were the cow's shoulder blade and turtle's shell. At the moment of divination, the king's diviner first recorded the charge or marginal notation which detailed the question and purpose of a given divination. It was then inscribed onto the surface of the bone and shell. After that, a series of hollow pits were bored or chiselled into the back or inner surface of the bone or shell. Heat was then applied to the hollow pits. Scorching of the bone or shell caused 卜-shaped cracks to fan out on the surface. The hollow pits decreased the thickness of the bone or shell, making it easier to crack. Once the crack formed, they were presumably "read" by the diviner or the king himself. Sometimes, especially if the result was efficacious, it was also inscribed onto the bone or shell near the original charge.

The bones and shells are called oracle bones, and a great number of the antiques of Shang Dynasty were unearthed in Henan Province about 100 years ago. In 1977 and 1979, many oracle bones of West Zhou Dynasty came to light at *Zhouyuan*, in Shaanxi Province. The writings carved on the bones or shells are known as oracle bone inscriptions.

▶ A turtle plastron and a bovid scapula used in divination

殷墟卜用龟腹甲和牛胛骨

xū

需 甲 　 金 　 霈 霏 古 　 霏 篆 霈

9700 — to need, want.

儒, 孺, 蠕, 薷, 顬, 嚅, 濡 rú.

Glyph 霈 = 需 xū shows a priest or diviner taking a shower before performing divination or other ritual. 而 ér.16 is derived from 天 tiān.4. PLC, 濡 rú: to immerse. ☞ 雨 yǔ.35, 儒 rú: learned man.

象人沐浴之形。古人占卜或祭祀之前要进行沐浴，以示诚敬。

bǔ

卜 甲 　 金 　 卜 卜 古 　 卜 九 卜、九，古文 篆 卜

535C — to divine; predict, foretell; divination; a surname.

补=補 bǔ, 讣, 赴 fù; 咎 jiù; 钋 pō; 朴 pò; 扑=撲 pū; 仆=僕 pú; 朴= 樸 pǔ; 外 wài; 蘿蔔=萝卜 luó bo.

Portrays the 卜-shaped crack formed on the oracle bone or shell due to scorched on the other side, and borrowed the sound of the 卜 bǔ broken. Generally in the divination, the branch goes up for lucky, 卜 and K are not good.

借烧灼甲骨而成的兆之形，借卜骨开裂成兆之声。

guǎ

冎 甲 　 金 　 W 古 　 篆

518E — to scrape meat off bone.

冎=剮=剐 guǎ; 骨 gū; gǔ; 堝, 锅, 涡 guō; 過=过 guò; 滑, 猾 huá; 禍 huò; 娲 wā; 挝, 涡, 莴, 窝, 蜗 wō.

Drawing of the cow's shoulder blade used for divination. Note the small 卜 bǔ on the bone. PLC, 骨 gǔ; bone; with human body radical 肉 ròu.128. 骨 gǔ is also a radical. ☞ 卜 bǔ.

象占卜用牛胛骨之形。在骨上有卜纹。剮=别，分解。牌骨。

dǎi

歹 甲 　 篆 　 参 　 死，古文

6B79 — bad, wicked; bad deed.

歼=殀=死 sǐ: to die.

Drawing of a rotten bone. It may derive from 冎 guǎ, see above. 歺 =歹 dǎi is a radical for bone, disabled or death.

象残骨形。歺，古文歹。一说象木杙残裂之形。

zhēn

貞=贞 甲 　 金 　 古 　 篆

8C9E＝8D1E— divination; loyal, faithful; (of woman) chastity or virginity.

侦, 祯, 桢zhēn; 帧zhèng.

A kind of bronze tripod used for heating the bronze rod and to scorch the bone or shell during divination. The upper part 卜bǔ: divination, and 贝bèi the simplified form of 鼎dǐng: tripod.

从鼎从卜，表示卜问。鼎在占卜中用于烧灼加热。

zhēn

眞＝真甲

771E＝771F — true, real; clearly.

缜zhēn; 镇zhèn; 嗔chēn; 滇, 颠, 巅, 癫diān.

This common character derives from 贞zhēn; 真人zhēnrén: literally true man, wizard.

真源于贞。𣅀，古文。鼎，金文真，读若鼎。

shòu

受甲

53D7 — to receive, accept.

授, 绶shòu.

Depicts the taking or delivering of a divination plate by hands. Later, the plate was simplified. When a bone or tortoise shell was ready to be used or accepted by the oracle, it was placed on a large plate. No person was then allowed to touch the bone or shell. ☞ 授shòu: award, teach, 爪zhǎo, 又yòu.17.

用手传递放有占卜用甲骨的大盘。一说登舟授手，形声兼会意字。

zhèn

朕甲

6715 — sign, omen; I, the sovereign.

勝＝胜shèng; 謄＝誊, 滕, 藤, 腾téng; 媵yìng; 送sòng: to give.

㳇＝关zhuàn shows the diviner holding a heated bronze rod to scorch the bone or shell in order to form the crack. The left part 月yuè derives from the drawing of the divination plate. ☞ 受shòu.

㳇＝尖＝关表示占卜者双手持青铜棒加热甲骨，月或舟源于占卜时放置甲骨的大盘。朕＝朕表示烧灼甲骨以求朕兆。

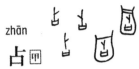

zhān

占 甲

5360 — to divine.

沾，毡，粘zhān；战=戰，
站zhàn；掂diān；點=点，
踮diǎn；店，惦，阽，坫，
玷diàn；占jī；拈niān；黏=
粘，鲇=nián；苫shān；帖，
萜，贴tiē；帖tiē，tiè；
砧zhēn；钻=鑽zuān, zuàn.

Drawing of the ⼘-shaped crack on a scapula or shoulder blade of ox combined with a small □kǒu.13: mouth, means to ask the oracle. ☞ ⼘bǔ.

《说文》占，视兆问也。就卜骨上形成的卜兆，审视、询问结果。觇=覘=觇=觇 chān，窥视。詀，多言。生絀，生絹。鉆=鉗，以铁有所镊取。痁，瘧疾。佔伥字篆作觇。

7. 2. 2—Sacrificial Offerings 祭祀

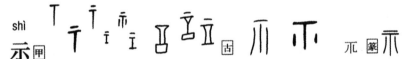

shì

示 甲

793A
— to show,
notify.
标=標biāo；
际=際jì.

A T-shaped sacrificial altar, or an abstract symbol of the marrow, ghostly Hell and the broad, bright Heaven, see the scenes on the silk-painting. The strokes surrounding the T were later additions, used to balance or embellish the T-shaped altar. 示 shì is also a radical for offering sacrifices and religion-related.

象 T 形祭台，或被解释为神主。古文字示、主一字。兀，古文。

▶ Lady Dai's funeral banner with tassels is an illustration of the character 示 shì. The T-shaped red silk banner painting came to light from the Han Tomb No. 1 at *Mawangdui*, Changsha, Hunan Province in 1972. This banner depicts Lady Dai's ascent to heaven. The bottom section portrays the ghosts in hell and the offerings made to them. The next section shows Lady Dai and her maids, while just above her are two guardians waiting at the gate of heaven. The heavenly paradise at the top consists of the moon, the sun, two dragons and the primordial ancestor Fuxi with a long serpent tail. Lady Dai was a minor official's wife in the Han dynasty. (*From Fagan, p. 260, drawing by David Buck, copied from Changsha Mawangdui Yihao Hanmu 1973. Length 205cm, width 92—47.7cm.*)

马王堆一号汉墓出土的软夫人升天彩绘帛画，为当时葬仪中所用的裌幡。

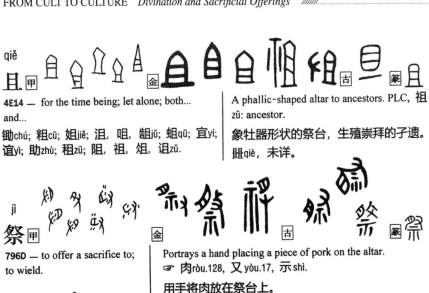

qiě

且 甲 ... 金 ... 古 ... 篆

4E14 — for the time being; let alone; both... and...

铡chú; 粗cū; 姐jiě; 沮, 咀, 龃jǔ; 蛆qū; 宜yí; 谊yì; 助zhù; 租zū; 阻, 祖, 俎, 诅zǔ.

A phallic-shaped altar to ancestors. PLC, 祖 zǔ: ancestor.

象牡器形状的祭台，生殖崇拜的孑遗。龃qiě，未详。

jì

祭 甲 ... 金 ... 古 ... 篆

796D — to offer a sacrifice to; to wield.

Portrays a hand placing a piece of pork on the altar.
☞ 肉ròu.128, 又yòu.17, 示shì.

用手将肉放在祭台上。

zōng

宗 甲 ... 金 ... 古 ... 篆

5B97 — ancestral temple, ancestor, clan.

棕, 腙, 综, 鬃, 踪zōng; 粽zòng; 崇chóng; 淙, 琮cóng.

Shows an altar inside the ancestral temple.
☞ 六liù.97 or 宀mián, 示shì.186.

宗庙中的祭台。

xiōng

兄 甲 ... 金 ... 古 ... 篆

5144 — elder brother.

觋, 况kuàng; 祝zhù.

A person facing the sky and praying. The direction of mouth indicates the upward face. PLC. 祝zhù: wish, hope.

象人仰面张口祈祷形。倪、佳、觋，并金文兄。

mǐn

皿 甲 ... 金 ... 古 ... 篆

76BF — vessel, utensil.

盥guàn: to wash hands.

A plate or vessel with a tall pedestal and attached handles. 皿mǐn is a lower radical for vessels.

象有耳高足的器皿形。䀁、㿻，金文皿。盁，同匜。

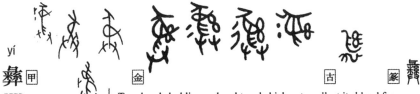

yí

彛 甲 金 古 篆

5F5D

— sacrificial.

Two hands holding a slaughtered chicken to collect its blood for sacrifice. The chicken is strung, and the 米 mǐ.45 represents the drops of blood. The top 彑 jì is a phonetic. ☞ 糸 mì.93, 又 yòu.17 or 共 gòng.157.

以鸡为牺，杀鸡取血用于祭祀。

xuè

血 甲 金 古 篆

8840 — blood; blood lineage.

血 xiě; 恤, 洫 xù.

A ritual vessel with blood. The dot represents the blood used for sacrificial rites. It is a radical for a few characters. ☞ 皿 mǐn.

象盛血的祭盘。盟、盟，古文盟，从血，今俗从皿。

mèng

孟 金 古 篆

5B5F — eldest (brother); the first month (of a season); a surname.

猛，锰，蜢，艋 měng.

A combination of 八 bā.85: to cut, 子 zǐ.26: son and 皿 mǐn: a ritual vessel. Early Chinese once offered their first baby, as the most precious thing, to the Gods. The practice of infanticide, a callous and atrocious custom, appeared in ancient China.

从八从子从皿。

níng

寧 = 宁 甲 金 篆

5BE7 = 5B81 — quiet; tranquil; would rather.

柠，拧，咛，狞 níng; 拧 nǐng; 宁，泞 nìng.

A ritual vessel containing a heart on a T-shaped sacrificial altar, and being kept in a temple. The heart element appeared later; it may be a radical. ☞ 宗 zōng, 皿 mǐn, 心 xīn.5.

象贮藏器物于室内形。安宁之宁篆作寍，宁可之宁亦作甯。

jìn

盡=尽 甲

76E1=5C3D — to the highest degree or the utmost limit; all; to come to an end; to use up completely.

烬, 荩, 赆jìn; 盡=尽jìn.

A hand holding a brush to clean the 皿mǐn.188: ritual vessel. ☞ 聿yù.198.

手持刷子涤器形。《说文》从皿羣jìn声。

yì

義=义 甲

7FA9=4E49 — righteousness; human relationship; adopted.

议yì; 仪yí: ceremony; 蚁yǐ.

A ram 羊yáng being slaughtered by 我wǒ.148, a saw-ax for sacrifice. ☞ 犠=牺xī: sacrifice.

从羊从我，表示杀羊祭祀。

7. 3   The Cradle of Civilization   文明的摇篮

7. 3. 1—Quipu—keeping Records by Weaving Knots   结绳记事

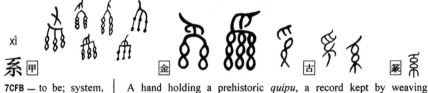

xì

系 甲

7CFB — to be; system, series; relate to.

繋=系jì: tie.

A hand holding a prehistoric *quipu*, a record kept by weaving patterned knots. ☞ 又yòu.17 or 爪zhǎo.20, 糸mì.93.

象手持史前记事的结绳。兹=絲，金文系，族徽。

sūn

孫=孙 甲

5B6B=5B59 — grandson; a surname.

狲sūn, 逊xùn.

A combination of 子zǐ.26: son and 系xì: *quipu*. The upper knot stands for the son, while the lower knot represents the son's son.

指示子孙相承关系的结绳。愻=逊=逊xùn，顺从。

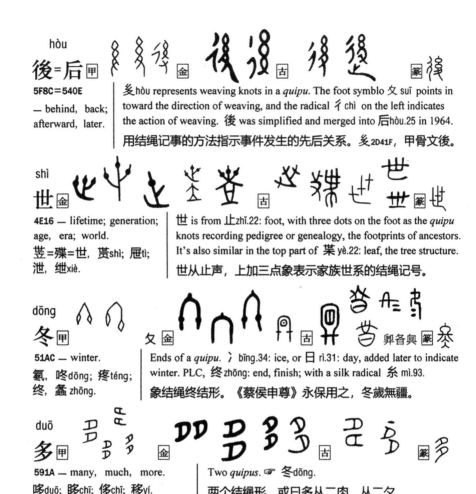

hòu

後＝后 甲 金 古 篆

5F8C＝540E

— behind, back;
afterward, later.

夌 hòu represents weaving knots in a *quipu*. The foot symblo 夊 suī points in toward the direction of weaving, and the radical 彳 chì on the left indicates the action of weaving. 後 was simplified and merged into 后hòu.25 in 1964.

用结绳记事的方法指示事件发生的先后关系。夌 2D41F，甲骨文後。

shì

世 金 古 篆

4E16 — lifetime; generation;
age, era; world.

�＝殜＝世，赳shì；屉tì；
泄，绁xiè.

世 is from 止zhǐ.22: foot, with three dots on the foot as the *quipu* knots recording pedigree or genealogy, the footprints of ancestors. It's also similar in the top part of 葉 yè.22: leaf, the tree structure.

世从止声，上加三点象表示家族世系的结绳记号。

dōng

冬 甲 夊 金 古 舅各奥 篆

51AC — winter.

氡，咚dōng；疼téng；
终，螽zhōng.

Ends of a *quipu*. 冫 bīng.34: ice, or 日 rì.31: day, added later to indicate winter. PLC, 终zhōng: end, finish; with a silk radical 糸 mì.93.

象结绳终结形。《蔡侯申尊》永保用之，冬歲無疆。

duō

多 甲 金 古 篆

591A — many, much, more.

哆duō；眵chī；侈chī；移yí.

Two *quipus*. ☞ 冬dōng.

两个结绳形。或曰多从二肉、从二夕。

7. 3. 2—Numbers and Symbols   数字和符号

The earliest uses of glyphs were not to convey ideas, experience or otherwise, but to keep records of hunting, harvest, fabricated goods and booty. The arithmetical reckoning was an even greater feat than the capture.

文字的出现首先从简单的数字符号开始。汉字中还保留着中国人的祖先积画成数的原始计数方法。但是，用积画成数的方法不便于表示大的数目，因此大于四的数字就使用假借的方法来表示了。

yī

一 甲 金 一 古 篆 一

4E00 — one, a.

壹 58F9.yī; 噎 yē;
殪, 饐, 黳, 撎,
曀, 瘱, 墲 yì.
弌, 古文一。
醫, 与一同。

One stroke. This glyph is one of the most common characters in the Chinese language. The horizontal stroke is a symbol of carrying numbers, used in the units of numbers such as 十 shí: ten, 百 bǎi: hundred, 千 qiān: thousand and 萬＝万 wàn.49: ten thousand.

算筹形。一画为一。在十百千万诸字中，一表示进位。鼠，金文一，从鼠一。《中山王方壶》曾乚鼠夫之救。读若竟无一夫之救。羆，一字别体。《鄂君啟車節》戠罷返。读若岁一返，即返节年检。一是汉字中出现频率最高的字，组词能力也很强。

èr

二 甲 金 古 篆 二

4E8C — two.

仁 rén; 貳 èr; 膩 nì;
佞 nìng; 竺 zhú.

Two strokes.

积画成二，会意字。貳，金文貳。《郜大叔斧》呂大弔之貳車之斧。

sān

三 甲 金 古 篆 三

4E09 — three.

叄 sān.

Three horizontal strokes.

积画成三。弎、弎，古文三。毵、毿，同仁。蒲松龄《蓬萊宴·第一回》賓客密如麻，東毵毵，西毵毵，八百席一霎安排下。又蒲松龄《增補幸雲曲·第十一回》好丫頭笑嘻嘻，勸姐姐休撒急，我有一條絕妙的計。咱毿同到玉火巷，你可藏的嚴實實，俺毿上樓把你替。

wǔ

五 甲 金 古 篆 五

4E94 — five.

伍, 捂, 牾 wǔ;
吾, 浯, 梧, 齬
wú; 悟, 晤, 焐,
寤, 瘉 wù; 衙 yá;
语 yǔ.

Creating numerals by adding strokes is a good method for one two three. But it falls when representing numbers larger than four or five. Early Chinese used a cross to indicate the number five; it has been seen on Chinese Neolithic pottery inscriptions. Note that five is the middle point between one and none. ☞ 四 sì: four.

借叉号乂表示五。五是一、九之间的中数。

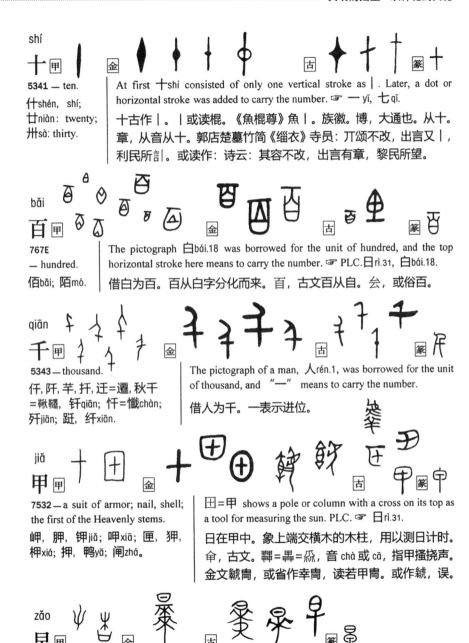

shí

十 甲 金 古 篆

5341 — ten.

什 shén, shí;
廿 niàn: twenty;
卅 sà: thirty.

At first 十 shí consisted of only one vertical stroke as 丨. Later, a dot or horizontal stroke was added to carry the number. ☞ 一 yī, 七 qī.

十古作丨。丨或读棍。《魚棍尊》魚丨。族徽。博，大通也。从十。章，从音从十。郭店楚墓竹简《缁衣》寺员：丌颂不改，出言又丨，利民所訃。或读作：诗云：其容不改，出言有章，黎民所望。

bǎi

百 甲 金 古 篆

767E
— hundred.

佰 bǎi; 陌 mò.

The pictograph 白 bái.18 was borrowed for the unit of hundred, and the top horizontal stroke here means to carry the number. ☞ PLC. 日 rì.31, 白 bái.18.

借白为百。百从白字分化而来。百，古文百从自。会，或俗百。

qiān

千 甲 金 古 篆

5343 — thousand.

仟, 阡, 芊, 扦, 迁 = 遷, 秋千 = 鞦韆, 釺 qiān; 忏 = 懺 chàn; 歼 jiān; 跹, 纤 xiān.

The pictograph of a man, 人 rén.1, was borrowed for the unit of thousand, and "一" means to carry the number.

借人为千。一表示进位。

jiǎ

甲 甲 金 古 篆

7532 — a suit of armor; nail, shell; the first of the Heavenly stems.

岬, 胛, 钾 jiǎ; 呷 xiā; 匣, 狎, 柙 xiá; 押, 鸭 yā; 闸 zhá。

田 = 甲 shows a pole or column with a cross on its top as a tool for measuring the sun. PLC. ☞ 日 rì.31.

日在甲中。象上端交横木的木柱，用以测日计时。㐀，古文。羁 = 畾 = 㐀，音 chà 或 cā，指甲搔挠声。金文䩞冑，或省作幸冑，读若甲冑。或作鞃，误。

zǎo

早 甲 金 古 篆

65E9 — morning; early, in advance; long ago. 草cǎo.

This character shows the sun rising on the top of a 甲jiǎ, a tool for solar observation. PLC. ☞ 日rì.31.

日在甲上。甲骨文或以艸为早，后又作从日枣声。

shì

是 金 古 篆

662F — correct, right; yes, OK; to be. 匙shi, chí; 提, 堤dī; 提, 醍tí.

A combination of 早zǎo and 止zhǐ.22: footprint, a symbol of movement and a phonetic as well. PLC. ☞ 早zǎo, 止zhǐ.22.

从早从止，止亦声。

shí

時=时 甲 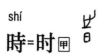 金 古  篆

6642＝65F6— time, days; hour; current, present. 鲥，埘shí; 莳shì.

The ancient glyph 旹 shí time, is a combination of 日rì: the sun, and 之zhǐ.23: footprint, and the 寺sì is a phonetic introduced later.

时从日之声，后寺声，表示太阳的运动。

xī

昔 甲 金 古 篆

6614 — former times, the past. 腊，惜xī; 醋cù; 措, 错cuò; 籍，藉jí; 藉jiè; 腊，蜡là; 鹊què; 蜡zhà.

Perhaps early Chinese carved zigzag lines to count days. The 日rì: sun, day, is a meaning element. Some people the upper part of 昔 stands for the great flood that occurred in the time of noah.

史前人类多用刻画短线来计日。昔可能源于史前的"日历"。或以为从水从日，指过去大禹治水的往昔年代。醋，俗鹊。

zhōng

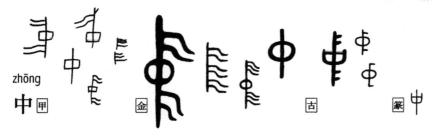

中 甲 金 古 篆

4E2D — center, middle; China; in, among.

忠、盅、衷、钟=鐘zhōng; 肿=瘇、种=種zhǒng; 中、仲、种zhòng; 冲=衝、忡chōng; 种chóng; 冲chòng.

Drawing of a pole with some decorative streamers. The pole was placed in the center of a circle or dial so that a shadow cast by the sun on a calibrated dial could measure solar time, such as the gnomon or style of a sundial.

日晷测时树立起的杆子，即圭表测影的表。

guī

 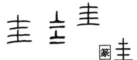

圭 金

572D — the dial of a sundial.

硅、闺、鲑guī; 桂、guì; 卦、挂、褂guà; 恚huì; 佳jiā; 街jiē; 奎kuí; 畦qí; 窪=洼、哇、蛙wā; 娃wá; 哇wa; 鞋xié.

Shows one part or section of the graduated lines on a sundial.

象圭上的一段刻度之形。

shàng

 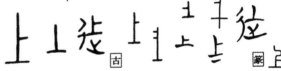

上 甲 　金　　　　　　　　古　　　　　篆

4E0A — upper, up; higher; to go up.

忐tǎn; 让=讓ràng.

A dot above a horizontal stroke.

横上一点。古文作二、辻、⊥。𡴞，金文上，从上尚聲。

xià

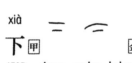 

下 甲 　金　　　　　　　　古　　　　　篆

4E0B — down, under, below; lower; to descend.

吓xià; 忑tè; 卡kǎ; 虾=蝦xiā.

A dot below a horizontal stroke. ⊥, ⊤ were useful characters on maps, and the short horizontal stroke on the left was introduced idiomatically as 上, 下 to prevent confusion.

横下一点。古文作⊤、二。统一在上下右侧加短横，系避免在诸如地图等不能判断行文上下时产生混淆。

qū

曲 甲 　金　　古

66F2 — bent, crooked; curve; unjustifiable.

蛐、麯=曲qū; 曲qǔ.

Shows a crooked or concave thing. PLC.

象物曲折之形。𠃊、𧰨，同曲。玉，声符。

195

7. 3. 3—Education　教育

yáo

爻 甲 金 古 篆

723B — in *The Book of Changes* 《易经》 yì jīng, the basic continuous line —268a or 阳爻 yáng yáo or *male yao* and broken line --268B or 阴爻 yīn yáo *female yao* used in divination trigrams.

The two crosses which appear also in 教 jiāo and 学 xué represent bamboo counting-rods 筹 chóu. The notations by rods were of two types, and they were used consecutively. ☞ ╳ =五 wǔ.192.

两组相交的算筹形。燚3E1A.lǐ，燚尔，稀疏明朗貌。

Counting-rods（筹）place value

	0	1	2	3	4	5	6	7	8	9
vertical	(gap)	Ⅰ	Ⅱ	Ⅲ	ⅢⅠ	Ⅲ‖	⊤	Ⅱ⊤	Ⅲ⊤	Ⅲ‖⊤
horizontal	(gap)	—	＝	≡	≣	≣	⊥	⊥	⊥	⊥

suàn

算 篆 算 算 算 籠 祘

7B97 — to count; to plan, calculate; accounting; number.

籑 cuàn; 籑 zuǎn; 祘 suàn.

Both hands 廾=収 gǒng calculating with some bamboo counting-rods, and the whole is topped by a bamboo-radica 竹 zhú.46. The middle part in 算 is resemble an abacus; however, the Chinese invented the abacus in the 14th century, not in the *Han* Dynasty.

双手持筹计算之形。圜2D375=圜2D36B. suen，古壮字，园子。

jiāo

教 甲 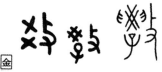 金 古 篆

6559 — to teach.

教 jiào: education, religion.

A hand holding a pointer and teaching a child a lesson, which is designated by the two crosses 爻 yáo.196. 爻 yáo is considered to be a phonetic component as well. ☞, 子 zǐ.26: son, 父 fù.157: father.

手持教鞭教子之形。手持教鞭为"父"，所指教内容为"爻"。

xué

學=学 甲 金 篆

5B78＝5B66
— to learn.

A child arranging the counting-rods in a house. ☞ 教jiāo, 臼jū, 六liù.

象子双手持筹仿效之形。《说文》作敩=教, 觉悟也。學, 篆文敩省。

shān

彡 甲 金 篆

5F61 — line ornamentation.
杉, 钐, 衫shān.

A radical implying pattern and adornment, for instance in 彩cǎi: color, pigment; 影yǐng: shadow; 形xíng: form; etc.

彡表示笔画或装饰的纹样。

dān

丹 甲 金 古 篆

4E39 — red; cinnabar; pill (of immortality sought by alchemists), elixir vitae.

坍tān, 彤tóng.

𠄌=丹 shows a piece of cinnabar, the dot, placed in a tray or palette to be used as red pigment.

调色盘中放有朱砂用作红色颜料。𠄌彤彤同, 古文。

qīng

青 金 古 篆 叁 家靖=寂靜

9752 — blue or green; green grass; young (people).

清, 蜻, 鲭qīng; 情, 晴, 氰qīng; 请qǐng; 菁, 腈, 睛, 精jīng; 静, 靖jìng; 倩qiàn.

Represents the color of grass; the top 生shēng is a pictophonetic element, the lower 丹dān is a meaning element. ☞ 生shēng, 丹dān: palette, 井jǐng.

青字从生从井或丹, 表示青草的颜色。岺岺𡴀夽岺𡴀靑𡴀峉, 古文。

197

yù、

聿甲 金 古 篆

807F — then (written) .
律lǜ; 建, 健, 毽,
腱, 键jiàn; 键jiān.

A hand holding a Chinese writing brush. PLC, 筆=笔bǐ: pen; 書=
书shū: to write, a book; 畫=画huà: to paint, a painting;. ☞ 隶ll.

象手持毛笔形。

 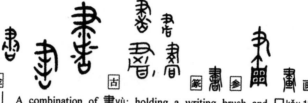

shū

書=书甲 金 古 篆 篆 画

66F8 = 4E66 — book;
to write, calligraphy.

A combination of 聿yù: holding a writing brush and 口kǒu.13:
mouth. A phonetic element 者zhě had been introduced in this
character..

从聿从口，表示记录语言。篆文作書。俗作卡。

cè

册甲 金 古 篆 篆

518C — book,
booklet; copy.

删: to delete, cut out,
姗, 珊, 栅, 跚shān;
栅zhà: railings, bar.

Bamboo-slip book. Before paper had been invented, Chinese people
wrote characters on bamboo slips, and tied them together at their ends
like冊=冊=冊=册, then forming as a scroll. Therefore, Chinese
developed the habit of writing and reading vertically because of the
position of the bamboo slips.

编简成册。篳，古文册。饕2B8EE，从冊从収余聲。古文敘。

diǎn

典甲 金 古 篆 典

198

5178 — established or traditional system,
institution or law; classic; dictionary;
literary allusion or reference; a surname;
to mortgage, pawn.

碘diǎn; 腆tiǎn.

Both hands holding a 冊cè: bamboo-slip book.
☞ 冊 cè.

双手捧册之形。篆文作畀 畀，此典谟之典。
典守之典篆作敂。

lún

4F96＝4ED1 —logical sequence,
coherence; to ponder.

伦, 沦, 抡, 囵, 论, 纶,
轮lún; 论lùn to discuss, view;
抡lūn.

Shows 冊cè: a bamboo-slip book, placed in a room. Or
someone believes that the ∧ is the mouth, and 冊 is the
bamboo flute, thus, 侖 lún has the same story of 龠 yuè.178
☞ 六 liù.97.

从∧从册，屋下有书。侖，篆文。侖、侖，古文。

Cang Jie, the legendary inventor of Chinese writing. He got
his ideas from observing the human body, plants, animals
and birds as well as other natural phenomena; thus, it was
said he had four eyes.

仓颉，相传为文字始创者。

Design on a bronze wine jar, Warring States Period.

战国铜器图案。

音序检字表　Index for Characters

图书在版编目(CIP)数据

汉字字源入门 / 王宏源著. --修订本. --北京:
社会科学文献出版社,2019.4
ISBN 978-7-5201-4278-6

Ⅰ.①汉… Ⅱ.①王… Ⅲ.①汉字-字源 Ⅳ.
①H12

中国版本图书馆CIP数据核字(2019)第028210号

汉字字源入门(修订本)

著　　者 / 王宏源

出 版 人 / 谢寿光
责任编辑 / 王　绯
文稿编辑 / 尹传红

出　　版 / 社会科学文献出版社·社会政法分社 (010)59367156
　　　　　　地址:北京市北三环中路甲29号院华龙大厦　邮编:100029
　　　　　　网址:www.ssap.com.cn
发　　行 / 市场营销中心 (010)59367081　59367083
印　　装 / 三河市东方印刷有限公司

规　　格 / 开　本:787mm×1092mm 1/16
　　　　　　印　张:13.75　字　数:245千字
版　　次 / 2019年4月第1版　2019年4月第1次印刷
书　　号 / ISBN 978-7-5201-4278-6
定　　价 / 98.00元